The Art of
LOW-CALORIE
COOKING

The Art of
Low-Calorie
Cooking

Sally Schneider

Photography by
Maria Robledo

Stewart, Tabori & Chang

New York

To Chris and Felicia, who were there
at the beginning

Text copyright © 1990 Sally Schneider
Photographs copyright © 1990 Maria Robledo

Prop stylist: Anita Colero

Published in 1990 by
Stewart, Tabori & Chang, Inc.
575 Broadway, New York, New York 10012

Library of Congress Cataloging-in-Publication Data

Schneider, Sally.
The art of low calorie cooking
Sally Schneider; photography by Maria Robledo.
ISBN 0-916103-12-9
Previously ISBN: 1-55670-157-8
1.Cookery.   2.Low-calorie diet.   I.Title.
TX652.S344   1990
641.5′635—dc20   90-34477   CIP

Food & Wine® Cookbooks
Distributed by
American Express Publishing Corporation
1120 Avenue of the Americas
New York, New York 10036

Printed in Japan
10 9 8 7 6 5 4 3 2 1

Many of the recipes in this book have appeared, in slightly
different form, in Food & Wine magazine.

Page 3: Peach Ice Cream, recipe on page 219

Contents

. . . .

Introduction

. . . .

*L*ow-calorie cooking is a grim subject and one that, for the food person, speaks of betrayal. "You're doing a book on low-calorie food?" colleagues ask warily, as if I'd sold my soul—passion and integrity instantly lost. Where is the woman who reported having mystical experiences eating foie gras alone in Paris, who created a chestnut chocolate cake so rich it could be served in slivers only one half inch thick, who made yearly treks down south to revel in the cuisine of corn bread and cracklings? Still here. Still do. But other realities assert themselves now too. When self-contempt rather than joy is the outcome of indulgence, it is time to revise the plan. My body says no to a daily diet of rich food; my psyche and self-image say no to overweight.

I have written this book for those like myself who want delicious food that nurtures both body and soul. I want wonderful food to eat every day, to feed my friends, to keep me a thin and healthy person who can still occasionally indulge in those inimitable, inherently fattening, and sublime "other" worlds of unknown and limitless calories. When my friend Irene in the mountains of West Virginia invites me over for buckwheat dumplings with onions fried in bacon fat, I'll go, and weigh them in the balance of my other, also delicious, low-calorie ways.

I have been passionate about food for as long as I can remember. As an adult, this passion led me to wander kitchens both private and professional to discover the joys of foie gras, cassoulet, and *gâteau Marjolaine* in France; the pleasures of risotto and *tiramisù* in Italy; and doughnuts and chicken pot pie at home right here in America.

After spending years working in restaurant kitchens whose pantries and walk-in refrigerators were loaded with fattening culinary marvels—myriad chocolates and fresh creams, eaux-de-vie, honeys, cheeses, fresh game meats, and wild mushrooms—I had the opportunity to pursue and oversee the development of low-calorie recipes for a national magazine. Anatomy being destiny, the opportunity coincided with and, I suspect, was secretly prompted by my desire and need to reconcile indulgence and healthy eating. I set about to re-create the food I adore, the foods of my travels and professional life, and to accommodate my desire to eat healthy, low-calorie meals. It is, I found, no easy feat, but it is possible, and that exploration is what this book is about.

My approach to creating low-calorie recipes is more about cooking creatively than it is about dieting, more about pleasure than denial. I have endured the same

Radicchio, Orange, and Grilled Onion Salad ➤

austere, unsatisfying diet fare everyone else has, food that asks us to pretend the experience rather than have it: yogurt as a substitute for whipped cream, and crackers for corn bread. The food may make great sense on paper, but not on our palates and in our hearts. There is more to a healthy diet than nutrition. Enjoyment and a sense of wonder are vital ingredients. There is the ritual of sitting at table with good friends, sharing wonderful food, wine, and conversation, the feeling of well-being and harmony, and the enduring memory that such a moment becomes. To me, the point of cooking, low calorie or not, is to connect us to the moment and to nurture our bodies and our souls.

There was a time, not long ago, when a half-pound steak was considered a healthy single serving, accompanied by a baked potato with plenty of butter and sour cream, a salad with blue cheese dressing, and cheesecake for dessert. More was better, protein was the key to life, and fat had no consequence other than to make things taste good. As a society we are now paying for our proclivity for high-fat diets with a host of maladies, from heart disease to cancer.

There is so much contradictory information about food and diet these days. People joke that they don't know what to eat anymore, that if it tastes good, it's probably bad for you. Government nutritionists from the National Academy of Sciences have recommended that we eat a wide variety of foods in moderate amounts, in order to consume a broad range of nutrients without overdoing any one, as well as to avoid large quantities of allergens or pesticide residues. Their message is that too much of anything is not good for you and that the bad stuff is only bad when we eat it in quantity. It seems a fair conclusion drawn from the increasing evidence of the cause-and-effect relationship of food and illness. They also recommend that our daily diet include a greater proportion of fiber-rich foods, such as vegetables, legumes, and grains, and a good deal less protein, fat, and refined sugar, for those are the culprits that, in abundance, pose a variety of health risks.

These dietary recommendations also stress the importance of exercise in a sensible regimen. Research has shown that exercise increases the metabolism and propels the body to burn calories more efficiently. Anyone who has tried knows that it is very difficult to lose or maintain one's ideal weight without exercising. It seems to help reduce cholesterol levels, stress, cravings, and the propensity for binging. Simply put, exercise is an essential component of healthy eating.

The balance of food and exercise represents, in effect, a more European way of eating, as I discovered on trips to Italy and France many years ago. There I ate everything I wanted: triple crème cheese, bread, pasta, rich sauces. I was initially surprised that I lost weight, until I realized that I ate only moderate amounts of these foods. Dishes were often simply prepared, yet so fully flavored, owing to the quality of ingredients and artful preparation, that I was perfectly content to eat portions that by American standards would be considered skimpy. Desserts and sweets were minimal; frequently, just fresh or poached fruit was served. Since I walked everywhere, I was getting plenty of exercise.

Generally speaking, my low-calorie recipes draw upon the flavors and techniques of the provincial French and Italian kitchen. This culinary palette accommodates sound nutritional principles yet also affirms the sensual and celebratory experience of eating and cooking.

About Creating Low-Calorie Recipes

The great challenge in low-calorie cooking is to build in enough flavor and texture so that no one knows calorie-laden ingredients are missing. This calls for reflecting on the richness derived from cream, butter, and sugar, for example, and on the qualities that touch us deeply and make us remember a dish for years—in short, on the real nature of fulfillment and the wonderful food that truly satisfies our hunger.

One finds, in analyzing the most notoriously fattening and enduring recipes, from pâtés to chocolate truffles, that they usually contain large quantities of cream, butter, oils, and animal fats. The fats play a major role in the chemical interactions of food. They are the medium by which flavors are harmonized. But fats are the most calorie-dense foods, with twice as many calories by weight as proteins or carbohydrates.

Fats are also too delicious to do without. In fact, I have found that for many people, total denial sends them reeling into overeating. Since the danger of fats lies in their being eaten in quantity, the basic principle of my cooking is to use them very judiciously, by applying classic techniques in new ways. I use them for crucial processes like sautéing or caramelizing or to augment, finish, or act as a flavoring agent. So, for example, I have learned to sauté shallots in a fraction of the oil cookbooks routinely recommend. In my low-calorie cassoulet, a small amount of goose fat is used only to flavor the beans, which have been cooked in a richly flavored and gelatinous stock rather than in the quantities of goose and pork fat used in a traditional cassoulet. The essence of successful low-calorie cooking is to favor low-calorie and high-fiber ingredients, while using just enough high-calorie or high-fat ones to achieve the desired effect.

Pure protein, such as meat, poultry, and seafood, also tends to be quite high in calories, so servings of protein rarely exceed four ounces per person. This amount is satisfying both aesthetically and nutritionally, within the context of an imaginatively composed dish.

Portions tend to be generous but not overindulgent, and ample within the context of a whole meal composed of a first course or salad, a main course, and a dessert. By checking the calorie counts at the end of each recipe, it is easy to formulate wonderful three-course meals for less than 660 calories.

On Using the Best Ingredients

The first time I traveled to France, I was struck by how easy it was to achieve wonderful results in the kitchen. I will never forget roasting a chicken with tarragon at a friend's house in Paris. It was, by all accounts, a startlingly delicious roast chicken, despite its simplicity. If one lives and cooks there for any length of time, the reason becomes obvious: raw ingredients are of such high quality, and so readily available, that one doesn't have to work to make them taste good. In America, this translates into buying the highest quality ingredients, searching out sources for them if need be.

There is an interesting economy both of money and calories in buying the best, even if it is more expensive. Generally, the more flavor something has, the less one needs to use. So, for example, a small amount of a pungent, fruity, extra-virgin olive oil will have more impact than a greater quantity of a less aromatic type.

The value of buying locally grown foods cannot be overestimated for the joy of cooking with seasonal ingredients and because, simply, foods have more flavor when they are harvested ripe and eaten quickly thereafter. We have all had the experience of biting into a beautiful-looking peach and finding it has no taste. In supermarkets, foods have no season anymore. We have asparagus year-round and summer fruits like blueberries and cherries in winter. The products of a far continent's growing season are picked green to weather the long distance. Yet they are often bred only to *look* ripe; their taste is disappointing. When fruits and vegetables are truly ripe, they have a lush flavor and perfume that are inherently satisfying and sensual. My rule of thumb in buying fruits and vegetables is that if it does not smell wonderfully like itself, it is not worth eating. In general, I rely on seasonal local fruits and vegetables whenever possible, buying them at produce stands, farmers' markets, or health food stores. I augment my supply, when necessary, with high-quality "imported" produce that has been picked ripe in its own growing season—the California strawberries or Hawaiian pineapples, for example, that appear in New York's winter markets. Happily, many supermarket chains carry organic produce, which will almost always be flavorful and pesticide-free. Herbs, lettuces like endive and radicchio, certain wild mushrooms, and yellow bell peppers do especially well under cultivation.

About these Recipes

No one will know the recipes you cook from this book are low calorie unless you tell them. I had two inviolable criteria for whether a recipe would be included in this book:

—It must match my memories of its delicious high-calorie counterpart.

—It must stand on its own with no excuses. If I ever get the comment "It is good—considering it is low calorie," I reject the recipe.

The recipes in this book are organized into traditional food groups with sample menus on pages 246–249 to illustrate the range of possibilities for a variety of occasions. Included with each recipe are notes, wherever possible, on keeping properties, serving suggestions, and advance preparation. Many recipes include variations on the basic recipe to increase its applicability and encourage improvisation. Nutritional information, including the calorie, protein, fat, and carbohydrate counts, can be found at the end of each recipe and used to target specific dietary needs.

Wines and Alcoholic Beverages

Wines and alcoholic beverages have suffered the same fate as other foods that are perceived to be very caloric: They are avoided altogether. To eliminate these beverages, wines in particular, is to wall off a world of flavor nuances, especially those that occur in their exquisite interplay with foods.

A glass of wine is an invitation to engage the senses in discerning not only the qualities of the wine but its relationship to the food you are eating. It can extend the simplest dish to a greater dimension. A glass of Champagne with a Lobster and Corn Bread Sandwich—consumed on a lush summer day—offsets the flavors of the sandwich. Its perfume mingles with that of the various ingredients and of the warm lazy air. The wine completes the meal.

Like the calories of any other element of a menu, those in wine, beer, and other alcoholic drinks are quantifiable. The danger simply lies in drinking too much of these beverages. Moreover, they should be carefully chosen for their qualities as well as their calories. A fragrant eau-de-vie paired with the fruit from which it is made might be more pleasing than an elaborate dessert. A glass of chilled manzanilla sherry might be perfect with some shellfish. Or, once in a blue moon, a dry Martini might be just the thing. Selected to reflect upon and enjoy, wines and alcohol become an integral part of the art of eating well and healthfully.

Stocking the Pantry

. . . .

The following ingredients compose the foundation of my low-calorie cooking. They are the staples I rely on and keep on hand to catalyze the markets' offerings into healthy meals. Since some, like butter, are quite unorthodox in low-calorie cooking, I have included my reasons behind using these foods and explanations of the roles they play in the chemistry and aesthetics of this kind of cooking.

OILS

All fats have about the same number of calories. Although research about the healthfulness of various kinds of fats is inconclusive and often contradictory, it is clear that some are significantly healthier than others. Generally the less processed and adulterated the oil, the healthier and better-tasting it will be. Commercially processed vegetable oils are often extracted with chemical solvents and then treated with additives of questionable safety.

In most of the recipes in this book, olive is the oil of choice because of its healthfulness, its cooking properties, and its wonderful flavor. It is rich in monounsaturated fat, considered to be the healthiest fat in the fight against cholesterol and heart disease. It is widely available in an unrefined form, termed extra-virgin, which indicates that oil from premium quality olives has been extracted by pressure rather than with solvents, and that by law it is less than one percent acidity. From year to year, extra-virgin olive oils can vary in flavor, from buttery to fruity to nutty, and color, from golden yellow to deep green, depending on the climates in which the olives are grown and the method of production. Their costs also vary considerably; high price and elegant packaging do not necessarily indicate a spectacular oil. One can become familiar and learn one's preferences only by tasting. Excellent olive oils are produced in France, Spain, Greece, Italy, and California. I usually keep at least two kinds on hand: the finest oil for preparations in which flavor is critical, a less expensive oil for light sautéing and for sweating vegetables.

I use peanut oil when I need to sauté at a higher heat than olive oil can withstand. It is a bland, neutral-flavored oil with slight peanut overtones. Cold-pressed varieties available in health food stores or those imported from France have the least chemical residue and a cleaner flavor. Canola oil, made from the rapeseed (in the mustard family), is another excellent, virtually neutral-flavored oil.

Nut and seed oils are used for flavoring rather than cooking, since they break down easily under intense heat. They are invaluable in low-calorie preparations since they are not calorie dense like the nuts they are made from. Aromatic walnut and hazelnut oils

impart their flavor and aroma most spectacularly in baked goods, such as Hazelnut Espresso Genoise, which is redolent of hazelnuts without containing any. Because the hazelnut oil I use is of such extraordinary quality, only a teaspoon is necessary to flavor the entire cake. Nut oils are also wonderful in salad dressings for bitter leaves, such as endive and radicchio, as well as for such fruits as pears or oranges. Though expensive, these oils need be used only in small amounts and so will last a long time. Since they are quite volatile, they must be stored in the refrigerator once opened. Look for imported French nut oils with the honest flavor of roasted nuts. The best French walnut and hazelnut oils I have ever found were produced by J. LeBlanc, imported by Select Vineyards, Ltd.

Toasted sesame oil is commonly used in Asian cooking. It is an excellent and potent flavoring in salad dressings, sauces, and marinades. A little goes a very long way, so it must be used sparingly. It is available in health food stores as well as in the Oriental food section of supermarkets.

BUTTER

Unlike most calorie-conscious cooks, I never cook with margarine (the only exception being Paul Prudhomme's Seafood Filé Gumbo recipe). Flavorwise, it is a poor substitute for butter, and there are concerns as to its healthfulness. All margarines are composed of significant amounts of partially hydrogenated oils as well as emulsifiers, coloring agents, and preservatives. Hydrogenation of fats is a process by which liquid vegetable oils are biochemically altered into a more saturated man-made compound solidified to mimic the texture of butter. There is a great deal of controversy regarding the chemical changes that occur as a result of this process and the effect of partially hydrogenated oils in the body. The oils are suspected of everything from interfering with fat metabolism to enhancing fatty deposits in the arteries.

The present fear of eating butter is based on the fact that it is a saturated fat and therefore is thought to contribute to elevated cholesterol levels and heart disease. Such studies are based on the diet of the average American, whose consumption of fats has increased by 30 percent in the past 70 years, as has consumption of high-fat meats and cheeses, as well as plasticized shortenings, such as margarine. The simple point is that it is not the butter that is the problem, it is the quantity of fat we eat. The positive side of butter is that it is a sublime-tasting natural product, made without additives. Used judiciously, within the context of a healthy diet, the occasional indulgence in butter poses no danger. And it can contribute manyfold to the pleasure of eating and to satiety.

◄ Flavoring olive oil

I usually buy unsalted butter made from certified raw cream, available at health food stores. It has a richer, fresher flavor than commercial butters do.

DUCK, GOOSE AND HAM FAT

Occasionally, I will use a small amount of duck or ham fat when I am cooking with these meats. Because they are saturated, they are normally totally off limits to dieters. Like butter, these fats are so flavorful that even a minute amount can add delicious character to a recipe at no more calories than margarine.

CREAM

On rare occasions I will use cream in my recipes. I have spent a lot of time trying to figure out ways to get around using cream altogether, and to a large degree I have. But there are effects cream, and nothing else, can achieve. In the alchemy of cooking, it bonds with other flavors in the purest way, yielding an inimitable silkiness and richness. Again, as in the case of butter, moderation is the secret. A small amount of the taboo ingredient when and where it is really needed significantly diminishes the calorie/cholesterol threat while increasing the pleasure and deliciousness of a dish.

SOUR CREAM

Tasting far more caloric than it is, sour cream has about half the calories and fat of heavy cream and can often lend a creamy quality that is perfect for sauces or for enrichments. A little goes a long way. It can also be mixed with buttermilk for an even lower-calorie and lower-fat substitute (see Double Sour Cream). A tiny amount of sour cream can lift food out of the realm of "diet" into the sphere of indulgence.

BUTTERMILK

Traditional, or authentic, buttermilk, rarely available commercially, is literally the liquid left over after butter is churned. Commercially produced buttermilk is milk, usually skim, cultured with various bacteria—similar to the way yogurt is made—to mimic the slightly tart flavor and thick consistency of the original. I always keep buttermilk on hand in a glass jar in my fridge, since it lasts for weeks and is an excellent low-calorie substitute for milk in many recipes. I use it frequently in conjunction with sour cream as a base for sauces and salad dressings. I find it less acidic and more delicately flavored than yogurt. It is wonderful in baked goods, since it not only has leavening properties when mixed with baking soda, which reduces the quantity of eggs needed, but it also produces a fine, tender crumb.

C H E E S E

Since most cheeses are extremely high in fat, I use them sparingly. I will eat a cheese course at the end of the meal, but only when the meal has been spectacular and I know the cheeses will be too (see Fruit and Cheese, page 185). I use cheese more as a flavoring element than as a main ingredient unto itself and in doing so find that a strongly flavored cheese can do little caloric harm since not much is needed. I always keep a chunk of true Italian Parmesan, Parmigiano-Reggiano, or other hard dry cheese, such as aged Gouda, Sapsago, or the Spanish Manchego, on hand for shaving or grating. A little goes a long way, and its flavor can add great dimension to a dish of pasta, risotto, steamed asparagus, or fennel salad. Other strongly flavored softer cheeses, such as aged chèvres like Bucheron or blue-veined cheeses like Gorgonzola or Roquefort, can be blended with a mild low-fat fresh cheese, such as ricotta or cottage, to increase their volume and use their flavor to best advantage with fewer calories. Certain cheeses can be used in lieu of other fatty foods in a dish, as in the case of an oil-less buttermilk-based blue cheese salad dressing or a baked polenta in which melted Gorgonzola adds flavor and creaminess. Semisoft cheeses like Raclette, Appenzeller, Gruyère, and Fontina or those of the Cheddar family like Cheshire, Cantal, and Mimolette can be melted into casseroles, gratins, and sandwiches, adding protein and hearty flavor. Grating or shredding these cheeses helps to extend their volume and to allow even melting.

S W E E T E N E R S

I do not use artificial sweeteners, a common staple of dieting, because their healthfulness remains suspect and their flavors and interactions in cooking are never as vibrant or successful as natural sweeteners. There is also some evidence that they actually increase cravings for food. Such sweeteners as sugar, honey, and molasses, like any of the other forbidden foods of dieting, are not harmful in small amounts, and they provide a great deal more satisfaction and appeal. Indeed, many nutritionists agree that a small amount of sugar is necessary to achieve satiety.

V I N E G A R S

Vinegars have virtually no calories and can provide a bright note to salad dressings and sauces. Their natural acid content works like lemon juice to intensify the flavors of a dish and therefore to reduce the amount of salt needed. Well-made vinegars, naturally fermented from good wines or fruit juices, tend not to have the characteristic harsh bite of the most common commercial vinegars. The less adulterated and refined they are the better. There is, for example, a noticeable difference between commercial cider vinegar and a good quality organic one, the latter having more body and the flavor of ripe apples. Because one uses them sparingly, vinegars last a long time and only get better with age.

It is well worth investing in a variety of interesting vinegars—at the very least Champagne, sherry, cider, rice wine, and red wine. Balsamic vinegar is a red wine vinegar with a sweet, round, mellow flavor that is a boon to dieters because it is so mild and pungent it can be used with a minimum of oil in salad dressings. Fruit-flavored vinegars, such as raspberry or blueberry, can lend the bouquet of ripe berries to the dishes they touch, and a few drops will enhance the fresh fruit itself. Quality vinegars may be purchased in the gourmet sections of supermarkets, specialty, and health food stores. Vinegars with herbs, fruit peel, berries, garlic, or shallots can easily be made at home for a fraction of the cost of store-bought (see page 234).

SALT

I consider salt to be essential to good cooking and use it sparingly throughout the recipes in this book. The amounts may be reduced as your taste or dietary needs dictate. The various salts have strikingly different flavors. Common household salt, obtained from mining rock salt deposits of ancient seabeds, is highly processed with additives in the form of anticaking agents, whiteners, and iodine and has a stale, flat, almost chemical flavor when compared with a good sea salt, which is made from evaporating seawater. Sea salts, particularly the English and French ones, have a clear, fresh flavor that can truly enhance the flavors of a recipe. They tend to be more intense, so one must use them sparingly. Kosher salt, widely available in supermarkets, is a refined salt that is more coarsely ground than common table salt. Because it does not contain additives, its flavor is much better. Its special texture is important to several of the recipes in this book.

FRESH HERBS

Herbs add a wonderful flavor dimension to recipes and provide infinite possibilities for variation. Since most herbs have a crisp, clear flavor that tends to lift and focus the taste of a dish, they can replace some of the salt in recipes. Over the years, fresh herbs have become increasingly available in supermarkets. Italian flat-leaf parsley, basil, dill, coriander (also called cilantro), and mint are now commonplace, with fresh thyme, tarragon, chives, chervil, sage, and rosemary more and more visible. All of these kitchen herbs can easily be cultivated in a window box or flower pot in a moderately sunny window.

Saffron threads crushed in a mortar for Saffron Pasta ➤

I have yet to read a description of herbs that conveys the flavor, aroma, or effect adequately. The recipes in this book will provide a good guide as to how to use many herbs. Experimentation—simply buying some and tasting them, and letting your imagination guide you as to where to use them—is the best way to become acquainted with them.

DRIED SPICES AND HERBS

I have an entire drawer in my kitchen devoted to spices and herbs, the bottles standing upright with their tops labeled for easy identification. They deepen the flavor of everything they touch, from delicate poaching liquids for fresh fruits to the bouquet garni for stocks and braises. My basic inventory includes:

allspice	ginger
bay leaves, imported	mace
cayenne pepper	mustard, ground
chili powder	nutmeg, whole
cinnamon	oregano
cloves	paprika
coriander	peppercorns, black, white, and
crushed hot red pepper	Szechuan
cumin	rosemary
curry powder	saffron
fennel seeds	sage
five-spice powder	thyme

Tarragon, chervil, parsley, and basil do not translate well when dried, so I use only fresh. Dried spices and herbs lose their potency over time and should be replaced about every six months.

FRESH CHILES

I have found that the addition of minced fresh chiles, such as the readily available jalapeño and serrano chiles, to most savory dishes can reduce or eliminate the need for salt for those who must restrict their salt intake. The amount used, usually from one half to one teaspoon minced chile, should be just enough to lend a piquant, not fiery, flavor to the food. Fresh jalapeño and serrano chiles are readily available in the produce section of most supermarkets. They are smooth-skinned, dark green, oval peppers about 2 inches long, serrano being slightly narrower. Use only the flesh of the chile; discard the seeds, stem, and membrane. In handling chiles, take care to wash knives, cutting board, and hands carefully to avoid transferring the hot flavor to other foods. Since the chile's oils often linger on the skin after working with it, do not rub your eyes or you can irritate them.

VANILLA

Whether bean or extract, vanilla is a staple ingredient in low-calorie desserts, for it can draw out the natural sweetness of the other ingredients, particularly fruits, giving the illusion of greater sweetness without the calories. Whole vanilla beans are preferable to vanilla extract, since they give a fuller flavor to desserts. They can be found two or three to a jar in the spice section of supermarkets. To use in cooking, split the bean lengthwise and scrape out the seeds, then add both seeds and bean to the dish as indicated. Remove the beans before serving. Vanilla extract should be added after cooking, except in baked goods, since it loses much flavor when exposed to heat.

CHICKEN STOCK

Very few people have time to make homemade chicken stock anymore. Chefs I know bemoan the fact yet admit that they rarely make it at home themselves. Yet there are myriad uses for good chicken stock in low-calorie cooking, whether it is to add body and flavor to a sauce or soup or to act as the perfect neutral medium for braising. Although I do make chicken stock sporadically (see Chinese Chicken Stock), and love having it on hand in the freezer, there are often times when my freezer is bare as well. So I have found three strategies that will do in a pinch. 1) Often gourmet stores or sections of super-markets offer acceptable frozen chicken stocks. It is worth searching them out, trying several different brands until you find one you like. Then stock up on it. (They can vary radically in quality, claiming to use the best ingredients, but not achieving even the level of canned broth.) 2) Explore local Chinese restaurants. Often Chinese vegetable and won ton soups are made with real chicken broth and can be carried home in quart containers as takeout. Drain and eat the vegetables or won tons and use or freeze the broth. 3) Finally, there is canned broth. Some of the "natural" salt-free chicken broths, such as Hain, available at health food stores, are quite acceptable and can be used as is. If you have time, chicken parts or aromatics can be boiled in canned broth for a half hour to fortify the flavor. Commercial supermarket brands tend to have quite a bit of salt and a tinny flavor and should be diluted by at least two times as much water.

LIQUORS

Although I rarely drink more than wine, my liquor cabinet is extensive. Wines and spirits are, in essence, distillations of flavors that are important in low-calorie cooking. They can be transformed into rich sauces or marinades for poultry, seafood and meat or simple flourishes for fresh fruit desserts. When cooked, alcohol, from wine to Cognac, loses its alcoholic content as well as most of its calories, leaving only its flavor behind. Because of its potency, only small amounts of uncooked alcohol are necessary to add wonderful flavor, but not many calories. A few drops of kirsch or Cognac, for example, will greatly enhance dishes featuring fresh tomatoes. The following list covers the basic alcohols I use frequently. They last quite a long time and may be bought in half bottles or nips if space is a consideration.

Rainwater Madeira or Marsala	dry red and white wine
tawny port	French Sauternes or Barsac,
dry sherry	Muscat de Beaumes de Venise
white vermouth	Irish whiskey
Cognac	vodka
eaux-de-vie: pear, framboise, kirsch	tequila
liqueurs: Grand Marnier, Frangelica,	bourbon
Sambuca, or Anisette	

T H I C K E N E R S

Although starch-thickened sauces have gone out of fashion during the past few years in favor of reductions and butter-mounted essences, I find they have been unjustly abandoned. The gentle thickeners, such as arrowroot and potato starch, can provide the delicate liaison to give a wine or stock reduction body without a starchy flavor or thick texture. And they are very easy to use, requiring only that they be mixed with a small amount of liquid before being stirred into the sauce. Because both of these starches thicken upon contact with hot liquid and do not have to be cooked to remove rawness, they should be added just before serving.

Arrowroot is perfect for last-minute thickening, as in the recipe for Turkey Marsala with Wild Mushrooms, since it breaks down if it is held for more than 15 minutes or if it is reheated. It is available in the spice section of supermarkets.

Potato starch produces a smooth, light, neutrally flavored gel that holds up well but will lose its thickening power if heated for too long at the boiling point. It can be found in the kosher food section of supermarkets.

Equipment
. . . .

The recipes in this book require basic tools that are commonly used in the practice of good cooking and found in any well equipped kitchen: mixing bowls, vegetable parer, salad spinner, spatulas, measuring cups and spoons, as well as a blender or food processor. An accurate scale that weighs from fractions of an ounce up to several pounds is essential for measuring ingredients, as well as for learning portion sizes. High quality, heavy duty pots, baking sheets, and frying pans, particularly seasoned cast iron, aid in cooking with a minimum of fat without scorching and, unlike nonstick or lightweight pans, provide an excellent exterior texture and greater depth of flavor. Unlike most low-calorie cooks, I use nonstick pans only occasionally for cooking foods that might stick otherwise and which do not require a crisp surface, such as omelets, pancakes, or crêpes.

Because the way foods are sliced and presented can greatly enhance the visual appeal of a dish, as well as contributing to a sense of abundance, texture, and flavor, an array of sharp knives, including one with a long, thin flexible blade such as a salmon slicer, facilitate much greater control and creativity. A slicer-julienner, also known as a mandoline, is indispensable for cutting vegetables, fruit, cheese, or other semi-firm foods quickly into consistent slices, julienne, shavings, or shreds to create interesting and unusual textures with a minimum of effort.

A Miscellany of Indispensable Foods

The following is a rather personal list of foods that I rely on constantly and keep on hand to expand single recipes into pleasurable whole meals. For example, tossing Garlic Fried Greens with a cup of pasta and a couple of tablespoons of Parmesan results in a wonderful earthy supper. I include alcoholic beverages in this list as well.

	CALORIES		CALORIES
Olive and nut oils,		Prosciutto, 1 ounce	60
1 teaspoon	40	Shrimp, 3 ounces,	
Unsalted butter,		peeled, cooked	84
1 teaspoon	34	Smoked salmon, 1 ounce	33
Sour cream,		Caviar, 1 ounce	71
1 tablespoon	31	Cookie, 1 amaretti	27
Heavy (whipping) cream		Granulated sugar,	
1 tablespoon	51	1 teaspoon	16
2 tablespoons whipped	26	Dark brown sugar,	
Ricotta, 1 ounce, whole		1 teaspoon	17
milk	49	Confectioners' sugar,	
1 ounce, part skim	39	1 teaspoon	10
Goat cheese, 1 ounce	105	Honey, 1 teaspoon	22
Parmesan, 1 ounce	111	Maple syrup, 1 teaspoon	17
1 tablespoon, grated	28	White wine or	
Mozzarella, 1 ounce	80	Champagne, 4 fluid	
Pasta, 2 ounces dry	210	ounces	80
1 cup cooked	197	Red wine, 4 fluid ounces	85
Potatoes, 3 ounces,		Dessert wine, 2 fluid	
cooked	73	ounces	92
Rice, ½ cup, cooked	132	Beer, 6 fluid ounces	73
Wild Rice, ½ cup,		Vodka, whiskey, rum,	
cooked	83	86 proof, 1 fluid	
Bread, 1 ounce	82	ounce	70

o o o

Hors d'Oeuvres, Appetizers, and Salads

o o o

Artichoke Bottoms and Chicory with Warm Walnut Dressing

· ·

When I first started cooking professionally, the cookbooks I read were the classics of French cooking. The recipes were simply notations of ingredients, technique was merely implied. I remember being astonished at the number of recipes that included artichoke bottoms, and how extravagant that seemed, for in modern kitchens they have long since been forgotten. The *Larousse Gastronomique*, Prosper Montagne's monumental encyclopedia of French cooking, includes more than 45 preparations for artichoke hearts or bottoms, from appetizers to garnishes, and suggests possibilities for at least 50 more. It is rare that one is served fresh artichoke bottoms these days—I imagine because of the perception that they are a lot of work to prepare. Instead we rely on frozen or canned ones, whose briny flavor bears no relation to the real thing. Once the basic technique of paring the artichoke is mastered, they are quite simple to prepare and present wonderful possibilities for unusual side dishes, soups, and salads, for they are very low in calories. This recipe marries the flavors and contrasting textures of endive and artichoke bottoms. Boiling together white vermouth and shallots with walnut oil yields a savory, lightly emulsified sauce with a buttery quality. The calories of the vermouth are burned off when heated. The dressing is also delicious on boiled noodles, as well as on other boiled or steamed root vegetables, such as potatoes, turnips, and parsnips.

Artichoke Bottoms and Chicory with Warm Walnut Dressing

. . . .

Juice of 1 lemon
¾ teaspoon salt
4 large artichokes
¾ pound total Italian chicory or curly endive and Belgian endive, leaves separated
¼ cup plus 2 tablespoons white vermouth
1 tablespoon minced shallots
2 teaspoons Champagne vinegar or white wine vinegar
1 tablespoon plus 2 teaspoons walnut oil
Scant ¼ cup coarsely chopped walnut halves
1 tablespoon minced Italian flat-leaf parsley or fresh tarragon
Freshly ground pepper

Fill a large saucepan about two-thirds full of water. Stir in the lemon juice and ½ teaspoon of the salt. Cut the stems off the artichokes. Pull off the tough outer dark leaves until you reach leaves with a touch of pale yellow. (Discard the stems and outer leaves or save for another use. For instance, boil or steam them and eat with a dipping sauce.) Using a long sharp knife, slice the artichokes in half crosswise. Using a sharp paring knife, trim around the artichoke bottom to remove the outer layer of green skin, exposing the pale yellow flesh.

Place the pared artichokes in the saucepan and bring to a boil over moderately high heat. Cover, reduce the heat to moderately low, and cook until the artichokes are tender when pierced with a knife, 30 to 35 minutes. Drain, rinse under cool water, and drain well.

Pull off the leaves from the artichoke bottoms. Using a small spoon, scoop out the fuzzy choke and discard. Place the artichoke bottoms in the center of each of 4 salad plates. Place the chicory in a medium bowl and set aside.

In a small heavy saucepan, combine the vermouth, shallots, and the remaining ¼ teaspoon salt. Bring to a boil over moderately high heat. Using a long kitchen match, ignite the vermouth and cook until the flames die down, 1 to 2 minutes. Add the vinegar and walnut oil and boil vigorously until the oil and vermouth are combined, about 1 minute.

Spoon half of the dressing over the chicory and toss to coat. Arrange the chicory around the artichoke bottoms. Spoon the remaining dressing into the center of the artichokes. Top the salads with the walnuts, parsley, and pepper to taste.

4 Servings   132 Calories   3.7 gm Protein
8.4 gm Fat   13.2 gm Carbohydrate per Serving

Buttermilk Slaw

Like barbecued meat and corn bread, coleslaw is a quintessentially American food, the preparation of which every cook claims to know the one true way. There are slaws with sweet vinegar dressings, others with mayonnaise or sour cream or Worcestershire sauce, some in which celery seed, grated onion, chopped tomato, or sweet pickles are the critical element. Based on data collected on yearly eating treks down south, this coleslaw recipe rolls several slaws into one, fudging on the fattening ingredients.

Most slaw recipes feature dressings with half a cup of mayonnaise or more, close to 1000 extra calories in fat alone. This recipe uses less than one tablespoon of sour cream per person along with low-fat buttermilk to produce a creamy slaw at enormous savings of calories and fat. It complements ham or pork dishes, as well as grilled seafood or poultry, and can be used in lieu of mayonnaise, lettuce, or tomato for many sandwiches.

¼ cup plus 1 tablespoon sour cream
¼ cup buttermilk
1 tablespoon cider vinegar
1 teaspoon Worcestershire sauce
2 to 4 dashes of hot sauce
1¼ teaspoons sugar
1 teaspoon celery seed
½ teaspoon salt
½ teaspoon freshly ground pepper
1 small head of cabbage (1 pound), tough outer
   leaves removed
¼ cup plus 2 tablespoons chopped red onion
¼ cup chopped parsley
2 tablespoons chopped fresh basil (optional)

In a small bowl, whisk together the sour cream, buttermilk, vinegar, Worcestershire sauce, hot sauce, sugar, celery seed, salt, and pepper.

Quarter the cabbage; cut out the core. Using a mandoline or a thin sharp knife, slice the cabbage lengthwise into ¼-inch-wide shreds.

In a large bowl, toss the cabbage with the red onion, parsley, and the dressing. *(The recipe can be made up to 1 hour before serving; refrigerate.)* Add the basil, if desired, at the last minute.

6 Servings   59 Calories   1.9 gm Protein
2.8 gm Fat   7.4 gm Carbohydrate per Serving

Cheese Straws

．．．．．．．．．．．．．．．．．．．．．．．．．．．．．．．．．．．．．．．

I have a friend who keeps a tin of cheese straws under her bed. She claims not to eat them all the time but likes to have them there for those moments when life is too much. Phone off the hook, she retreats to bed with a book and the comfort of a few old-fashioned, puff-pastry cheese straws. She says they revive her, renew her faith in life, and restore her spirits.

I put great store in this kind of ritual—the power of certain foods to revive flagging spirits and fortify the body, to offer respites from the demands of a stressful world. For me, these respites take the form of impromptu gatherings with friends over a glass of Champagne or a martini and a snack of something wonderful, like this low-calorie version of the inimitable cheese straw. They lend that element of indulgent comfort to the weary for few calories. They can be made ahead and then pulled out at a moment's notice.

To my mind, the best cheese straws are made with all-butter puff pastry. My attempts to fashion other kinds of doughs have yielded various permutations of crunchy cheese crackers, but not the melting, buttery cheese straw. So I returned to puff pastry. However, since I was unwilling to make it, I bought a good commercial variety at my local gourmet market. The puff pastry is rolled thin, sprinkled with Romano cheese, sweet paprika, and black pepper, then cut into long strips and baked. The flavor of sweet butter within the pastry mellows the effect of the savory-salty exterior. As is its nature, the puff pastry inflates with air, yielding double the volume but half the calories of other pastry crusts. These dramatic 15-inch cheese straws have fewer than 35 calories apiece.

Commercially prepared puff pastry, made with butter, is available in the freezer section at gourmet markets and some supermarkets. These straws are best served the day they are baked, but if made ahead, store them in an airtight tin and simply crisp them in the oven for a few minutes before serving. The recipe can be easily doubled or tripled. The unbaked strips can be kept frozen for a couple of weeks.

1 ounce Romano cheese, finely grated (about ½ cup)

1 tablespoon imported sweet paprika

½ teaspoon freshly ground pepper

¼ pound prepared puff pastry dough, defrosted according to package directions

All-purpose flour, for dusting

1 egg white lightly beaten with 2 teaspoons of water

Preheat the oven to 400°. Line 2 large baking sheets with parchment, cut so that 1 inch of the metal is exposed at each short end of the pan. In a small bowl, combine the Romano cheese, paprika, and pepper and set aside.

Place the puff pastry on a lightly floured work surface and dust lightly with flour. Roll the dough into a 12-by-10-inch rectangle, about ¹⁄₁₆ inch thick. Brush the dough with a little bit of the egg wash. Sprinkle half of the cheese mixture evenly over the surface, spreading and smoothing it with your fingers. Lightly roll the dough with a rolling pin. Fold the dough in half crosswise to enclose the cheese, forming a 7½-by-10-inch rectangle. Brush the top of the dough with more egg wash, sprinkle half of the remaining cheese mixture over the surface, spreading evenly; roll lightly with a rolling pin. Turn the dough over and repeat the procedure on the other side with the remaining egg wash and cheese.

With a long sharp knife, or with a pastry wheel and ruler, slice the folded dough crosswise into twenty ½-inch-wide strips. Picking up 1 folded strip at a time, unfold it and place it across the prepared baking sheet, stretching gently so that the ends of the strip reach the exposed metal edges of the baking sheet. To prevent the straw from curling while baking, press the ends firmly onto the baking sheet so that the dough sticks to the pan. Repeat with the remaining strips, spacing them about ½ inch apart on each pan. Freeze for 5 minutes before baking. (The unbaked strips can be left on their baking sheets, covered securely with plastic wrap, and frozen for up to 2 weeks.)

Bake the straws for about 10 minutes or until golden. Transfer the baking sheets to a rack to cool.

Variation: Each baked cheese straw can be cut into three 5-inch lengths, at 11 calories each.

Makes 20 Cheese Straws   33 Calories
1.0 gm Protein   2.0 gm Fat
2.7 gm Carbohydrate Each

Skordalia

. . . .

*S*kordalia is a Greek garlic sauce similar to the French *aioli* commonly made with a base of mashed potatoes. It is one of life's perfect foods because the simplest elements combine to produce a hauntingly earthy flavor. Eaten on peasant bread or with cold vegetables, it can be a healthy little supper on its own. It is wonderful with many kinds of cocktails and wines. This recipe is roughly based on one my great-grandmother used to make, pounding garlic by hand with an old wooden pestle, which I have inherited.

The skordalia that follows uses only about one-quarter of the standard amount of olive oil yet retains the character of the sauce. To save on calories, the potatoes are mashed to the correct consistency with some of their own flavorful cooking water instead of olive oil. At the end of this process, a small amount of olive oil, contributing its singular texture and flavor, is added. It coats the potatoes rather than being absorbed by them.

I often serve cold sliced beets with this sauce, but it is equally good with any number of other vegetables, such as artichoke hearts, asparagus, bell peppers, cherry tomatoes, endive, or fennel. It is delicious on cold poached chicken or fish and on Pan-Grilled Bread.

Use the freshest, firmest garlic possible. If you have garlic that has sprouted, slice each clove in half and remove the bitter green sprout with a paring knife.

Don't use a food processor to mash the potatoes. It will make them gummy.

. . . .

1½ pounds red or yellow boiling potatoes, peeled and sliced into 2-inch chunks

1 teaspoon coarse (kosher) salt

5 garlic cloves, minced

¼ cup extra-virgin olive oil

Salt and freshly ground pepper

In a medium saucepan, combine the potatoes and ½ teaspoon of the coarse salt with enough water to cover by ¼ inch. Bring to a boil over high heat, reduce the heat to moderately high, cover, and simmer for about 15 minutes. If the water has evaporated by more than 1 inch, pour in enough hot water to cover the potatoes. Cook the potatoes until tender when pierced with a sharp knife, about 10 minutes longer.

Meanwhile, mash and scrape the minced garlic with the remaining ½ teaspoon coarse salt against a work surface with the side of a large knife until it is reduced to a paste. Alternatively, pound the garlic and salt in a mortar with a pestle.

Using a slotted spoon, transfer the cooked potatoes to a large mixer bowl. Reserve the cooking liquid. Beat the potatoes at low speed until coarsely broken apart. Alternatively, beat with a potato masher. Stir in the garlic paste. Gradually beat in some of the cooking liquid, ¼ cup at a time, until the potatoes have the texture of a soupy puree. Stir in 3 tablespoons of the olive oil and season with salt and pepper to taste. *(The recipe can be made up to 1 day ahead; cover and refrigerate. Let sit at room temperature 2 hours before serving or microwave briefly to warm it up. The intensity of the garlic and the balance of salt will change as the sauce sits. Add a little garlic or salt to taste if necessary.)* Serve the *skordalia* warm or at room temperature. Just before serving, drizzle the remaining 1 tablespoon olive oil on top.

**8 Servings (About 3½ Cups)   120 Calories
1.4 gm Protein   11.0 gm Fat
13.4 gm Carbohydrate per Serving**

. . . .

Julienned Leeks and Sliced Beets with Beurre Noisette

. . . .

Beurre noisette, or browned butter, is a sauce that has traditionally accompanied such classic French dishes as calves' brains, skate wings, and shirred eggs. In this recipe, it is used as a vinaigrette to make a kind of warm vegetable salad. The toasted butter gives it a flavor of roasted hazelnuts, while the balsamic vinegar contributes a slight sweetness and an acidity that brings out the earthy flavors of the leeks and beets. It is so pungent that only a small amount is necessary to dress and season the vegetables. The leeks are finely julienned, to create a texture similar to pasta, and surrounded with disks of sliced beets. *Beurre noisette* is delicious on other warm root vegetables, such as parsnips and turnips, as well as on steamed artichokes.

Serve these vegetables warm or at room temperature, but pour the hot butter over them at the last minute.

Julienned Leeks and Sliced Beets
with Beurre Noisette

2 medium beets (about 10 ounces total), trimmed
  of greens
½ teaspoon salt
6 medium leeks
1 tablespoon plus 1 teaspoon unsalted butter
1 tablespoon plus 1 teaspoon balsamic vinegar
Freshly ground pepper
12 small sprigs of chervil or Italian flat-leaf
  parsley, for garnish

In a medium saucepan, place the beets, ¼ teaspoon of the salt, and enough water to cover by 1 inch. Bring to a boil over high heat, reduce the heat to moderate, and cook the beets until tender, about 1 hour (or 30 minutes for small beets). Let cool, then peel and slice ¼ inch thick. (The beets can be prepared up to 2 days ahead; cover and refrigerate.)

Trim the roots and tough green tops from the leeks, leaving about 1 inch of pale green on the white stalks. Slice the leeks crosswise into 3- to 4-inch lengths. Then slice each section lengthwise into thin julienne strips. Rinse the leeks in a bowl of cold water to remove any grit, then drain. (The leeks can be prepared to this point up to 4 hours ahead and kept in the bowl of cold water.)

In a steamer or in a medium saucepan with a steamer basket, bring 1 inch of water to a boil over moderately high heat. Add the leeks, toss with the remaining ¼ teaspoon salt, cover, and steam until tender, about 5 minutes. Transfer the leeks to a medium bowl and cover. Add the beets to the steamer, cover, and steam until warmed through, about 2 minutes.

In a small heavy skillet, cook the butter over moderate heat until it begins to brown, about 2 minutes. Turn off the heat and add the balsamic vinegar. The butter will sputter and darken in color. Add 2 teaspoons of the *beurre noisette* to the leeks and toss. Place a mound of leeks on each of 4 warmed salad plates; arrange the beets decoratively around the leeks. Spoon an equal amount of the remaining *beurre noisette* butter over the beets. Season with pepper to taste. Garnish with the chervil.

4 Servings   85 Calories   1.5 gm Protein
4.0 gm Fat   11.8 gm Carbohydrate per Serving

Rillettes of Duck

Classically, rillettes are made with pieces of pork—or sometimes goose, duck, or rabbit—that are cooked in fat, pounded in a mortar, packed into small stone jars, and covered with a thin layer of lard. Like *confit d'oie*, rillettes fall into the category of delicious, hearty, fat-preserved preparations from the farmhouse cookery of France. In the days before refrigeration, the high fat content of these dishes worked as a preservative by sealing out the bacteria in the air. These foods provided needed calories for long work and cold weather. The flavor of rillettes—rich, slowly cooked pork or rabbit, goose, or duck, liberally seasoned with pepper— evokes their rustic origin. I have many friends with a passion for this specialty but, by virtue of its usual 50 percent fat content, a fatalistic attitude about eating it that slightly dampens the experience. In this recipe, duck legs and carcasses are braised slowly in wine and aromatics to create a rich, gelatinous stock that is then defatted and reduced. The stock, which has a concentrated duck flavor, forms the binding for the shredded meat and produces the smooth, creamy texture normally achieved by using quantities of duck fat. Although it is a bit of work, this recipe yields a generous five cups, or about 20 servings. You can freeze any leftovers in an airtight container.

Ducklings are readily available in supermarkets. To save time, ask the butcher to prepare the ducks according to the instructions below. The tender duck breasts will not be used in this recipe since they cannot stand up to long, slow braising. They can be reserved for another use; I like to sear them quickly and serve them rare, as in the recipe for Pan-Fried Duck Steaks.

Spread the rillettes on slices of French bread and serve with cornichons, Pickled Cherries, grilled and caramelized onions, or even prunes that have been steeped in black tea.

2 ducklings (about 4½ pounds each)
½ pound onions, chopped
1 shallot, thinly sliced
2 garlic cloves, smashed
2 cups dry white wine
1 bay leaf
3 allspice berries, crushed
½ teaspoon dried thyme
2 teaspoons salt
¼ teaspoon ground allspice
About 1 tablespoon freshly ground pepper

Remove the giblets from the ducklings and set aside, reserving the livers for another use. Rinse the ducklings inside and out and pat dry. Using a thin sharp knife, strip all the skin from the ducklings, trimming away any excess fat clinging to the flesh. Discard all but ¼ cup of the duck fat. Carefully cut the breasts off the rib cage and reserve for another use. Separate the legs and thighs from the carcass. Using kitchen shears, cut each carcass into 4 sections, leaving the rib bones intact.

Preheat the oven to 300°. In a large heavy skillet, heat the reserved duck fat over moderate heat until it is melted and very hot, about 7 minutes. Add the duck legs and thighs and cook until browned, about 4 minutes on each side. Using a slotted spoon, transfer the duck to a large heavy casserole. Add the carcass pieces and giblets to the skillet. Reduce the heat slightly if the fat is too hot. Cook until browned, about 4 minutes on each side, and transfer to the casserole. Add the onions, shallot, and garlic to the skillet and cook over moderate heat, stirring, until soft and browned, about 8 minutes. Transfer them to the casserole.

Pour off all the fat from the skillet and add the wine; scrape the bottom of the skillet with a wooden spoon to loosen the browned bits. Stir in 4 cups of water and bring to a boil. Pour the boiling liquid over the duck in the casserole. Add the bay leaf, allspice berries, thyme, and 1 teaspoon of the salt. Place a double layer of heavy-duty aluminum foil over the casserole, cover

tightly with the lid, and bake for 3 hours or until the meat is falling off the bones.

Using a slotted spoon, transfer the meat and bones to a colander placed over a bowl. Strain the casserole liquid through a fine-mesh sieve into a large jar or measuring cup; discard the residue. Let the stock cool to room temperature, then freeze for about 30 minutes. Using a spoon, skim as much fat as possible from the surface of the stock.

Pour the stock into a heavy medium saucepan. Bring to a boil over moderately high heat, then move the pan so it is sitting over just half of the burner. Reduce the heat to moderately low and simmer for about 40 minutes, frequently skimming the impurities and fat that rise to the surface on the cooler side of the pan. Pour the stock into a heatproof measuring cup. You should have 2 cups. If you have more than this, return the stock to the saucepan and continue to reduce the liquid.

Meanwhile, when the duck is cool enough to handle, strip all the meat from the bones with your fingers and place in a large bowl. Discard the bones. Pinch and rub the meat between your fingers to shred it and to pick out any small bones.

When the stock is reduced to 2 cups, slowly pour it over the duck, stirring to combine. Stir in the ground allspice, 1 tablespoon of the pepper, and the remaining 1 teaspoon salt. Season with additional pepper to taste. Pack the rillettes into a crock (or more than one if you wish to freeze some for future use), cover with plastic wrap and refrigerate until completely chilled, about 4 hours. Stir before serving. (These rillettes will keep for up to 5 to 6 days in the refrigerator; let stand at room temperature at least an hour before serving. Or freeze for up to 3 months and defrost in the refrigerator overnight. If the rillettes become a little dry, stir in some warm water to restore the original creamy texture.)

20 Servings (About 5 Cups)   91 Calories
9.2 gm Protein   5.1 gm Fat
1.4 gm Carbohydrate per Serving

Roasted Peppers with Caramelized Garlic

. . . .

*B*ell peppers roasted over an open flame and peeled take on a sweet smoky flavor and are wonderful as an hors d'oeuvre served with thin garlic croutons, as an appetizer, or as an accompaniment to cold roasted meats or grilled fish. Or, for a light lunch, add one and a half ounces of thinly sliced fresh mozzarella cheese or the same amount of individual bocconcini to each serving.

. . . .

4 medium yellow and red bell peppers, in any combination
2 tablespoons extra-virgin olive oil
18 garlic cloves, peeled and sliced
4½ tablespoons balsamic vinegar
2 sprigs of fresh thyme
¼ cup coarsely chopped Italian flat-leaf parsley or basil
Freshly ground black pepper

Roast the bell peppers directly over a gas flame or under a broiler as close to the heat as possible, turning until charred all over, about 5 minutes. Enclose the peppers in a bag to steam for 10 minutes. Using a thin knife, scrape the skin off the peppers and remove the core, seeds, and ribs. Cut the peppers lengthwise into 1-inch strips.

In a small skillet, combine the olive oil and garlic. Cover and cook over very low heat until the garlic is very tender, about 7 minutes. Uncover the pan, increase the heat to moderate, and cook the garlic until lightly browned. Stir in the vinegar. Strip the leaves off the thyme branches and add them to the pan. Simmer for 1 minute.

Arrange the pepper strips in a fan or criss-crossing pattern on a platter or on individual salad plates. Spoon the caramelized garlic and dressing over the peppers. Sprinkle the parsley and plenty of black pepper on top. Serve at room temperature. *(The salad will keep refrigerated for 3 days.)*

4 Servings   102 Calories   1.6 gm Protein
7.4 gm Fat   9.2 gm Carbohydrate per Serving

Mesclun Salad and Mixed Green Salads

. . . .

*L*ately, my local farmers' markets, and even some supermarkets, have begun carrying something I had seen only in markets in the south of France—wonderful salade mesclun. Mesclun simply means a mixture of baby lettuces, fragile young greens, herbs, and sometimes edible flowers whose flavors range from peppery to mild to herbal.

Mesclun is an extremely satisfying and versatile salad full of eclectic flavors, colors, and textures, which, because the lettuces are picked young, are not overpowering. It is wonderful served with a wide variety of foods as a garnish or side dish, or as a "green salad" either before or after the main course. It is the ultimate convenience food: the greens are already picked over and washed.

Even if mesclun is not available, the basic concept of mixing an assortment of tender greens is easy to execute with the lettuces commonly sold at produce markets. Belgian endive, curly endive or frisée, the Italian chicories (including radicchio), watercress, Oak Leaf, sorrel, Bibb, arugula, basil, chervil, chives, coriander, mint, Italian parsley, the tender hearts of Boston and romaine are all good choices. Keep an eye out for lettuces that appear seasonally, or new offerings, such as the Japanese *mizuna*, with its lacy pungent leaves, or delicate *mâche*, which has the faint scent of rose petals. The tops of baby beets and turnips are delicious as well. Spinach,

Swiss chard, and dandelion should be young and tender. Generally, you will want to have a good balance of mildly flavored lettuces with some bitter or peppery ones, as well as some herbs. Pick the smallest leaves from the greens, discarding any tough stems. Wash well and spin them dry in a salad spinner. Wrapped in a damp kitchen towel and placed in a plastic bag, the cleaned lettuces will keep refrigerated for 3 to 4 days.

To create a variety of other mixed salads, experiment with lettuces and herbs found in your local markets. Combining just two or three elements can result in a surprising contrast of flavors and textures, such as Belgian endive leaves with beautiful fernlike red Treviso chicory (a variety of radicchio) or Oak Leaf, Belgian endive, and peppery watercress. Edible flowers, such as nasturtiums, chive blossoms, roses, violets, and day lilies might also be included.

A simple dressing, such as Champagne Vinaigrette, is best with mesclun as well as the milder greens. It won't detract from the flavors of the lettuces. Hazelnut or Walnut Oil Dressing is best on salads made up mainly of more assertive lettuces with peppery or bitter flavors.

. . . .

1 tablespoon plus 2 teaspoons Champagne
  Vinaigrette (page 237)
4 cups cleaned young greens, lettuces, and herbs,
  in any combination
Freshly ground pepper

Pour the vinaigrette in a large salad bowl. Add the lettuces and herbs and toss until lightly coated with dressing. Season with pepper to taste and toss again. Serve at once.

4 Servings   48 Calories   1.0 gm Protein
4.5 gm Fat   1.8 gm Carbohydrate per Serving

Warm Mesclun Salad with Pan-Fried Tuna

. . . .

The flavors of mesclun are well suited to main course salads. When pan-fried or grilled tuna, duck breast, or salmon is added, the meat's natural juices become part of the dressing, wilting the greens slightly. This recipe illustrates the method using a tuna steak, and the variations that follow replace the tuna with other recipes from this book. Pan-Grilled Bread, with its slight flavor of wood smoke, is a wonderful accompaniment.

1 recipe Mesclun Salad
1 tablespoon crushed black peppercorns or fresh
    rosemary leaves (or 1 teaspoon dried)
½ pound tuna steak
1 teaspoon olive oil
Pinch of salt

Arrange half of the Mesclun Salad on each of 2 dinner plates. Rub the peppercorns or rosemary over the tuna. In a heavy medium skillet, heat the oil over moderate heat until hot. Add the tuna steak and cook until the tuna is browned on the outside and still rare on the inside, about 2 minutes on each side. Transfer the tuna steak to a cutting board. Using a thin sharp knife, slice the steak ¼ inch thick. Season lightly with salt.

Arrange half of the slices over each salad, pour any juices over the greens, and serve at once.

Variation: Omit the peppercorns or rosemary and olive oil. Substitute ½ recipe of Pan-Fried Duck Steaks for the cooked tuna. Arrange the sliced breasts over the mesclun as directed. 209 calories per serving.

Or substitute ½ recipe Divine Inspiration Pan-Smoked Salmon for the cooked tuna. Arrange ½ salmon steak in one piece over the mesclun. 244 calories per serving.

2 Servings   287 Calories   28.8 gm Protein
16.9 gm Fat   5.6 gm Carbohydrate per Serving

Fennel and Parmesan Salad with Aromatic Pepper and Orange Zest

In Italy's Tuscany, fennel is held in such high esteem that it is often eaten raw with only a little extra-virgin olive oil and some salt to dress it. It is also eaten in that country as a dessert with cheese and fruit. In supermarkets in America, as I am buying it, I am frequently asked what this mysterious vegetable is and what one does with it. Fennel, with its sweet anise flavor and its texture a cross between celery and apple, is a versatile vegetable—wonderful both raw and cooked. To my mind, the combination of raw fennel, shaved Parmesan, and olive oil is one of the greatest of food affinities. It is extremely low in calories and is perfect as an accompaniment to cocktails or as a first course to a rich meal. This salad goes the dish one better with the addition of aromatic pepper and orange zest for greater flavor dimension. Paired with an ounce or two of thinly sliced prosciutto, it makes a light and well-rounded lunch or supper.

In supermarkets in France, it is commonplace to find mixtures of black and white peppercorns and Jamaican pepper, or allspice. I keep a pepper mill filled with this mixture and use it often in place of black or white pepper; it adds an interesting, subtle note to simple foods, such as this salad.

Fennel and Parmesan Salad with Aromatic Pepper and Orange Zest

2 teaspoons white peppercorns
2 teaspoons black peppercorns
1 teaspoon allspice berries
1 tablespoon plus 1 teaspoon fresh lime juice
Pinch of sugar
1 tablespoon plus 1 teaspoon extra-virgin olive oil
1 pound fennel bulb (1 large)
2 strips of orange zest (2 by ½ inches), cut into thin julienne strips
1½ ounces Parmesan cheese

To make aromatic pepper, combine the white and black peppercorns and the allspice berries. Grind to a fine powder in a spice grinder or pour into a pepper mill to grind as needed.

In a small bowl, whisk together the lime juice and sugar. Slowly whisk in the olive oil to form a vinaigrette.

Using scissors, snip enough fine feathery fronds from the fennel stalks to measure 6 tablespoons; discard the green stalks. Quarter the fennel bulb lengthwise through the root. Using a mandoline, a fine vegetable slicer, or a thin sharp knife, cut each fennel quarter into paper-thin slices. Place in a medium bowl and toss with the vinaigrette, orange zest, fennel fronds, and ½ teaspoon or more of the aromatic pepper. Divide evenly among 4 salad plates.

Shave the Parmesan into paper-thin slices and arrange on top of each salad. Grind an additional pinch of aromatic pepper over the cheese (save the remaining pepper for another use) and serve.

4 Servings   109 Calories   5.3 gm Protein
7.6 gm Fat   5.9 gm Carbohydrate per Serving

Radicchio, Orange, and Grilled Onion Salad

. . . .

A happy outcome from experimenting one afternoon in the kitchen was the surprising discovery that grilled, slightly charred red onions taste more like duck cracklings than onion when added to a refreshing radicchio and orange salad. They lend an autumnal flavor. This dish makes a stunning visual presentation, either on individual salad plates or on one large serving platter.

. . . .

4 medium navel oranges (about 10 ounces each)
2 teaspoons sherry vinegar or red wine vinegar
¼ teaspoon salt
Freshly ground pepper
1 tablespoon plus 2 teaspoons extra-virgin olive oil
1 large head of radicchio (about ½ pound), shredded into ¼-inch strips
1 medium red onion (about 5 ounces), sliced crosswise ⅛ inch thick with slices kept intact

Preheat the broiler. With a vegetable peeler, remove eight 2-by-½-inch strips of zest from the oranges, leaving behind the bitter white pith. With a small sharp knife, cut the zest into thin slivers and set aside. Remove the remaining zest and white pith from the oranges and discard. Holding the oranges over a bowl, cut between the membranes to release the sections. Squeeze the membrane to extract all the juice.

Strain the orange juice into a small bowl. Whisk in the vinegar, ⅛ teaspoon of the salt, and pepper to taste. Whisk in 1 tablespoon plus 1 teaspoon of the olive oil until incorporated.

In a medium bowl, toss the radicchio with half of the dressing and half of the slivered orange zest. Toss the orange segments with the remaining dressing and plenty of pepper. Arrange the radicchio on 4 salad plates. Mound ¼ of the oranges and the remaining zest in the center of each salad. Or arrange the radicchio and oranges on a large serving platter. *(The recipe can be prepared to this point up to 1 hour ahead; refrigerate until ready to serve.)*

Preheat the broiler. Just before serving, brush the onion slices lightly with the remaining 1 teaspoon olive oil and season with the remaining ⅛ teaspoon salt. With a spatula, transfer the onion slices to a broiler pan. Broil as close to the heat as possible until the onions are soft and just beginning to blacken, 2 to 4 minutes. Arrange the onion slices on top of the salads and serve at once.

4 Servings   163 Calories   3.1 gm Protein
6.3 gm Fat   27.4 gm Carbohydrate per Serving

Prosciutto with Figs and Raspberries

. . . .

*I*taly's prosciutto di Parma is perhaps the best known of the world's air-cured, uncooked hams. The unique curing process gives these hams—like France's Jambon de Bayonne, Spain's Serrano, and America's Smithfield—a dense, chewy texture and a sweet, nutty flavor. They are best served in transparently thin slices, and at 60 calories or less per ounce—about two to three slices—are a naturally low-calorie food. The aromatic meat requires no preparation other than pairing it with good bread, salad greens, or fruit. Any of the aforementioned hams will work equally well in this recipe. Domestic prosciuttos are acceptable but do not have the complex flavor of true prosciutto di Parma. To cure your own prosciutto-style ham at home, see the recipe on page 123.

This first course, simplicity itself, consists of the classic combination of fresh figs and prosciutto embellished with a burst of summer flavors: basil, lime, and raspberries.

. . . .

6 ounces prosciutto, very thinly
   sliced and trimmed of excess fat (about 12
   slices)
Freshly ground pepper
4 medium, fresh figs
1 cup fresh raspberries
1 lime, cut into 6 wedges
8 to 12 small fresh basil leaves

Loosely fold the slices of prosciutto into free-form rosette shapes. Place 3 rosettes in a row across the center of each of 4 large dinner plates. Dust with several grinds of pepper.

Quarter each fig or cut lengthwise into 4 slices. Place 1 cut fig at the base of the prosciutto on each plate. Scatter ¼ cup of the raspberries around each of the figs. Garnish each plate with 1 lime wedge and 2 to 3 basil leaves. *(The recipe can be prepared up to 3 hours in advance; cover and refrigerate until ready to serve.)*

Just before serving, squeeze a few drops of lime juice from the remaining lime wedges over the fruit on each plate.

4 Servings   136 Calories   12.5 gm Protein
3.8 gm Fat   13.6 gm Carbohydrate per Serving

Corn, Tomato, and Vidalia Onion Salad

. . . .

This refreshing salad rolls two great food traditions of summer into one: corn on the cob and tomatoes with basil. Summer corn is usually so tender and sweet that cooking really is not necessary; the raw kernels give this salad its crunch. Juices from the ripe tomatoes become part of the dressing. Vidalia onions are mild, sweet onions from Georgia that are increasingly available around the country in the summer. If unavailable, sweet Bermuda onions will do. If you cut the tomatoes into half-inch dice rather than wedges, this salad can also act as a salsa for grilled fish and poultry.

. . . .

3 very ripe medium tomatoes, cored and diced (2½ cups)
1 medium Vidalia onion or sweet Bermuda onion, peeled and chopped (½ cup)
3 medium ears of fresh corn
1 tablespoon plus 1 teaspoon balsamic vinegar
⅛ teaspoon salt
1 tablespoon extra-virgin olive oil
15 large basil leaves
Freshly ground pepper

In a medium bowl, combine the tomatoes and onion. Using a sharp knife, slice the corn kernels off the cobs. Scrape the cobs with the dull side of the knife to release any milky corn juice. (You should have 1 cup of corn and juice.) Add the corn to the tomato and onion mixture.

In a small bowl, combine the vinegar and salt. Slowly whisk in the olive oil. Stack the basil on a work surface and slice into fine shreds. Add the basil and dressing to the vegetable mixture and toss well to combine. Season with pepper to taste. Cover the salad with plastic wrap and refrigerate for at least 1 hour and up to 2 days before serving.

4 Servings   99 Calories   2.9 gm Protein
4.3 gm Fat   15.6 gm Carbohydrate per Serving

Chick-Peas with Indian Spices

Chick-peas have a rather exotic and illustrious past that is not known to many. They have been found in prehistoric ruins of the neolithic period in Sicily and Switzerland. They were grown in the Hanging Gardens of Babylon and were stored in amphorae in Pompeii for export throughout Roman territory. However, like most legumes, in modern times they have generally been regarded as food of the poor. They are consumed largely in impoverished areas of India, Africa, and South America, for they are extremely nourishing, cheap, and easy to cultivate.

Like a variety of legumes, chick-peas are gaining popularity in America of late because of the spectacular nutritional value they offer. They seem tailor-made for the government's nutritional guidelines. Legumes are high in protein as well as B vitamins and such minerals as iron, magnesium, zinc, and copper. Unlike animal protein, they contain no cholesterol and are very low in fat, sodium, and calories. They provide one of the highest concentrations of fiber of any plant food, and thus they are extremely filling.

In this recipe, chick-peas are simmered with a fragrant mixture of onions, ginger, garlic, and a blend of Indian spices, including coriander, curry, cardamom, and cloves. The chick-peas become glazed with sweet, spicy, and savory flavors. They are excellent warm or cold as a first course or as an accompaniment to a variety of simply cooked meats, poultry, and seafood. A serving makes an excellent, healthy, and satisfying midday snack.

This recipe works very well with either dried chick-peas or rinsed canned chick-peas.

Chick-Peas with Indian Spices

2 cups dried chick-peas or 2 cans (16 ounces each) cooked chick-peas (garbanzos), rinsed
2 teaspoons ground coriander
2 teaspoons sweet paprika
2 teaspoons granulated sugar
1 teaspoon curry powder
1 teaspoon ground cumin
1 teaspoon ground cardamom
1 teaspoon salt
¾ teaspoon crushed hot red pepper
¼ teaspoon ground cloves
2 teaspoons vegetable oil
2 medium onions, chopped (1½ cups)
10 garlic cloves, sliced
¼ cup tomato paste
2 tablespoons fresh lemon juice
1½ tablespoons freshly grated ginger

To prepare dried chick-peas: In a heavy medium saucepan, place the dried chick-peas and add enough water to cover. Bring the water to a boil and cook for 2 minutes. Cover, turn off the heat, and let stand for 1 hour. Strain off the soaking water and then add 8 cups of fresh water. Bring to a boil over moderate heat and simmer until the peas are tender but not mushy, 2 to 2½ hours. Drain well and set aside. *(The chick-peas can be made up to 1 day ahead.)*

In a small bowl, combine the coriander, paprika, sugar, curry powder, cumin, cardamom, salt, crushed hot red pepper, and cloves; set aside.

In a large skillet heat the oil over moderately low heat. Add the onions and garlic and cook, stirring constantly, until golden brown, about 10 minutes. Add the reserved spice mixture and cook, stirring, for 15 seconds. Add 1 cup of water, tomato paste, and reserved cooked or canned chick-peas. Cover, reduce the heat to low, and simmer for 7 minutes. Uncover and stir in the lemon juice and ginger. Cook until most of the liquid has evaporated and the chick-peas are glazed, 3 to 4 minutes.

8 Servings   179 Calories   6.7 gm Protein
2.8 gm Fat   33.0 gm Carbohydrate per Serving

Buttermilk Mashed Potatoes

These wonderful lumpy mashed potatoes (with the skins left on) taste as if they have far more butter than one-half teaspoon per serving. Adding the small amount of butter at the end creates a buttery finish. Buttermilk and baking soda react to lighten the potatoes and make them very fluffy. For an even more buttery look and taste, use yellow Finnish potatoes if available.

1¼ pounds all-purpose white potatoes, unpeeled
   and scrubbed, or peeled if desired
1½ teaspoons salt
¾ cup warm buttermilk
½ teaspoon baking soda
2 teaspoons unsalted butter
Freshly ground pepper

Place the potatoes and 1 teaspoon of the salt in a medium saucepan; add enough cool water to cover. Bring to a boil over high heat. Reduce the heat to moderate and simmer until the potatoes are tender when pierced with a fork, about 45 minutes. Drain, reserving a few tablespoons of the cooking liquid.

Place the potatoes in a large bowl and mash with a potato masher or fork until fairly smooth (with some lumps remaining). Combine the buttermilk and baking soda and beat into the potatoes with a wooden spoon until thoroughly incorporated. If you prefer creamier potatoes, add the reserved cooking liquid. Stir in the butter, the remaining ½ teaspoon salt, and plenty of pepper to taste.

Variation: Mashed Potatoes and Root Vegetables, 149 calories per serving. Replace 6 ounces of the potatoes with pared chunks of turnip, celery root, or parsnips and 3 whole garlic cloves.

4 Servings   147 Calories   4.5 gm Protein
2.5 gm Fat   27.7 gm Carbohydrate per Serving

Oven Fries

These crisp potato sticks are a close match to traditional french fried potatoes but are made with much less fat. Each serving contains only one and a half teaspoons of butter.

3 tablespoons unsalted butter
1 pound large red or white all-purpose potatoes
½ teaspoon salt

Preheat the oven to 450°. In a small saucepan, melt the butter over low heat. Skim the foam off the top and discard; set the butter aside.

Peel the potatoes and slice into julienned strips about 2 to 2½ inches long by ¼ inch thick. Soak the cut potatoes in a bowl of cold water for 5 minutes. Drain the potatoes and rinse thoroughly under cold water. Sandwich between several layers of paper towels and pat dry. Transfer the potatoes to a medium bowl.

Skim off 2 tablespoons of the clear yellow part of the reserved melted butter and discard the white milk solids in the bottom of the pan. Pour the clarified butter over the potatoes and toss to completely coat the potatoes.

Spread the potatoes on a large baking sheet, making sure they don't stick together. Bake for 15 minutes in the top of the oven, then toss the potatoes with the salt and rearrange them with a metal spatula to brown evenly. Bake for 5 minutes longer, toss again, and bake for another 5 minutes until the potatoes are brown and crisp. Serve at once.

4 Servings   149 Calories   2.2 gm Protein
6.7 gm Fat   20.4 gm Carbohydrate per Serving

Winter Squash and Gruyère Gratin

. . . .

As chilly weather sets in, I hanker for a thick country soup, almost a gratin, such as the one made famous by Paul Bocuse. He layered pumpkin with Gruyère and grilled bread and cooked it in the pumpkin with lots of cream and no regard for calories. This recipe is a rough adaptation of Bocuse's, taking the essential notion and many liberties to recreate the effect of a warm gratin. The squash is layered with leeks, French bread, and Gruyère cheese, moistened with chicken stock and milk, and baked.

The cream in the original soup is an unnecessary extravagance, for the squash and Gruyère need only a little milk to form a rich mixture that is almost thick enough to hold a spoon upright.

. . . .

2 medium butternut squash (1½ pounds each)
¾ teaspoon salt
¾ teaspoon freshly ground pepper
1 medium leek (white part only), chopped
1 teaspoon olive oil
½ cup dry white wine
½ cup chicken stock or low-sodium canned broth
1 can (12 ounces) evaporated skim milk (see Note) or 1 cup whole milk
½ teaspoon sugar
2 ounces of a baguette (thinly cut into 8 small slices) or 2 slices of peasant bread (cut into 4 equal pieces), toasted
4 ounces Gruyère cheese, grated (about 1 cup)
1 tablespoon plus 1 teaspoon grated Parmesan cheese
8 basil leaves, shredded

Preheat the oven to 400°. Slice the squash in half lengthwise and remove the seeds. Place the squash, cut side up, in a baking pan. Season with ½ teaspoon each of the salt and pepper and cover tightly with aluminum foil. Bake until the squash are tender but not mushy, about 1 hour. Set aside.

Meanwhile, in a medium saucepan, combine the leek, olive oil, and 2 teaspoons of water. Cover and cook over moderately low heat until the leek is soft and translucent, about 5 minutes. Remove the lid and stir in the wine. Increase the heat to high and boil until the liquid is reduced to approximately 3 tablespoons, about 3 minutes. Stir in the stock, milk, sugar, and ¼ teaspoon each salt and pepper. Remove from the heat.

Using a big spoon, scoop the flesh from the squash in large pieces. Place in a medium bowl. *(The recipe can be prepared to this point up to 3 hours ahead. Set aside at room temperature.)*

To assemble the gratin, preheat the oven to 400°. Bring the leek mixture to a boil. Spoon half of the squash into a 6- to 8-cup ovenproof casserole. Ladle half of the leek mixture over the top and cover with half of the toast and half of the Gruyère cheese. Repeat the layers with the remaining squash, leek mixture, toast, and Gruyère. Sprinkle the Parmesan over the top.

Bake the gratin for 30 minutes or until the top is browned and bubbly. Garnish with the basil and serve.

Note: *Evaporated skim milk is whole milk from which half the water and most of the fat have been removed. It contains twice the nutrients and protein of regular skim milk.*

4 Servings 397 Calories 21.2 gm Protein 12.0 gm Fat 55.5 gm Carbohydrate per Serving

. . . .

Warm Black-Eyed Peas with Onions and Bacon

These spicy black-eyed peas are a far cry from the traditional southern black-eyed peas that most of us are accustomed to, the dried peas boiled with a ham hock to a delicious soupy mush. This is more of a warm salad, served with a balsamic vinegar dressing flavored with bacon and caramelized sweet onions. It is made with frozen black-eyed peas, which have a fresher flavor and firmer texture than the dried ones.

2 packages (10 ounces each) frozen black-eyed
  peas, thawed
½ teaspoon salt, plus more for seasoning
½ ounce of thick bacon, cut into ½-inch dice
2 medium red onions, thinly sliced
1 bay leaf
½ teaspoon sugar
Freshly ground pepper
¼ cup balsamic vinegar
2 teaspoons olive oil

In a medium saucepan, combine the peas, salt, and 2 cups of water over moderate heat. Bring to a simmer, cover, and cook until tender but not mushy, about 20 minutes; drain.

Meanwhile, place the bacon and 2 to 3 tablespoons of water in a heavy medium skillet. Cover and cook over moderate heat until the fat begins to render from the bacon, about 5 minutes. Uncover, reduce the heat slightly, and continue cooking until the water has evaporated and the bacon is lightly browned, about 2 minutes.

Add the onions, cover, and cook until wilted, about 5 minutes, adding 1 tablespoon of water, if necessary, to prevent sticking. Remove the lid and continue cooking until the onions are translucent and beginning to brown, about 4 minutes. Stir in the black-eyed peas, bay leaf, sugar, and salt and pepper to taste. Add the vinegar and ¼ cup of water, cover, and simmer for 15 minutes longer. Stir in the olive oil. Let cool slightly before serving.

6 Servings 178 Calories 9.4 gm Protein 3.6 gm Fat 28.1 gm Carbohydrate per Serving

Grilled Vegetables and Fruits

How is it that when we could easily flip a switch to warm the oven or heat the broiler, there are times when we turn to the most primitive form of cooking—grilling over fire. Funny that we still cook the way our forebears did more than a million years ago.

The French avant-garde playwright Antonin Artaud noted that with every convenience and labor-saving device we embrace, a part of life is lost. It seems to me that the refined conveniences of our modern kitchens, with their high-tech ovens and microwaves, have almost stripped us bare of the experience of fire, the prime mover in cooking. We have lost our connection to fire, and to the meals, transmuted and imbued with its flavor, that were cooked over it. So we grill to rekindle that connection.

My style of grilling is influenced by grills I had in Tuscany. Generally unadorned except for a brush of olive oil and the simplest of seasoning, the food is transformed by the fire, which seals in the juices and concentrates the natural flavors while adding its own. Sauces are unnecessary and added fat is minimal, keeping calories low.

I am so enamored of grilling that I have installed a grill-stand from Tuscany in my New York fireplace. I have tried grilling just about everything, including many vegetables and fruits that people generally don't consider cooking this way. Grilled vegetables, beyond the usual onions and peppers, are delicious, easy to make, and add great dimension to a simple meal.

Surprisingly, a variety of fruits, except supersoft ones like berries, take well to grilling. Their flavors intensify, yet their sweetness is attenuated by the smoke. Grilled fruits can add an unexpected accent to a meal, taking the place of a sauce or condiment.

What follows is more of a guide than a recipe. It indicates the best ways to grill specific fruits and vegetables, whether whole or sliced, as well as approximate cooking times, which vary depending on the hotness of the coals and the texture of the foods. The vegetables and fruits may be placed on the grill along with the foods they are accompanying. It is worth investing in a grill basket, which sandwiches small pieces between two wire racks, making turning easier.

All grilled foods, whether cut or whole, need to be brushed lightly with a fat to protect them from sticking to the grill or drying out. I use olive oil for both fruits and vegetables, since its flavor complements both. Do not peel the vegetables and fruits unless indicated. Sprinkle the vegetables with a little coarse (kosher) salt before serving if desired.

Grilled Vegetables and Fruits

Grilled Vegetables

Slice ¼ inch thick on a diagonal and grill for about
  4 to 6 minutes on each side:

Bell pepper, 1 medium (8 ounces) 57 calories

Eggplant, ¼ medium (4 ounces), 29 calories

Fennel stalks, trimmed and halved lengthwise, ½
  bulb (8 ounces), 34 calories

Meaty mushroom, such as porcino (cèpe) or
  portobello, 1 large (3 ounces), 21 calories

Potato, 1 medium (3 ounces), 67 calories

Sweet potato, 1 medium (6 ounces), 179 calories

Zucchini and summer squash, 1 medium (4
  ounces), 16 calories

Halve through the stem and grill for about 4
minutes on each side:

Belgian endive, 1 head (5 ounces), 21 calories

Mushroom: shiitake, Roman, or white button,
  1 large (½ ounce), about 4 calories

Radicchio, 1 head (6 ounces), 31 calories

Leave whole and grill for about 7 minutes on
each side, turning once:

Asparagus, 1 medium (1 ounce), 6 calories

Baby beets, 4 small (1 ounce), 12 calories

Baby carrots, 4 small (1 ounce), 12 calories

Baby turnips, 4 small (1 ounce), 8 calories

Baby zucchini, 4 small (1 ounce), 4 calories

Japanese or baby Italian eggplant, 1 medium
  (2 ounces), 15 calories

Leek, white part only, 1 medium (3 ounces), 52
  calories

Mushrooms: oyster (pleurotte) and smaller
  shiitake and white button (½ ounce), about 4
  calories

Scallion, 1 medium (1 ounce), 7 calories

Corn in the husk (12 ounces), 105 calories:
Carefully peel open the green husk and remove
the silk. Close the husks back over the cob and
soak in cold water for 10 minutes. Tie the corn in
several places with kitchen string to secure the
husk. Grill for about 15 minutes, turning
frequently.

Whole vegetables roasted in the coals: Brush
the vegetables with oil and wrap them individu-
ally in aluminum foil punched with 5 or 6 holes.
Bury the packages in the coals. Roast for about
30 minutes:

Artichoke, 1 quartered lengthwise (8 ounces), 46
  calories

Garlic, 1 head (about 3 ounces), 127 calories

New potatos, 3 small (3 ounces), 69 calories

Onion, 1 medium (about 4 ounces), 34 calories

Parsnip, 1 medium (2 ounces), 43 calories

Sweet potato, 1 medium (6 ounces), 178 calories

Grilled Fruits

Grill the fruit cut side down to start, turning
once, and continue to grill until the fruit is soft
but not mushy. Test fruit for doneness after grilling 3 to 5 minutes on each side, unless specified
otherwise.

Slice ½ inch thick:

Apple, ½ (about 4 ounces), 54 calories

Mango, ½ (5 ounces), 64 calories

Pineapple, peeled, 1 slice (2 ounces), 28 calories

Halve and pit:

Apple, 1 small (7 ounces), 108 calories

Apricot, 1 medium (3 ounces), 38 calories

Nectarine, ½ medium (5 ounces), 38 calories

Peach, ½ medium (about 4 ounces), 32 calories

Pear, ½ medium (about 4 ounces), 54 calories

Plum, 1 medium (4 ounces), 59 calories

Whole fruits: Grill a banana in its peel, turning
once, until it is very soft, about 10 minutes. Slice
open the peel and scoop out the flesh. Half a banana (2 ounces), 68 calories.

  Sandwich whole cherries in a grill basket. Grill
for about 2 minutes on each side. 4 cherries
(1 ounce), 18 calories.

Zucchini Noodles

. . . .

*I*n this recipe, zucchini or yellow squash is sliced into long thin julienne pieces, either on a mandoline or by hand. They are then sautéed in olive oil and garlic with the traditional herbs of Provence: thyme, rosemary, parsley, and lavender. The effect of eating them cut this way, as opposed to the usual disks or chunks of squash, is quite different. They are more like an exotic noodle, with Provençal flavors. They make an excellent vegetable side dish, particularly for lamb and grilled seafood. Although it doesn't take long to cut the squash, they are just as delicious sliced crosswise ⅛ inch thick for a more ordinary presentation.

. . . .

8 medium zucchini or yellow summer squash, or a combination (2½ pounds), trimmed
½ teaspoon coarse (kosher) salt
1½ teaspoons chopped fresh thyme or ½ teaspoon dried
¾ teaspoon fresh rosemary leaves or ¼ teaspoon crumbled dried
¼ teaspoon lavender (optional)
1 tablespoon extra-virgin olive oil
3 garlic cloves, thinly sliced
2 to 3 tablespoons minced Italian flat-leaf parsley
Freshly ground pepper

Using a thin sharp knife, slice the zucchini lengthwise ⅛ inch thick. Stack a few of the slices together at a time and cut them lengthwise into ⅛-inch-thick julienne strips, discarding the pulpy core. Or alternatively, using a mandoline or vegetable cutter, slice the squash lengthwise into thin julienne strips, again discarding the pulpy core. Place the julienned squash in a colander set over a plate. Toss it with the salt and set aside for 20 minutes. The salt will wilt the squash slightly and draw out some of its juices. Pat the squash dry with paper towels.

In a small bowl, combine the thyme, rosemary, and lavender.

In a medium skillet, combine the oil and the garlic. Cook gently over moderately low heat until the garlic is translucent, about 3 minutes. Increase the heat to moderately high and add the squash, 1 teaspoon of the herb mixture, and 2 tablespoons of water. Toss the squash several times. Cover the pan and cook, shaking the pan occasionally, until the zucchini is crisp-tender, about 2 minutes. Remove the lid and season with the parsley and pepper to taste. Continue tossing and cooking the squash until tender and wilted, 1 to 2 minutes longer.

Variation: These zucchini noodles make a lovely pasta and vegetable dish, 328 calories per serving. Toss each portion of zucchini noodles with 1 cup cooked pasta and ½ ounce thinly shaved Parmesan or goat cheese.

4 Servings   75 Calories   3.5 gm Protein 3.9 gm Fat   9.3 gm Carbohydrate per Serving

Giambotta

. . . .

I first learned of the wonders of *giambotta*, the Italian vegetable stew, from my friend Anne Disrude when she was working on an article about it and was excitedly developing one recipe after another based on its simple yet mysterious principle. In reading about *giambottas* one would never guess they would yield such divine and incredibly satisfying results. A mess of vegetables are gently boiled together with herbs, seasonings, and some olive oil and water. The boiling together causes the olive oil and vegetable juices to emulsify, melding the flavors into a rich essence while at the same time preserving the character of each vegetable. The *giambotta* is a revelation: it is easy to make, everything is cooked in one pot, and the possible combinations of vegetables are infinite. The results are invariably sublime and hearty.

Served with peasant bread and a salad, this dish is a meal in itself. If you wish, one-half ounce of Parmesan or hard goat cheese can be shaved on top of each serving. Fish and poultry may be cooked directly on top of the *giambotta* as in the variations below.

This recipe is the direct result of an October morning's shopping at an open-air farmers' market, for the *giambotta* takes well to spontaneous inspiration and seasonal offerings. Other vegetables may be substituted; the ones you can't find may be left out. The only ones I avoid completely in making a *giambotta* are broccoli and cauliflower because their flavors get too strong when left to sit.

Giambotta

1 medium red onion, sliced
2 leeks (white and tender green parts), sliced crosswise on a diagonal ¼ inch thick
2 yellow or red bell peppers, or a combination, cut into 1-inch strips
2 plum tomatoes, diced
1 fennel bulb, sliced ½ inch thick
1 carrot, sliced crosswise on the diagonal ½ inch thick, or 3 ounces baby carrots
1 small celery root (celeriac), cut crosswise into 1-inch pieces
1 medium parsnip, sliced crosswise on the diagonal ½ inch thick, or 3 ounces baby parsnips
2 turnips, sliced ½ inch thick, or 3 ounces baby turnips
½ small butternut squash, peeled and cut into 1-inch chunks
1 zucchini or yellow squash, sliced crosswise ½ inch thick
6 ounces Swiss chard, coarsely chopped
9 garlic cloves, chopped
1 teaspoon salt
2 imported bay leaves
½ teaspoon oregano
½ teaspoon thyme
½ teaspoon fennel seeds
½ teaspoon sugar
½ teaspoon crushed hot red pepper
¼ cup extra-virgin olive oil
2 tablespoons white wine vinegar
1 cup chopped fresh basil
¼ cup chopped fresh Italian flat-leaf parsley
¼ cup chopped fresh chervil (optional)
Freshly ground black pepper

In a large flameproof casserole, combine all the ingredients except ½ cup of the basil and the parsley, chervil, and black pepper. Add 1 cup of water, cover, and cook, stirring occasionally, over moderately high heat until the butternut squash is soft, about 30 minutes. Remove and discard the bay leaves. *(The recipe can be prepared to this point up to several days ahead. Let cool, then cover and refrigerate. Reheat before proceeding.)*

Sprinkle the reserved ½ cup basil and the parsley, chervil, if desired, and plenty of black pepper on top before serving.

Variations: *Giambotta* with Fish, 350 calories per serving. Five minutes before the giambotta is done, place four 5-ounce fish fillets, such as salmon, halibut, or swordfish, on top of the vegetables, cover, and cook over moderately high heat. Check the fish for doneness, re-cover, and cook for a few more minutes if necessary. Sprinkle the reserved herbs on top just before serving.

Giambotta with Chicken, 360 calories per serving. Serve 3 ounces of broiled or roast chicken directly on top of each serving of *giambotta*.

4 Servings   286 Calories   6.5 gm Protein
15.2 gm Fat   37.6 gm Carbohydrate per Serving

Greens with Rice from Patience Gray

....

*W*andering with a professional forager known as Wild Man Steve Brill through a park in the Bronx, I once spent hours looking for dinner. We feasted that evening on a variety of delicious wild foods, including Hen of the Woods mushrooms and a host of greens, berries, and nuts. Brill claimed to live on the foods he found in the parks around New York City, a declaration that heartens me. I am glad to know that wild foods exist nearby, even if only for the rare few who take the time to find them.

My daily life in the city precludes foraging for my supper, although I find myself drawn to foods that retain their wild origins even in their cultivated form—particularly greens. My neighborhood's Portuguese and Italian markets carry those wonderful bitter greens, such as dandelion, broccoli rabe, escarole, and chicory, that are easily transformed, even in the tame city, into earthy meals that hail from rougher origins and simpler times when wild greens were eaten for their health-giving properties.

In her beautiful and very personal cookbook, *Honey from a Weed*, about living in Mediterranean countries, Patience Gray includes a chapter called "Edible Weeds." It is some of the most illuminating writing on greens I have read. She describes what she was taught by her neighbors about the great array of wild edible greens, how to identify them, their culinary and medicinal uses, their ancient lore. This recipe is adapted from one she roughly notated, without quantities, which she attributes to a friend, Kyria Agapi, in Macedonia. Its last line states simply "Weeds promote energy."

Any green that has a strong, bitter flavor will work well in this recipe. The greens are cooked with shallots, olive oil, and long-grain rice into a homely and delicious mass. They have an indescribable quality reminiscent of much of my own Greek grandmother's cooking.

As is, this mixture makes an excellent side dish to lamb, chicken, or fish. With a tablespoon or two of grated Parmesan cheese, or an ounce of shaved sheep's milk cheese, it becomes a simple yet hearty lunch.

. . . .

1 teaspoon extra-virgin olive oil
4 to 5 shallots, chopped (½ cup)
2 garlic cloves, minced
¾ pound coarsely chopped dandelion, chicory, beet, or turnip greens, stems removed (about 8 cups)
¼ pound long-grain rice (¾ cup)
½ teaspoon salt
Freshly ground pepper

In a heavy medium pan, heat the oil over moderate heat. Stir in the shallots and garlic, cover, and reduce the heat to low. Cook the mixture, stirring occasionally, until the shallots are soft and translucent, about 4 minutes.

Add the greens, cover, and increase the heat to moderately low. Cook, stirring occasionally, until wilted, about 4 minutes. Add the rice, salt, and 1½ cups of water. Cover and simmer until the liquid is absorbed and the rice is tender, about 25 minutes. Stir in pepper to taste.

4 Side-Dish Servings   167 Calories
4.8 gm Protein   1.9 gm Fat
33.9 gm Carbohydrate per Serving

. . . .

Roasted Garlic

. . . .

The great chef Louis Diat considered garlic to be the fifth element, as important to existence as air, earth, fire, and water. He claimed that without it, he would not care to live.

Garlic evokes intense passion. Some people are passionate in their fear of it, as though it possessed malevolent power. They have usually experienced it badly handled—either raw in excessive amounts or burned until acrid—and have been rendered helpless against its odoriferous reverberation. Those who love garlic think it has healing properties and consider it as essential to life as love. They know that its greatness lies in its subtler manifestations, the result of gentle cooking that leaves it sweet and aromatic, devoid of antisocial aftereffects.

Generally, garlic is thought of as a flavoring agent, bound to contribute its inimitable presence to the greater good of a recipe. Roasting whole heads of garlic, however, makes them as soft and mellow as a baked potato. Spooned out of its skin and spread on bread, garlic becomes a delicacy in its own right, a true balm for any garlic lover's passion. When my friend Vicki Beth returns exhausted from her round-the-world business trips, she comes to my house to eat roasted garlic. She eats several heads at a sitting, sighing as the tensions of her complicated life fade.

This is the recipe I make when Vicki Beth and others come to my house in need of comfort. It makes a lovely lunch or light supper paired with a salad of bitter leaves, such as endive and Treviso, and an ounce or so of goat cheese.

The success of this recipe depends on using the freshest garlic possible. Look for firm white heads of garlic with no trace of mold or sprouting.

Roasted Garlic

. . . .

4 large heads of garlic or 8 small ones
   (about 14 ounces)
½ teaspoon extra-virgin olive oil
¼ teaspoon salt
Freshly ground pepper
Eight ½-inch sprigs of fresh thyme, or
   ¼ teaspoon dried

Preheat the oven to 400°. Place the garlic heads sideways on a work surface. Slice each head in half crosswise, through the circumference. Separate the halves and place each cut side up. Brush each cut surface with olive oil and sprinkle with the salt and pepper. Place 2 sprigs of thyme on each bottom half, or sprinkle with a little dried thyme. Fit the garlic halves back together and wrap each one in aluminum foil.

Bake the garlic heads until the flesh is soft, about 35 minutes for the large heads and 25 minutes for the small ones. Remove the foil and place one whole head of garlic on each plate, separating the halves if desired.

4 Servings   116 Calories   4.7 gm Protein
.9 gm Fat   24.5 gm Carbohydrate per Serving

Roasted Garlic with goat cheese and salad of endive and Treviso ➤

Garlic-Fried Greens

This is about the best way I know of eating greens: simply sautéed in olive oil with lots of garlic. The method works well for many of the late-season greens that need blanching to soften their toughness or bitterness: dandelion, escarole, kale, turnip, chicory, beet, Swiss chard. Occasionally I find young and tender greens, such as baby bok choy or turnip tops, at farmers' markets in early summer. In this case omit the blanching and add 2 to 3 tablespoons of water to the skillet after cooking the garlic and chile and before adding the greens. The dish may be eaten hot, at room temperature, or cold with a squeeze of lemon as the Greeks do. It's also a great topping for pasta.

½ teaspoon salt
2 bunches of dandelion greens, tough stems
   removed (about 1 pound cleaned greens)
1 tablespoon plus 1 teaspoon extra-virgin
   olive oil
15 garlic cloves, thinly sliced
1 teaspoon minced fresh jalapeño or serrano chile
   (optional)
Freshly ground black pepper

Bring a large pot of water to a boil over high heat. Add ¼ teaspoon of the salt. Wash the greens well. Add to the boiling water and cook for 30 seconds; drain and rinse under cold running water. Squeeze out any excess water and blot dry with paper towels.

In a large heavy skillet, heat the oil until hot, about 1 minute. Add the garlic and chile, if desired, and cook over low heat until soft but not browned, about 4 minutes. Add the greens and toss to coat with the oil. Cover and cook until the greens are hot and tender, about 5 minutes. Remove the lid and cook over moderate heat until all liquid has evaporated, about 2 minutes. Reduce the heat and cook for 1 minute longer. Season with the remaining ¼ teaspoon salt and black pepper to taste.

**4 Servings   96 Calories   3.3 gm Protein
5.3 gm Fat   11.7 gm Carbohydrate per Serving**

Summer Corn and
Chile Pepper Soup

. . . .

The greatest cooks I know are independent souls. Cooking without cookbooks, they follow some internal thread of knowing all their own. They express a personal sensibility, often quite subtle, that is as much about how they live as it is about food: making the most with what is on hand, what the season or life offers, culling ideas from memories, and accommodating various needs of family and friends to eat well and joyfully. Raw ingredients and flavors become a kind of vocabulary.

My friend Margot Wellington is one such cook and the creator of this corn soup. Like most of her inventions, there is no written recipe for it. She gave me the gist scrawled on a napkin and left me to figure it out. The dish is typical of her cooking. Made to feed the hungry weekend horde, it was literally thrown together one day to use up some summer corn that had been in the fridge for a few days too long. Having undertaken to pare calories and fat from her cooking, for the sake of her family's health and waistlines, she used a minimum of fat in the creamy soup, while building in a maximum of flavor. A simple soup to make, it is as rich and thick as a stew, with flavors that reflect her years of living in Mexico: sweet corn, chiles, and coriander. Fresh tomato is stirred in at the last moment for contrast and added dimension.

To save on time, frozen corn can be used in place of fresh. If desired, serve with 1 tablespoon of sour cream on top.

Summer Corn and Chile Pepper Soup

6 ears fresh corn, shucked or 2 packages (10 ounces each) thawed frozen corn kernels

1 teaspoon olive oil

2 medium onions, chopped (2 cups)

2½ cups chicken stock or 2 cups canned low-sodium chicken broth mixed with ½ cup water

2 cups whole or low-fat milk

4 garlic cloves, minced

2 jalapeño or serrano chiles, seeded and minced

¾ teaspoon salt

½ teaspoon plus an optional pinch of sugar

2 medium tomatoes—peeled, seeded, and cut into medium dice

½ teaspoon balsamic vinegar

1½ ounces country ham, such as Smithfield or tasso, coarsely chopped

1½ to 2 tablespoons fresh lime juice

½ cup fresh coriander or basil, coarsely chopped

2 tablespoons snipped chives (optional)

¼ cup plus 2 tablespoons sour cream (optional)

Over a large bowl, using a thin sharp knife, slice the corn kernels from each cob; scrape the cobs lengthwise to extract any juices. Reserve the corn kernels and cobs separately.

In a large heavy saucepan, combine the olive oil and onions. Cover and cook over low heat, stirring occasionally, until the onion is translucent, about 5 minutes. Stir in the reserved corn kernels, cover, and cook for 4 minutes longer. Stir in the chicken stock, 1 cup of the milk, the gar-

lic, chiles, salt, and the ½ teaspoon sugar. Nestle the reserved cobs into the mixture. Bring to a boil, reduce the heat to moderately low, cover, and simmer until the corn is tender, 15 to 25 minutes. (Older, or winter, corn will take longer than young summer corn.)

Meanwhile, in a small bowl, toss the tomatoes with the vinegar. Stir in the pinch of sugar, if desired, to bring out the flavors. Cover and refrigerate until ready to use.

Remove the cobs from the soup and discard. Stir in the remaining 1 cup milk. Using a slotted spoon, scoop out about ¾ cup of the corn-and-onion mixture from the broth and set aside. Working in batches if necessary, transfer the soup to a food processor. Puree to a coarse consistency. Return to the saucepan and stir in the ham, lime juice, and reserved corn-and-onion mixture. *(The soup will keep refrigerated for 5 days and frozen up to 3 months.)*

To serve, heat the soup over moderate heat, stirring, until it just reaches the boiling point. Stir in the coriander. Ladle the hot soup evenly into each of 6 warm soup bowls. Mound about 2 tablespoons of the reserved diced tomato mixture into the center of each bowl and sprinkle the chives on top, if desired. If using, pass the sour cream separately.

6 Servings   161 Calories   8.5 gm Protein
5.5 gm Fat   21.8 gm Carbohydrate per Serving

Yellow Pepper and White Bean Soup with Sage

. . . .

This recipe began with the classic Italian Tuscan flavorings for white beans—garlic and sage—and evolved into a rustic soup, almost a stew, embellished with sweet bell pepper, tomato, and just a small amount of heavy cream. It is a meal in itself. The soup is extremely rich, yet has all the healthy virtues of beans, which are low in calories and high in fiber and protein. The two teaspoons per serving of heavy cream added at the end help to unify and mellow the diverse flavors but may be omitted if the added fat is a concern.

. . . .

14 ounces navy or Great Northern white beans
   (2 cups), picked over to remove any grit
1 tablespoon plus 2 teaspoons olive oil
3 yellow bell peppers, seeded and cut into ½-inch
   dice (3 cups)
1 medium onion, chopped (1 cup)
4 large garlic cloves, coarsely chopped
1 can (35 ounces) Italian peeled tomatoes, seeded
   and coarsely chopped, and their liquid
1½ cups chicken stock or canned broth
8 sage leaves, preferably fresh
¾ teaspoon salt
½ teaspoon sugar
¼ cup plus 2 tablespoons heavy cream
1 teaspoon balsamic or red wine vinegar
Freshly ground black pepper

Yellow Pepper and White Bean Soup with Sage

In a medium saucepan, soak the beans overnight in enough water to cover. Alternatively, in a medium saucepan, cover the beans with water and bring to a boil over moderately high heat. Cover, remove from the heat and let sit for 1 hour.

Drain the beans. Return to the saucepan and add cold water to cover by 2 inches. Bring to a boil, reduce the heat to a simmer, and cook until the beans are tender but not mushy, about 1 hour. Drain the beans.

In a large heavy saucepan or flameproof casserole, combine the oil, bell peppers, onion, and garlic. Cover and cook over low heat, stirring frequently, until the vegetables are soft but not brown, about 15 minutes.

Add the tomatoes and their liquid, the chicken stock, sage, salt, sugar, and cooked beans. Simmer until the soup begins to thicken and the beans are soft, 30 to 45 minutes.

Stir in the cream and vinegar. Season with black pepper to taste. *(This soup can be made ahead. Let cool, cover, and refrigerate for up to 4 days; or freeze for up to 3 months.)*

Variation: This soup also makes a sublime sauce for pasta, 351 calories per serving. For each serving, figure ½ portion (about ½ cup) of the soup per 2 ounces of dry pasta.

**8 Servings   282 Calories   13.4 gm Protein
8.0 gm Fat   41.0 gm Carbohydrate per Serving**

. . . .

Green Soup

. . . .

I'm always amazed to have made it through winter. In March, I find myself believing that the sun is never going to appear. In April my hibernating self wakes with the rest of the world, remembering the sensual side of life. In spring I start, shakily, to scrutinize my winter body from summer's point of view. I also begin to pick greens and am happy knowing that sorrel, with its incredible tartness, will be around from now until the fall. The best recipe I know for sorrel soup comes from bedtime reading of *Jane Grigson's*

Vegetable Book. In this volume, Grigson mentions her friend Margaret Costa, who discovered that adding raw sorrel puree to a potato and onion base at the last minute results in a great, simple spring soup. It tastes green and is simultaneously fresh, mellow, and acidic.

I have revised the recipe slightly to pare away some calories, and the tomato cream I've added provides a balance to the tart flavor of the sorrel. The small amount of cream also gives the illusion of the richness found in a traditional French sorrel soup (which comes close to 1000 calories of butter, egg yolks, and cream).

When served with a salad and dessert, this lively green soup makes a lovely light spring meal.

. . . .

1 teaspoon unsalted butter
1 medium onion, finely chopped (1 cup)
1 large boiling potato (8 ounces), peeled and diced
3½ cups homemade chicken stock or 1 can
    (13¾ ounces) chicken broth diluted with
    enough water to make 3½ cups
1¼ teaspoons sugar
⅛ teaspoon nutmeg
1 pound sorrel (about 4 cups), tough stems
    removed, coarsely chopped
¼ cup heavy cream
¼ teaspoon salt
½ teaspoon freshly ground pepper
2 tablespoons sour cream
½ teaspoon tomato paste
2 tablespoons chopped fresh chervil
1 tablespoon chopped fresh chives

In a heavy medium saucepan, combine the butter and onion. Cover and cook over low heat until the onion is soft but not brown, about 5 minutes.

Add the potato, stock, sugar, and nutmeg. Bring to a boil, reduce the heat, and simmer until the potato is soft, about 10 minutes.

In a food processor or blender, puree the soup in 2 batches, adding half of the sorrel with each batch. Return the soup to the saucepan and whisk in the heavy cream, salt, and pepper.

In a small bowl, whisk together the sour cream, tomato paste, and 2 teaspoons of water until creamy.

Heat the soup over low heat until hot (do not let boil). Ladle 1 cup of soup into each of 4 heated soup bowls. Swirl 1½ teaspoons of the tomato cream into the center of each serving. Sprinkle with the chopped chervil and chives and serve at once.

4 Servings   176 Calories   5.3 gm Protein
9.4 gm Fat   20.3 gm Carbohydrate per Serving

Root Vegetable Soup

. . . .

*T*his simple blend of winter root vegetables—celery root, potato, parsnip, and leek—simmered with chicken broth and thyme mysteriously yields far more than the sum of its parts. The fine puree has a velvety texture that is normally achieved only with a quantity of heavy cream. The flavor is rich and complex, with overtones of earth and spice.

. . . .

1 teaspoon olive oil
1 teaspoon unsalted butter
1 small celery root, thinly sliced (¾ cup)
1 medium yellow or red waxy potato, thinly sliced
(¾ cup)
2 small parsnips, woody core removed and thinly sliced (⅔ cup)
1 medium leek (white and tender green parts), thinly sliced (¼ cup)
2 garlic cloves, thinly sliced
1 sprig of fresh thyme or ¼ teaspoon dried
¼ teaspoon salt
¼ teaspoon sugar
3 cups homemade chicken stock or 2 cups canned broth diluted with 1 cup water
2 tablespoons minced Italian flat-leaf parsley (optional)
Freshly ground pepper
Pinch of freshly grated nutmeg

In a medium saucepan, combine the olive oil, butter, celery root, potato, parsnips, leek, garlic, thyme, salt, sugar, and ½ cup of water. Cover and simmer over moderate heat until the water is almost completely evaporated, about 15 minutes. Add the chicken stock, bring to a simmer over moderate heat, cover, and cook until the vegetables are very tender, about 15 minutes longer.

Transfer the soup to a food processor or blender and puree until perfectly smooth, about 1 minute. Return to the saucepan and bring to a simmer over moderately low heat. Add the parsley, if desired, fresh pepper to taste, and the nutmeg. Serve at once.

4 Servings   92 Calories   2.6 gm Protein
3.0 gm Fat   14.3 gm Carbohydrate per Serving

Risotto, Pasta, and Polenta

Fresh Tomato and Saffron Risotto

After Labor Day the weather often turns chilly, jarring us back to work and winter industry. But just as often it warms up again, and Indian summer arrives with its aura of subtly changing light and air. Then tomatoes—whether eaten sliced with a little basil, summer style, or cooked in hearty dishes that bespeak cooler days—are even more welcome as the bleak prospect of a tomato-less season looms.

This vividly colored risotto makes use of the last great tomatoes of summer. It combines the concentrated juices of tomatoes with rice's natural starch to produce an intense flavor and a creamy texture usually achieved only with an abundance of butter, cream, and cheese. This risotto is baked in the oven, eliminating the traditional stovetop stirring. The oil used to sauté the onion and rice is pared to a minimum, and only a little Parmesan cheese is used so as not to overpower the tomato-saffron flavor.

The presence of juicy, ripe tomatoes—charred over high heat to heighten their flavor—will easily overcome the flaws of canned chicken broth if homemade stock is not used. Be sure to dilute a canned broth with an equal amount of water to reduce its saltiness. Risotto's success depends on imported Italian arborio rice, available in specialty food markets and some supermarkets. Regular long-grain white rice will not yield the creaminess of a traditional risotto.

Fresh Tomato and Saffron Risotto

. . . .

2 pounds ripe tomatoes or 2 cans (28 ounces
   each) Italian peeled tomatoes—well drained,
   seeded, and chopped
1 tablespoon olive oil
2 small onions, chopped
2 large garlic cloves, minced
1 cup arborio rice
¾ cup dry white wine
¼ teaspoon saffron threads
1½ tablespoons tomato paste
2 cups hot chicken stock or 1 cup hot canned
   broth diluted with 1 cup water
Pinch of salt
Freshly ground pepper
½ teaspoon balsamic vinegar (optional)
2 tablespoons sour cream
½ cup (loosely packed) fresh basil leaves,
   shredded
½ cup freshly grated Parmesan cheese (about 1½
   ounces)

Preheat the oven to 350°. If using fresh tomatoes, spear one with a long-handled kitchen fork and roast it about 1 inch above a gas flame or electric burner set on high heat, turning slowly, until the skin bursts and begins to char all over. Repeat with the remaining tomatoes. When cool enough to handle, peel, core, and halve the tomatoes. Squeeze each half to extract the juices and seeds. Chop the tomatoes into ½-inch dice.

   In a heavy medium ovenproof saucepan, combine the olive oil, onions, and garlic. Cover and cook over moderately low heat until the onions are translucent, about 5 minutes. Uncover, increase the heat to moderate, and add the rice. Cook, stirring, to thoroughly coat with oil, about 1 minute. Add the tomatoes and cook, stirring, until thoroughly incorporated, about 1 minute longer. Stir in the wine, increase the heat to high, and bring to a boil. Add the saffron, tomato paste, and 1½ cups of the hot chicken stock; bring to a boil.

   Transfer the pan to the oven and bake the risotto for 10 minutes. Stir well and bake for another 5 minutes. Stir in ¼ cup of the chicken stock and bake for another 5 minutes. Stir in the remaining ¼ cup chicken stock and bake for another 5 minutes or until the risotto is creamy and the rice is tender but still firm to the bite. If the rice is still firm in the middle of the grain, add ¼ cup of water and cook for 5 minutes longer.

   Remove the risotto from the oven and season with the salt, pepper, and balsamic vinegar, if desired. Stir in the sour cream. Divide the risotto evenly among 4 warm shallow soup bowls. Sprinkle 2 tablespoons of the basil over each serving and pass the Parmesan cheese separately. Or serve the risotto in a large bowl or on a platter and top with wide shavings of fresh Parmesan cheese.

4 Servings   343 Calories   11.2 gm Protein
9.2 gm Fat   55.0 gm Carbohydrate per Serving

Risotto with Porcini and Shiitake Mushrooms

. . . .

In this recipe, intensely flavored dried porcini (or cèpes) are soaked in water to create a powerful mushroom liquor that will flavor the rice, along with red wine, sage, and shallots. Meaty shiitake mushrooms add the robust flavor and texture of fresh wild mushrooms. The result is an extremely rich, filling, and earthy risotto for the chill days of winter. Serve with a salad of bitter or peppery greens, such as arugula, radicchio, or another Italian chicory.

. . . .

1 cup boiling water
½ ounce dried porcini (cèpes) mushrooms
3 cups chicken stock or 2 cups canned broth mixed with 1 cup water
2 teaspoons unsalted butter
3 large shallots, chopped
1 garlic clove, minced
2 fresh sage leaves, chopped, or ¼ teaspoon rubbed dried sage
1 cup arborio rice
½ cup dry white wine
½ pound fresh shiitake mushrooms, sliced
½ cup freshly grated Parmesan cheese
Freshly ground pepper

In a small bowl, pour the boiling water over the dried mushrooms. Let soak for 30 minutes. Remove the mushrooms with a slotted spoon, rinse, and drain well. Chop the mushrooms coarsely and set aside. Strain the mushroom liquid through a fine-mesh sieve or a triple layer of cheesecloth and set aside.

In a medium saucepan, bring the stock to a boil over high heat; lower the heat to maintain a simmer until ready to use.

In a large heavy saucepan, melt the butter over moderate heat. Add the shallots, garlic, and sage and cook, stirring occasionally, until the shallots are translucent. Add the rice and cook, stirring constantly, until lightly toasted and coated with the oil, about 5 minutes. Do not allow the rice to brown.

Add the wine and cook, stirring constantly, until the wine is absorbed, about 3 minutes. Stir in the fresh mushrooms, the reserved chopped mushrooms, the mushroom liquid, and ½ cup of the simmering chicken stock. Simmer, stirring frequently, until the liquid is almost absorbed, 3 to 5 minutes. Continue adding the stock, about ¾ cup at a time or enough to just cover the rice, and cooking, stirring frequently, until the rice is tender but still firm to the bite and the mixture is creamy but not soupy, about 20 minutes.

Remove the saucepan from the heat and stir in ¼ cup of the Parmesan cheese and pepper to taste. Serve immediately, passing the remaining Parmesan on the side.

4 servings   305 Calories   11.8 gm Protein
7.3 gm Fat   48.0 gm Carbohydrate per Serving

Pasta with Swiss Chard, Cognac, and Cream

. . . .

Sophisticated in its simplicity, this pasta is reminiscent of the wholesome, elegant pastas I have eaten many times in Italy. The pasta is laced with Swiss chard greens that have been stewed with shallots, Cognac, cream, and a touch of walnut oil. It is a delicious example of the profound effect a little cream has on simple food—food that falls within the boundaries of a low-calorie meal. Harmonized with the light glaze of cream, the flavors meld to create a silky, rich pasta. Although there is only a small amount of cream in this recipe—one tablespoon per serving—I set out to find a way to replace it. Every attempt—milk lightly thickened with flour, pureed ricotta cheese, or vegetables—obscured the flavors and muddled the texture. I am not sure why. It was the cream in my original recipe that gave this dish its enormous complexity and elegance. Nothing else would do. When this pasta is served with dishes that have little added fat, such as Prosciutto with Figs and Raspberries as an appetizer and the Espresso Sorbet for dessert, the overall fat in the menu is negligible.

Pasta with Swiss Chard, Cognac, and Cream

. . . .

4 pounds Swiss chard, trimmed of stems—about
  2 pounds of leaves (see Note)
1½ teaspoons olive oil
1 cup finely chopped shallots (about 6 large)
¼ cup Cognac or Armagnac
¼ cup milk
¼ cup heavy cream
1 tablespoon walnut oil
¼ teaspoon salt
Freshly ground pepper
½ pound dried pasta, such as orecchiette or
  fettuccine

Rinse the chard leaves in several changes of cold water to remove every trace of grit. Drain the leaves well and set aside.

In a large flameproof casserole, combine the olive oil and shallots. Cover and cook over moderately low heat, stirring occasionally, until the shallots are softened, about 5 minutes. Uncover and continue cooking until the shallots are translucent, 1 to 2 minutes. Increase the heat to high and add the Cognac. Boil to cook off the alcohol, about 1 minute.

Add the milk and chard leaves to the casserole. Cover and steam over moderately low heat until the leaves begin to wilt, about 3 minutes. With a large kitchen fork, turn the chard leaves so that the uncooked leaves are on the bottom and the wilted leaves are on top. Cover and continue cooking, turning and stirring occasionally, until the chard is completely wilted, about 8 minutes longer. Uncover, increase the heat to moderately high, and boil to reduce the cooking liquid until rich tasting, about 3 minutes. *(The chard can be prepared to this point up to 3 hours ahead and refrigerated; reheat in the casserole before proceeding.)*

Stir in the cream, walnut oil, salt, and lots of pepper. Keep warm.

Cook the pasta in a large pot of boiling water until tender but firm, about 10 minutes. Drain well. Add the pasta to the chard in the casserole and toss over moderate heat until combined and warmed through.

Note: *Reserve the Swiss chard stems for a later use. Chard stems have a delicious flavor and a texture similar to celery; they can be steamed or sautéed.*

4 Servings   387 Calories   13.0 gm Protein
12.3 gm Fat   59.0 gm Carbohydrate per Serving

Shell Pasta with Stir-Fried Radicchio

Radicchio, the preeminent ruby-red member of the chicory family, has somewhat tough leaves and a markedly bitter flavor. It is usually used as an addition to mixed salads, or on its own, slivered and liberally dressed with olive oil and vinegar. Its assertive flavor takes well to cooking, particularly on the grill, where its bitterness mellows with heat and smoke. In this recipe, stir-frying the coarsely cut leaves until nearly wilted concentrates the sugars in the leaves, caramelizing them slightly and producing a complex sweet, smoky flavor. Garlic, pieces of smoked prosciutto, and a firm-textured pasta further attenuate the radicchio's bitterness and combine to make an unusually earthy and satisfying meal.

The radicchio itself has few calories. Smoked prosciutto, thinly sliced and chopped, contributes the protein element in the meal. If desired, sprinkle a tablespoon of freshly grated Parmesan cheese over a serving.

4 ounces imported dry shell or orecchiette pasta
1 tablespoon extra-virgin olive oil
8 garlic cloves—6 thinly slivered, 2 minced
¾ pound radicchio (2 medium heads), cored and sliced into 1-inch pieces
4 very thin slices of smoked prosciutto,* or dry-cured country ham, sliced into ½-inch strips (1 ounce total)
Freshly ground pepper
Pinch of salt
*Available in Italian or specialty food markets

Bring a medium saucepan of lightly salted water to a boil. Add the pasta to the boiling water and cook until tender but still firm, 8 to 10 minutes.

Meanwhile in a wok or a large heavy skillet, heat the oil over moderate heat. Add the slivered garlic and cook, stirring occasionally, until soft and just turning golden. Using a spoon, remove half the garlic and oil to a small bowl and set aside.

Add the radicchio to the wok and stir-fry, tossing continually, over moderate heat, until mostly wilted with some pinkish leaves remaining, about 3 minutes. Add the prosciutto, the minced garlic, and plenty of pepper; stir-fry for 30 seconds longer. Remove from the heat.

Divide the radicchio evenly between two plates, spreading it out slightly into a circle. Drain the pasta and toss with the reserved garlic oil, the salt, and more pepper to taste. Spoon half the pasta over each mound of radicchio. Serve at once.

2 Servings   326 Calories   12.7 gm Protein
9.3 gm Fat   48.3 gm Carbohydrate per Serving

Homemade Pasta

An inimitable quality of pasta that is made at home and cooked soon after is lacking in commercial brands. I suppose one could chalk it up to the mysterious alchemy of pasta making: the eggs and olive oil have a distinct though subtle presence, and there is a satisfying suppleness to the texture. Homemade pasta tastes better and different.

Pasta is quite easy to make if you use a hand-crank pasta machine to roll and cut the dough. My attempts at rolling pasta dough by hand, despite the optimistic directions of cookbooks, have produced only rather uneven, heavy pasta, which was charming by virtue of its extraordinary homeliness. The standard manual pasta machine is a worthwhile investment. It is so simple to use that making delicious pasta can become more of an everyday event than a valiant effort.

Once the dough is rolled, it can be cut into a variety of shapes. The pasta machine will cut it into linguine or fettuccine. Using a long chef's knife or pizza cutter, the dough may be cut into pappardelle (one-inch-wide strips), squares, or triangles of any size.

I adore saffron pasta and used to buy it as an occasional indulgence at a local gourmet store for $12.00 a pound. I now make my own at a fraction of the cost. See the Variation for instructions.

Making Saffron Pasta ➤

This pasta can stand on its own, with only the simplest of treatments—a Flavored Oil perhaps, plenty of fresh pepper, and some parmigiano-reggiano, or Cold Fresh Tomato Sauce—to make a delightful meal. As an accompaniment, these fresh noodles lend a hearty elegance to a simple ragout or braise, such as the Ragout of Duck Legs or Coq au Vin.

Homemade Pasta

1 cup plus ¼ cup unbleached all-purpose flour
2 eggs, at room temperature
½ teaspoon extra-virgin olive oil
⅛ teaspoon salt

Place the 1 cup of flour in a mound on a work surface. Make a well in the center of the flour so that the sides are about 1½ inches high. Add the eggs, olive oil, and salt to the well. Using a fork, beat the eggs lightly, gradually incorporating some flour from the inner rim a little at a time. Work the mixture with the fork until it forms a wet paste. Using a pastry scraper, scrape up the dough from the work surface and mash it together.

Sprinkle the remaining flour, a teaspoon at a time, over the dough to keep it from sticking and knead the dough until smooth and elastic, about 8 minutes. The dough will feel ever so slightly sticky. If the dough feels quite moist and sticky when pressed with a finger, knead a little more flour into the dough. Divide the dough into 4 sections and pat into ½-inch-thick disks. Wrap each in plastic wrap until ready to use.

Set the rollers of the pasta machine to the widest position. Feed 1 dough ball through the machine. Fold the dough into thirds and lightly flour the outside. Pass it through the machine 3 more times. Set the rollers to the next narrower setting. Pass the dough through the rollers. Repeat, moving the rollers 1 setting closer each time, until the pasta is very thin (one of the last 2 settings). Lay the ribbon of dough on kitchen towels laid out on the counter to dry for about 5 minutes. Repeat with the remaining dough balls.

The pasta is ready to cut when it is pliant but not so wet that it will stick to itself. If the pasta sheets appear to be drying too soon before you want to cut them, cover them with plastic wrap. Pass the sheets of pasta through the desired cutter on the pasta machine. Or cut the dough into desired shapes with a long chef's knife. Separate the cut noodles and lay them out on kitchen towels to dry for a few minutes or up to 3 hours before cooking. Or you can dry them completely to cook at another time. To dry fettucine or linguine, lay about 10 strands at a time parallel to each other and roll them into nests. Pasta that is thoroughly dried does not need to be refrigerated. Store in plastic bags or an airtight container.

Cook the pasta in plenty of salted boiling water. Fresh pasta takes literally only seconds to cook, so watch it carefully. Dried pasta takes a little longer.

Variation: Saffron Pasta. Add ¼ teaspoon ground saffron along with the eggs and olive oil. If you are using saffron threads, crush them in a mortar before measuring.

Makes About ¾ Pound Pasta or 4 Servings
184 Calories   7.1 gm Protein   3.4 gm Fat
30.0 gm Carbohydrate per Serving

Cold Spicy Sesame Noodles

. . . .

These sesame noodles, seasoned with an aromatic five-flavored sesame oil, have a fresher, more complex flavor than the sesame-paste-dressed noodles commonly available in Chinese restaurants. They are a snap to prepare once the flavored oil, which is the base for the dressing, is ready. Because the oil is so aromatic, only a small amount is necessary to season the noodles, keeping calories to a minimum. The noodles are an excellent accompaniment to Pepper and Salt Shrimp, Clove-and-Pepper-Cured Roast Pork, or grilled tuna. The noodles can also be quickly transformed into a satisfying, portable lunch with the addition of three ounces of cooked shrimp for an additional 100 calories.

. . . .

5 medium scallions, 4 thinly sliced
4 quarter-size slices of fresh ginger
1½ teaspoons Szechuan peppercorns
½ cup Oriental sesame oil
2 tablespoons peanut oil
½ teaspoon crushed hot red pepper
½ pound fresh Chinese or Italian noodles, ¹⁄₁₆ to ⅛ inch thick
1 tablespoon plus 2 teaspoons low-sodium soy sauce
1 tablespoon plus 2 teaspoons balsamic vinegar
½ teaspoon salt
½ teaspoon sugar
½ cup chopped fresh coriander
Scallion and red bell pepper slivers, for garnish

Using the side of a large knife, lightly crush the unsliced scallion and then slice into 1-inch pieces. Smash the ginger slices and quarter them. Combine the scallion, ginger, and Szechuan peppercorns in a bowl and set aside.

In a small heavy saucepan, heat the sesame and peanut oils over moderate heat. To test whether the oil is hot enough, drop a pinch of hot red pepper into the oil; the pepper should sizzle, and the oil should form a small ring of tiny bubbles.

Reduce the heat to moderately low and add all the hot red pepper. Cook for 5 seconds, then remove from the heat. Stir in the scallion, ginger, and peppercorn mixture. Cover the pan loosely with aluminum foil and set aside the five-flavored oil to steep for at least 1 hour or, preferably, overnight. Strain the oil into a clean jar and set aside. *(The five-flavored oil will keep refrigerated for several months.)*

In a medium saucepan of boiling, lightly salted water, cook the noodles until tender but still firm to the bite, 1 to 2 minutes. With a slotted spoon or a strainer, transfer the noodles to a bowl of cold water. Drain and rinse under cold water until the noodles are completely cool. Drain well.

In a medium bowl, combine the soy sauce, vinegar, salt, sugar, and 2 tablespoons of the reserved five-flavored oil. Add the cooked noodles, the remaining 4 sliced scallions, and the coriander; toss until well combined. Cover and refrigerate at least 1 hour before serving. Garnish with the scallion and red bell pepper slivers. *(The dressed sesame noodles will keep for up to 3 days.)*

4 Servings   293 Calories   6.9 gm Protein
14.9 gm Fat   33.0 gm Carbohydrate per Serving

Basic Polenta

Polenta, in an infinite array of dishes, is an essential element in the cuisine of Italy's Friuli region and neighboring Veneto. In Italian literature, there are many poetic descriptions of the rite of polenta-making in country kitchens: the tireless stirring of the cornmeal mush in an unlined copper kettle over a wood fire, the moment of joy when it was poured, steaming, onto a poplar or beechwood board, placed in the center of the table, and eaten then and there, or set aside to cool and slice for future preparations.

Polenta might seem to be the antithesis of a low-calorie food since it quite naturally loves butter and cheese, two high-fat nemeses of dieters. However, unadorned polenta is actually quite low in calories. It is extremely filling and nutritious as well. In my experiments with it, I found it actually does not take huge quantities of cheese or butter to produce wonderfully satisfying polenta dishes, which range from breakfast to main-course to side dishes.

The following recipe is a basic, foolproof method for making polenta that can be eaten as is or as a thick mush simply adorned with olive oil, Parmesan cheese, and fresh pepper or as a warming breakfast with ricotta cheese. The polenta can be molded and cooled for any of the recipe variations that follow. While traditional polenta recipes call for slowly sprinkling the cornmeal into boiling water to avoid lumping, my unorthodox method of mixing the cornmeal into cold water before cooking insures lumpless polenta without painstaking effort. There are two types of polenta flour, one fine-grained, the other coarse. I recommend using coarsely milled cornmeal, available in Italian specialty stores and gourmet markets, since it has a far more interesting texture and robust flavor than the fine does.

1 cup yellow cornmeal, preferably coarsely milled
1 teaspoon salt

In a heavy, medium saucepan, combine the corn-meal, salt, and 3½ cups of cold water. Bring to a boil over high heat, stirring constantly with a wooden spoon. Reduce the heat to moderately high and cook, stirring constantly to prevent scorching, until the polenta pulls away from the bottom of the pan, about 10 minutes. Serve the polenta piping hot or mold and chill as directed in the following recipes.

Variations: Garlic Polenta. Adding garlic to the cooking water adds a subtle depth of flavor to polenta that is wonderful in savory preparations. Stir in 3 cloves of finely minced garlic to the polenta and water before you bring it to a boil.

Polenta with Extra-Virgin Olive Oil and Parmesan, 159 calories per serving. For my money, the simplest and best way to embellish a bowl of hot polenta is with olive oil or butter, freshly grated Parmesan cheese, and plenty of fresh pepper. It takes only a few minutes to make and is just the right comforting meal in the midst of a demanding day. Divide the hot polenta evenly into 4 warm shallow soup bowls. Sprinkle 1½ teaspoons olive oil, 2½ tablespoons Parmesan cheese, and a generous amount of fresh pepper over each portion. Serve at once.

4 Servings   126 Calories   3.0 gm Protein
.6 gm Fat   26.8 gm Carbohydrate per Serving

Roasted Polenta

*I*n northern Italy, pan-fried or grilled slabs of polenta are the traditional accompaniments for roasted game birds and ragouts, such as the Wild Mushroom Ragout. In this recipe, the polenta is spread into a pan and cooled, cut into thin triangles, brushed lightly with olive oil, and baked at high heat in a heavy pan. The polenta, scented with garlic and rosemary, becomes crisp on the outside, still soft and melting on the inside.

Basic or Garlic Polenta (page 90)
2 teaspoons extra-virgin olive oil
2 garlic cloves, sliced
4 sprigs of fresh rosemary or 1 tablespoon dried
Salt and freshly ground pepper

Turn out the polenta onto a nonstick baking sheet and pat into a ½-inch-thick rectangle or square. Refrigerate to cool and firm up for about 30 minutes.

Preheat the oven to 500°. In a small bowl, combine the olive oil and garlic. Set aside to macerate for at least 15 minutes.

Slice the polenta into 4 equal rectangles or squares. Slice each piece diagonally into 4 equal triangles. Lightly brush the polenta triangles on each side with the garlic oil. Arrange on a heavy baking sheet or in 2 large heavy skillets (the heavier the utensil, the better the bottom will crisp). Pull the leaves off the sprigs of rosemary and sprinkle them over the polenta, pushing a few leaves underneath each slice. Season lightly with salt. Bake for 20 minutes in the top part of the oven. Season the polenta slices generously with pepper before serving.

4 Servings   150 Calories   3.0 gm Protein
3.0 gm Fat   27.6 gm Carbohydrate per Serving

Polenta Cakes with Gorgonzola and Fontina

. . . .

*O*nce cooled, polenta has a gelatinous consistency that offers many possibilities for molding or cutting into shapes that hold up well to frying, grilling, or baking. In this recipe, the polenta is molded into individual servings and cooled. It is then sliced horizontally, layered with a classic combination of Fontina and Gorgonzola cheeses, and baked. Although the cheeses are high in fat, they have so much flavor that only a small amount is required.

. . . .

Garlic Polenta (page 91)
¼ pound Italian Fontina cheese, shredded
2 ounces Gorgonzola cheese, crumbled
1½ teaspoons olive oil
2 teaspoons freshly grated Parmesan cheese
Freshly ground pepper
4 large sprigs of fresh basil, left whole or
chopped

Spoon ¼ cup of the polenta into each of four 1-cup soufflé dishes (about 4 inches in diameter). Pressing down with a knife to deflate any air pockets, smooth the surfaces. Set aside to cool and firm up for about 30 minutes. Then refrigerate, covered, for at least 2 hours. *(The recipe can be prepared to this point up to 2 days ahead.)*

Preheat the oven to 425°. Run a knife around the insides of the soufflé dishes and then invert to unmold the polenta cakes. If the cakes are wet, blot dry with paper towels. With a thin sharp knife, slice each cake horizontally into thirds. Combine the Fontina and Gorgonzola cheeses in a small bowl.

Brush a baking sheet with ¾ teaspoon of the olive oil. Arrange the bottom layers of the polenta cakes on the sheet and cover them with ½ of the Fontina and gorgonzola cheeses. Season generously with pepper. Repeat with the second layer of the polenta cakes, the other ½ of the Fontina and

Gorgonzola, and additional pepper. Top with the remaining polenta layers. Brush the tops with the remaining ¾ teaspoon olive oil.

Bake the assembled cakes for 12 to 15 minutes, until heated through and the cheese is melted. Top each of the cakes with ½ teaspoon of the Parmesan cheese and some more pepper and bake for about 1 minute longer, until the Parmesan is melted. Using a spatula, transfer the cakes to a warm serving platter or 4 warm dinner plates and garnish with the basil.

Variation: Polenta Cakes with Parmesan and Sage, 257 calories per serving. Substitute ¾ cup freshly grated Parmesan cheese for the Fontina and Gorgonzola and increase the amount of olive oil to 2½ teaspoons. Before beginning, combine the olive oil and 3 fresh sage leaves or ½ teaspoon ground sage in a small skillet. Cook over moderate heat until the sage is fragrant, about 2 minutes. Do not allow it to burn. Discard the whole sage leaves. When the polenta is ready to be layered, brush the baking sheet with ½ teaspoon of the sage oil. Brush each layer of polenta with a little olive oil. Then proceed as directed, layering with the Parmesan cheese and pepper.

4 Servings   309 Calories   13.7gm Protein
15.4 gm Fat   28.3 gm Carbohydrate per Serving

Wild Mushroom Ragout with Roasted Polenta

. . . .

There are certain foods that hold more mystery and magic than others, no matter how many times I eat them. Some are fiercely expensive, like truffles, some freely scavenged, like wild mushrooms. Perhaps their appeal has to do with the difficulty of obtaining them or the fact that they are perishable. They are always themselves, always somehow remaining close to their source—they taste wild. Their flavors and effect are profound. Is it mere coincidence that they are, for all that wild flavor, low in calories?

Increasingly, mushrooms that once could be found only in the wild are now being cultivated and can be found year-round in supermarkets, affording those of us who can't forage for our mushrooms the opportunity to cook with them. Even in their cultivated form, these mushrooms have an intense woodsy flavor that is a far cry from that of the ubiquitous button mushroom.

This wild mushroom ragout has the earthy flavors and rusticity of a rich game stew. Paired with crisp roasted polenta, it makes a sublime, warming meal for fall or winter.

The ragout is also a wonderful sauce for pasta. Figure two ounces of dried pasta per person at 210 calories, for a total of 485 calories.

. . . .

4 sun-dried tomato halves (see Note)
½ ounce dried wild mushrooms, such as porcini
   (cèpes), or morels
½ cup boiling water
1 pound fresh wild mushrooms, in any
   combination, such as cremini, morels, oyster,
   porcini (cèpes), or shiitake (golden oak)
1½ teaspoons olive oil
2 medium onions, chopped
3 garlic cloves, quartered
½ cup dry red wine
2 sprigs of fresh thyme or ¼ teaspoon dried
1 can (28 ounces) Italian peeled tomatoes—
   seeded and chopped—and their liquid
½ teaspoon salt
1 teaspoon sugar
Freshly ground pepper
Roasted Polenta (page 92)

In a small bowl, combine the sun-dried tomatoes, dried mushrooms, and boiling water, cover,
and set aside to steep for at least 15 minutes.
Using a slotted spoon, transfer the sun-dried tomatoes and dried mushrooms to a strainer. Rinse
under cool water to remove any grit. Press with
the back of the spoon to squeeze out any excess
water; chop coarsely. Set aside the chopped sun-
dried tomatoes and mushrooms and their soaking
liquid separately.

Pick over the fresh mushrooms, wiping off any
grit with a damp paper towel. Trim off the tough
ends. Cut the larger mushrooms ¼ inch thick;
leave the smaller ones (less than 1 inch) whole.
Set aside.

In a medium saucepan, combine the olive oil,
onions, and garlic. Cover and cook over moderate
heat until the onions begin to wilt, about 3 minutes. Uncover and cook until the onions are just
beginning to brown, about 2 minutes longer.

Without disturbing the sediment in the bottom of the bowl of mushroom liquid, spoon 5
tablespoons of the reserved liquid into the saucepan. Add the red wine and thyme and bring to a
boil. Boil for 1 minute, then add the reserved
fresh mushrooms. Stir to coat with the wine and
cook over moderate heat for 1 minute. Stir in the
tomatoes and their liquid, the chopped sun-dried
tomatoes and dried mushrooms, the salt, and the
sugar. Cover and simmer, stirring occasionally
and breaking up the tomatoes with the back of a
spoon, until the mushrooms are tender and the
ragout has thickened, 15 to 20 minutes. Season
generously with pepper. (*The ragout can be made
up to 4 days ahead; cover and refrigerate. If it
thickens too much, add a little red wine and boil for
1 minute to cook off the alcohol before serving.*)

Divide the ragout evenly among 4 warm shallow soup bowls. Arrange 1 portion of Roasted
Polenta on top of each serving. Serve at once.

Note: *If you can find only sun-dried tomatoes
packed in oil, simply rinse in hot water and then
proceed.*

4 Servings   275 Calories   8.6 gm Protein
5.9 gm Fat   50.8 Carbohydrate per Serving

Breakfast Polenta with Fresh Ricotta

. . . .

Polenta makes a delicious, warming, and highly nutritious breakfast. In this recipe, the polenta is topped with fresh ricotta cheese and drizzled with honey or maple syrup. The ricotta melts over the polenta, lending an extraordinary creaminess and added protein. Using a genuine whole milk fresh ricotta, available at Italian specialty and gourmet markets, is well worth the few extra calories. Part-skim ricotta can be used at a savings of 18 calories per serving and an attendant loss of richness.

. . . .

⅔ cup yellow cornmeal, preferably coarsely milled
½ teaspoon salt
¾ cup fresh ricotta cheese
1 tablespoon plus 1 teaspoon honey or maple syrup

In a heavy medium saucepan, combine the cornmeal, salt, and 2½ cups of cold water. Bring to a boil over high heat, stirring constantly with a wooden spoon. Reduce the heat to moderately high and cook, stirring constantly to prevent scorching, until the polenta pulls away from the bottom of the pan, about 10 minutes. Spoon ½ cup of the polenta into each of 4 warm shallow soup bowls. Spoon 3 tablespoons of the ricotta cheese over each portion and drizzle 1 teaspoon honey on top of each. Serve at once.

4 Servings   196 Calories   7.4 gm Protein
6.4 gm Fat   27.3 gm Carbohydrate per Serving

Fish and Shellfish

Grilled Red Snapper
with Pancetta and Herbs

. . . .

In this recipe a whole red snapper is stuffed with herbs and barded with pancetta, an Italian unsmoked bacon. Grilled over a wood fire, the herbs char slightly and perfume the fish, and the peppery pancetta bastes and protects the fish. The result is moist, succulent flesh with a crisp skin.

This method also works well when the fish is cooked under a broiler. It is one of my favorite ways to grill whole fish, especially in a city apartment, for it imparts an earthy flavor and texture that reminds me of the food of the Greek islands. Other white-fleshed fish of similar size, such as black bass or porgy, can replace the snapper.

. . . .

1 whole red snapper, about 2½-pounds (or 2 smaller fish, 1¼ pounds each), cleaned and scaled, head intact
½ teaspoon olive oil
¾ teaspoon coarse (kosher) salt
¾ teaspoon freshly ground pepper
8 imported bay leaves
4 sprigs of fresh rosemary
4 sprigs of fresh thyme
1½ ounces pancetta or bacon, cut into 4 thin slices

Rub the fish all over with the olive oil. Combine the salt and pepper and season the snapper, inside and out. Stuff 4 of the bay leaves and the rosemary and thyme sprigs into the cavity of the fish (2 bay leaves and 2 rosemary and thyme sprigs for each smaller fish).

Lay the fish flat on a work surface. Place 2 more bay leaves end to end along the length of the fish (1 each for smaller fish). Lay 2 overlapping slices of the pancetta on top of the bay leaves across the thickest part of the fish, leaving the tail and head exposed (use 1 slice of pancetta

for each of the smaller fish). Secure the pancetta with one hand and turn the fish over. Repeat the layering with the remaining 2 bay leaves and pancetta slices. Tie several bands of kitchen string snugly around the fish to secure the pancetta. *(The fish can be prepared to this point up to 4 hours before grilling. Cover with plastic wrap and refrigerate.)*

Light a wood or charcoal fire 30 to 40 minutes before grilling or preheat the broiler 15 minutes in advance. When the fire or broiler is hot, place the fish on a lightly oiled grill rack. (Alternatively, the fish can be sandwiched between two oiled grids of a grilling basket.) Grill the fish about 6 inches from the heat for 12 to 15 minutes per side for the larger fish, 8 to 10 minutes per side for the smaller fish. (The length of grilling time may vary depending on the heat of the fire.) The pancetta and the fish skin should be crisp and browned but not charred, and a fork inserted into the thickest part of the flesh should not meet with resistance until it hits the bone. If either the pancetta or fish skin begins to burn, move the rack farther from the heat source.

To serve, remove and discard the string. Discard the bay leaves. Cut the fish from the bone and serve warm or at room temperature.

Variation: A variation of this method also works well with fish steaks cut from a large fish, such as tuna, 214 calories per serving. Since fish steaks are best eaten rare or medium rare like a beef steak, you will not need the pancetta to keep them moist. As the fish cooks, the herbs tied to the steaks will smoke and flavor the flesh.

You will need 1¼ pounds of fish cut into two 1-inch-thick steaks. Place 2 sprigs each of rosemary and thyme and 1 bay leaf on each side of the steaks; secure with kitchen string as directed above. Brush each steak with ½ teaspoon olive oil. Grill the steaks for about 3 to 4 minutes, until the first side is seared, then turn the steaks and cook for 2 to 3 minutes longer. Transfer the steaks to a cutting board. Cut the string and discard. Using a thin, sharp knife, slice the fish ⅛ to ¼ inch thick and divide evenly among 4 plates.

**4 Servings   207 Calories   37.2 gm Protein
4.5 gm Fat   2.5 gm Carbohydrate per Serving**

Red Snapper Baked in Cider
with Mussels and Garlic Croutons

· ·

This recipe came about during a trip to Seattle's Pike Place Market. Like pieces of a puzzle, ideas linked together as I wandered among the high stalls of fresh produce and the tanks of live seafood. The main inspiration for this dish came when I found the locally made dry cider. It would become the poaching liquid for a mild fish fillet in a takeoff on the Normandy classic of sole poached in cider. I bought mussels to give flavor to the broth, in lieu of a fish fumet, as well as to provide a low-calorie visual and textural counterpoint. Tarragon and shallot temper the fruitiness of the cider. Garlic-brushed slices of baguette softened by the broth lend a rustic flavor to the dish.

The relative sweetness of hard cider varies and will make a considerable difference in cooking. I originally tested this with a Seattle microbrewery's very dry hard cider ale, which was like a pale ale or very dry Champagne with apple overtones. Its alcohol content was comparable to that of a dry white wine, about 11 to 13 percent. There are several varieties of dry hard cider with this alcohol content available at liquor stores, many of them American made. Some of the more commonly available French hard ciders, such as Purpom, have a much lower alcoholic content and are too sweet on their own, but mixing them half and half with dry white wine will cut the sweetness while retaining the apple flavor.

If you cannot find red snapper, fillets of farm-raised striped bass or halibut work equally well. The addition of one and a half teaspoons of heavy cream per serving lends richness—and 26 calories—to the sauce. However, if you wish to omit the cream entirely, the unadorned broth is still delicious.

· ·

½ cup finely chopped tart green apple
3 tablespoons minced shallots
2 teaspoons minced fresh tarragon (optional)
4 red snapper or halibut fillets (5 ounces each)
2 cups very dry hard cider (11 to 12 percent alcohol) or 1 cup hard cider plus 1 cup dry white wine
32 medium mussels (about 1½ pounds), scrubbed and debearded
2 ounces thin baguette, sliced ¼ inch thick
1 teaspoon olive oil
1 garlic clove, halved
¼ teaspoon salt
2 tablespoons heavy cream
2 tablespoons minced Italian flat-leaf parsley
1 tablespoon plus 1 teaspoon minced fresh basil or parsley
Freshly ground pepper

Preheat the oven to 425°. Scatter the apple, shallots, and tarragon, if desired, over the bottom of an 8-inch-square nonreactive baking dish. Arrange the fish fillets in the pan and pour the cider over them. Bake for 12 minutes, until fork tender.

Using a spatula, transfer the fillets to a plate and cover to keep warm. Strain the cooking liquid into a saucepan large enough to hold the mussels and bring to a boil over moderately high heat. Add the mussels and cover. Cook, shaking the pan occasionally, until the mussels open, about 4 minutes.

Meanwhile, arrange the bread slices on a baking sheet and brush the tops with the olive oil. Toast the bread in the oven for 2 to 3 minutes, until browned. Rub each slice lightly with the garlic and sprinkle the salt on top.

To serve, place one fish fillet in each of 4 soup plates. Arrange an equal number of mussels over each serving, along with 2 or 3 garlic croutons. Stir the cream, parsley, basil, and pepper to taste into the hot mussel broth and pour it over the fish. Serve at once.

4 Servings   282 Calories   36.9 gm Protein
7.3 gm Fat   14.7 gm Carbohydrate per Serving

Smoked Salmon Tartare

The idea for this very simple and surprising recipe came from chef Scot Carlsberg in Seattle, Washington, who is constantly experimenting with the Pacific Northwest's bounty. At one dinner he served a julienne of fresh marlin, caught that morning, dressed with extra-virgin olive oil and minced fresh herbs. The accompanying elements enhanced the sweet sea flavors of the marlin.

A wonderful tartare is made with smoked salmon; the dressing softens the smokiness and lends an appealing freshness to the cured fish. Although most of us do not have access to fresh marlin, salmon, tuna, and swordfish work equally well if they are of impeccably fresh sushi quality. Since tuna, swordfish, and smoked or fresh salmon contain less than 50 calories per ounce, the delicate, rich tartare is extremely low in calories and fat. It may be served on toast with cocktails as a first course or as a light lunch accompanied by a salad.

½ pound smoked salmon or fresh salmon, tuna, or swordfish
1 tablespoon extra-virgin olive oil
3 tablespoons minced chives
1 tablespoon plus 1 teaspoon fresh purple or green basil leaves, cut into chiffonade
1 tablespoon fresh chervil leaves (optional)
Freshly ground pepper
4 thin lime wedges

Slice the fish into small dice, about ¼ inch or smaller. Drizzle the olive oil and sprinkle half of the chives, basil, and chervil, if desired, over the fish. Season with 3 or 4 grinds of pepper and toss lightly to coat.

Divide the fish evenly among 4 salad plates and arrange in a mound in the center of each plate. Scatter the remaining chives, basil, and chervil on top, letting some fall onto the plate. Season with more pepper to taste and garnish with the lime wedges.

4 Servings   99 Calories   10.5 gm Protein
6.0 gm Fat   .7 gm Carbohydrate per Serving

Divine Inspiration
Pan-Smoked Salmon

. . . .

I am constantly trying to come up with ways to cook like an outdoors person—indoors. In a tiny tenement apartment, I once figured out a way to cure my own hams of pork and duck breasts (see Pork Loin Prosciutto and Goose or Wild Duck Prosciutto). My latest venture has been to make the flavors of wood-smoked fish accessible to apartment dwellers who have no access to a grill or a fireplace.

I don't know where it occurred to me that one could cook over smoke in a frying pan. My first attempt came about in seeking the extraordinarily satisfying pleasure of grilled bread, the perfect accompaniment to many hearty dishes (see Pan-Grilled Bread). It was when I turned my attention to applying the technique to salmon that the really dazzling effects began.

The method is simple. Wood chips or other smoking media are added to a hot cast-iron skillet, which can stand prolonged high heat. The salmon is placed over the chips on a rack. The pan is covered, and the fish cooks from the intense heat—the fat of the flesh basting, as it were, from the inside. The result is the most succulent salmon I have ever eaten. The flavor, enhanced by the smoke, is sweet and pure. Since only a small amount of wood chips is used, there is no need for any special ventilation procedure. One's apartment simply takes on the pleasing smell of wood smoke.

There are many woods commercially available for smoking or grilling. Mesquite chips are, at least during warmer months and barbecue season, readily available in supermarkets. Other aromatic grilling woods, such as grapevine and apple, can be bought at gourmet markets or through the mail. Grapevine produces a lovely mild smoke. I have bought rustic grapevine wreaths for a few dollars at florists and even supermarkets and then broken off pieces to smoke when needed. I have found that the flavors from hickory and sassafras, however, are too strong for the delicate salmon.

To cope with the unlikely possibility that a wood might not be available, I experimented with burning everything I could think of in an attempt to find a suitable alternate source of smoke. I tried cinnamon sticks and other dried spices, fresh herbs, and fruit peels, as well as dried fruits and tomatoes. A sudden inspiration made me try dried ancho chiles, on the hunch that their sweet flavor might translate well in smoke. The flavor imparted by this smoke surpasses even the fruitwoods for subtlety and deliciousness, lending a mild hint of sweet paprika to the salmon. (Hot chile peppers, on the other hand, produce an acrid smoke that will drive you out of the house.) Ancho chiles can be bought in the Mexican food section of most supermarkets as well as in Latin American markets. They last indefinitely and so can always be kept on hand.

From a diet and health perspective, this method of pan smoking adds only negligible amounts of salt, sugar, and oil to the salmon. The fish stands on its own with no need for sauces of any kind. Pan smoking produces a smoked fish, delicious hot or cold, without any nitrites.

This recipe serves four, with a four-ounce salmon fillet per person. Using the same pan, you can easily double the recipe to serve eight. Simply buy standard eight-ounce salmon steaks and cook them just about two minutes longer than the fillets. One steak will serve two people and should be divided after the steaks are smoked. Double the sugar, salt, and pepper. The amount of smoking medium remains the same regardless of the quantity of fish.

Divine Inspiration Pan-Smoked Salmon

2 teaspoons sugar
1 teaspoon coarse (kosher) salt
1 teaspoon freshly ground pepper
4 salmon fillets (4 ounces each)
Scant ½ tablespoon wood chips, or a 1-by-¼-inch chunk of wood, or 1 dried ancho chile
½ teaspoon olive oil

In a small bowl, combine the sugar, salt, and pepper. Place the salmon fillets on a plate and sprinkle ½ teaspoon of the mixture evenly on one side of each fillet. Turn the fillets over and sprinkle another ½ teaspoon of the mixture on the other side of each fillet. Cover with plastic wrap and refrigerate for at least 1 and up to 4 hours until ready to smoke.

If you are using an ancho chile and it is very dry and brittle, rather than rubbery and pliable, place it in a bowl and pour boiling water over to cover. Let soak until pliable, 1 minute or less. Drain and pat dry. Cut the chile into 2 pieces; discard the seeds and stem.

Line a 10- or 11-inch cast-iron skillet with aluminum foil. Using scissors, cut a 1½ inch hole out of the center (so that the wood or chile will lie directly on the bottom of the pan.) Heat the skillet over high heat until very hot, about 5 minutes. Line a heavy lid to fit the skillet with aluminum foil. Pat the salmon dry with paper towels and brush each side lightly with the olive oil. Place a round wire cake rack with 1-inch-high feet in the hot skillet. Add the pieces of wood or ancho chile to the exposed center of the pan. When they begin to smoke, place the salmon fillets on the rack and cover tightly. Reduce the heat to moderately low.

Smoke the salmon until a two-pronged fork inserted into a fillet meets with no resistance, about 9 minutes. Serve at once or refrigerate and serve cold.

**4 Servings   176 Calories   22.6 gm Protein
7.8 gm Fat   2.4 gm Carbohydrate per Serving**

Pepper-Cured Gravlax

. . . .

In Ireland I discovered the perfect lunch—full of clean subtle flavors, impeccably fresh, earthy, and elegant, and effortlessly low in calories. Served in tearooms and pubs along the southwest coast, that lunch consists of smoked Irish salmon, buttered Irish Brown Bread, and a salad, usually butterhead lettuce and tomatoes. The flawless quality of this simple lunch begins with the ingredients. The smoked native salmon is superb. Brown bread, while varying in style from cook to cook, is always chewy, flavorful, and satisfying. The wonderful butter and the salad vegetables are products of the surrounding countryside, for much of life there still centers around dairy and produce farming.

At my family's home in Ireland, the basic elements of this lunch are always on hand. The salmon, however, is not smoked; instead the fresh fish is cured with salt, sugar, and herbs to make a homemade gravlax. Since it freezes perfectly, there is always a side of gravlax on hand, in anticipation of the constant stream of hungry friends who visit. It is a food equally suited to special occasions or to simple lunches.

Gravlax in my book is as good a diet food as there is. It is extremely low in calories (about 50 an ounce) and fat and high in nutrients. Since the fish is rich and served in paper-thin slices, three or four ounces make an ample portion, economical in cost as well as calories. In the recipe below, the fish is seasoned with an aromatic pepper mixture rather than with the traditional herbs. Red snapper, black (sea) bass, or farm-raised striped bass may be substituted with good results.

The recipe calls for one-pound fillets of fish, rather than whole sides, substantially cutting down preparation time. This also makes it easier to freeze the gravlax in convenient amounts. Freezing provides the same safeguard for fish that cooking does, rendering powerless any possible toxins, including botulin or parasites, which can be found in fish. To insure the safety of eating a cured fish without cooking, freeze it at −10°F for at least three days. Gravlax will keep frozen indefinitely and refrigerated (at between 38°F and 40°F) for about one week.

In this recipe, a one-pound boneless fillet cures in about 24 hours. If you wish to cure two fillets cut from one fish, simply double the amount of cure and proceed as directed, wrapping each fillet separately.

1 pound boneless fillet of salmon, red snapper, black (sea) bass, or striped bass
3 tablespoons coarse (kosher) salt
1 tablespoon sugar
1 teaspoon Cognac or Armagnac
½ teaspoon whole black peppercorns
½ teaspoon whole white peppercorns
6 allspice berries
¼ teaspoon coriander seeds
¼ cup minced fresh herbs—parsley, chervil, chives, and up to 1½ teaspoons of tarragon (optional)
1 shallot, minced (optional)
Lime wedges, for garnish

Place the fillet skin side down on a large piece of plastic wrap. With tweezers or pliers, pull out any thin bones you can feel in the fish when you run your hand down its side.

In a small bowl, combine the salt and sugar. Rub the seasoning evenly over both sides of the fish. Wrap the fish in plastic wrap and then in foil like a package. Refrigerate for 12 hours or overnight, turning the package at least once.

Unwrap the fillet and rinse under cold water; pat dry. Place skin side down on a large piece of plastic wrap. Drizzle the Cognac over the fish and rub into both sides of the fillet.

With a spice grinder, blender, or mortar and pestle, coarsely grind the black and white peppercorns, allspice berries, and coriander seeds. Rub the pepper seasoning evenly over both sides of the fish. Wrap tightly in plastic wrap and again in aluminum foil. Sandwich the fillet between two small cookie sheets or flat platters. Place a 2- to 3-pound weight on top. Refrigerate for at least 6 hours or overnight to let the flavorings penetrate the fish. As an added precaution, freeze the fish at this point as directed above. To thaw, place in the refrigerator for at least 6 hours before proceeding.

To serve, unwrap and scrape off some of the pepper seasoning with the back of a knife. With a long narrow slicing knife held almost parallel to the fish, slice the fillet about ⅛ inch thick. Divide the slices evenly among 4 plates. Sprinkle with the herbs and shallot, if desired. Garnish each serving with 1 or 2 lime wedges.

4 Servings   180 Calories   22.4 gm Protein
7.2 gm Fat   4.0 gm Carbohydrate per Serving

Salmon Scallops with Hazelnut Vinaigrette

At New York City's Restaurant Le Petit Robert, where I worked many years ago, the signature dish was paper-thin slices of fresh salmon grilled directly on a dinner plate. This was brushed with a cold emulsion, in effect a mayonnaise, intensely flavored with mustard, vinegar, salt, and herbs and finished with a fine hazelnut oil whose perfume and taste mellowed and harmonized with the acidity. In this recipe, the salmon is sliced into elegant ¼-inch-thick scallops for ease of preparation and as a safeguard against overcooking. The sauce is made without the original egg yolks, but a complexity of flavors that complements the rich salmon remains. For further textural dimension, the salmon pairs beautifully with Salade Mesclun on the same plate—the salad will wilt slightly from the heat of the salmon—and crisp Oven-Fried Potatoes.

1 tablespoon plus 1 teaspoon balsamic vinegar
1 tablespoon Dijon mustard
2 teaspoons minced shallots
¼ teaspoon salt, plus more for sprinkling
1 tablespoon plus 1 teaspoon hazelnut or walnut oil
1 tablespoon plus 1 teaspoon minced fresh Italian flat-leaf parsley
Freshly ground black pepper
1 pound center-cut salmon fillet

Preheat the oven to 450°. In a small bowl, combine the vinegar, mustard, shallots, and salt. Gradually whisk in the hazelnut oil until the sauce has emulsified slightly. Stir in the parsley and the pepper to taste. (The sauce can be made up to 2 days ahead; cover and refrigerate.)

Using a long thin knife, preferably a salmon slicer, cut the salmon on the diagonal at a 45 degree angle into ¼-inch-thick scallops. Arrange the slices on a nonstick baking sheet. Season lightly with salt and pepper. Bake the salmon for about 5 minutes until opaque but still slightly undercooked in the center. Using a spatula, transfer 1 scallop to each of 4 hot dinner plates. Brush one quarter of the sauce over each portion and serve at once.

4 Servings   208 Calories   22.6 gm Protein
12.0 gm Fat   1.0 gm Carbohydrate per Serving

Kasu Salmon

. . . .

*M*y sister, Susy, came by this recipe at the vast and wonderful Japanese supermarket Uwajimaya in Seattle. She had gone there searching for sake kasu, the lees, or dregs, left over from the fermentation of sake, the Japanese rice wine. This was the base for a marinade for some black cod she had tasted at Cafe Sport in Seattle. She claimed it was the best fish she'd ever had. Having examined every bottle in the sake section, she was finally directed to the produce section by a compassionate clerk. There were the packages of kasu, looking like sand. The clerk spoke little English but through gestures and a few key words gave my sister the gist of this recipe, which further experimentation perfected. The kasu marinade firms up the texture of the fish and permeates it with a slightly sweet flavor. Broiling or grilling causes the surface of the fish to caramelize and form a glaze. The effect is spectacular.

The flavor of this dish is so unique and delicious that it is well worth the effort of searching out sake kasu, which is sold by the pound at Japanese specialty stores. It will keep indefinitely refrigerated (I kept some for more than a year) and may also be frozen. One pound will make at least eight times the recipe. The marinade works best with fatty fish, such as salmon, black cod (which is available only on the West Coast), and bluefish.

Kasu Salmon

. . . .

¼ cup sake
⅓ cup sake kasu*
¼ cup sweet white miso*
1 tablespoon dark brown sugar
1 tablespoon soy sauce
4 salmon fillets (4½ ounces each) or four ¾-inch-
   thick salmon steaks (6 ounces each)
1 teaspoon olive oil
*Available at Japanese markets

In a small saucepan, bring the sake to a simmer over high heat. Using a long kitchen match, ignite the sake. Reduce the heat to low and cook until the flames subside, about 45 seconds. Remove from the heat.

In a food processor, combine the sake kasu, miso, brown sugar, soy sauce, the warm sake, and ¼ cup of water. Process to a paste the consistency of wet sand, adding a little more water if necessary.

Spread about one-third of the paste over the bottom of a medium glass baking dish. Arrange the salmon fillets on top. Spread the remaining paste over the fillets to completely coat them. Cover with plastic wrap and refrigerate for at least 12 and up to 24 hours.

Preheat the broiler or light a charcoal or wood grill. Scrape the kasu paste from the salmon and pat dry with paper towels. Brush lightly with the olive oil. Broil or grill the fillets 3 inches from the heat for 3 to 4 minutes. Turn over and cook on the other side for 2 to 3 minutes or until you feel no resistance when you insert a kitchen fork into the salmon. Serve at once.

4 Servings   216 Calories   26.4 gm Protein
9.7 gm Fat   4.2 gm Carbohydrate per Serving

. . . .

Lobster and Corn Bread Sandwich

. . . .

This sandwich is seriously indulgent. A huge slice of rosemary-scented corn bread is spread with a pungent garlic sauce and piled high with the sensual delights of summer: lobster, ripe tomatoes, roasted peppers, peppery arugula, and basil. Only after inventing it did I realize that it derives from my memories of summers at the beach when my mother would make Crab Louis and serve it with corn bread, and from my longing for those pure summer flavors that are made more vivid by the sea air. It is a luxurious sandwich, a meal in itself really, despite its sensible healthiness.

The individual components of the sandwich are simple to prepare and may be done in advance, so that the sandwich can be assembled at the last minute. The availability of shelled cooked lobster meat from local fish markets makes preparation even easier. The method for cooking lobsters given in this recipe is from Jeremiah Tower. It yields succulent, tender meat.

The corn bread is best served still warm from the oven. If made the day before, it can be split and toasted before making the sandwich.

1 yellow bell pepper
Two 2-pound live lobsters (to yield 1¼ pounds shelled cooked lobster meat)
Crackling Rosemary Corn Bread (page 175)
Garlic Sauce (page 227)
¼ pound arugula, tough stems removed
2 ripe medium tomatoes, thinly sliced, or 20 yellow cherry tomatoes (7 ounces), thinly sliced
About 16 large basil leaves, preferably purple basil, shredded

Roast the yellow bell pepper directly over a gas flame or under a broiler as close to the heat as possible, turning until charred all over, about 5 minutes. Enclose the pepper in a bag to steam for 10 minutes. Using a thin sharp knife, scrape the skin off the pepper, rinse, and remove the core, seeds, and ribs. Cut the pepper into thin strips and set aside.

In a large pot place the lobsters and enough water to cover by 6 inches. Cook over high heat until just about to boil. Turn off the heat and let sit for 13 minutes. Remove the lobsters from the pot and place in a large bowl of ice water to cool. Working over a bowl, twist the lobster tail off the body. Let the coral, roe, and juices run into the bowl and set aside. Using scissors, cut through the soft cartilage on the underside of the tail. Separate the meat from the tail. Remove the

claws, wrap in a kitchen towel, and tap with a hammer to break the shell. Remove the meat and cut into ¼-inch slices. Set all the meat aside and discard the shells.

Slice the corn bread into 4 equal wedges and split each horizontally. Place 1 wedge of corn bread, with the pieces cut side up, on each of 4 dinner plates.

Stir the reserved lobster juices and roe into the Garlic Sauce, if desired. Spread each piece of corn bread with ½ tablespoon of the sauce.

Divide the arugula and arrange over each corn bread half. Place the sliced tomato over the arugula and top with the lobster meat. Dollop the remaining Garlic Sauce on each sandwich. Arrange the reserved pepper slices decoratively over the lobster. Garnish with the basil.

Variation: One and a quarter pounds of shelled cooked shrimp or crabmeat may be used in lieu of lobster. Or cook your own shrimp: bring a large pot of water to a boil, add 1½ pounds fresh shrimp, and cook until the water is just returning to the boil and the shrimp are pink and opaque, about 2 minutes. Drain the shrimp and let cool in a bowl of ice water. Peel and devein the shrimp, leaving the tails on.

4 Servings   450 Calories   38.4 gm Protein
15.4 gm Fat   39.5 gm Carbohydrate per Serving

Shrimp Ragout

This satisfying ragout is a testament to the profound practicality of crustaceans in low-calorie cooking. Like their cousins, crayfish and lobster, shrimp are extremely low in calories, and the shells yield much extraordinary flavor for free. A rich essence is made by grinding the shells and infusing them into an aromatic stock, or court bouillon. A small amount of cream, some asparagus, roasted peppers, and snipped herbs are then all that's needed to create a luxurious ragout that can play the starring role in an elegant dinner party. It is a bit of work but most of it can be done the day before and it is well worth the effort.

1 large onion, chopped (1 cup)
1 leek (white and tender green), chopped (¾ cup)
1 large carrot, chopped (½ cup)
1 sprig of fresh thyme or ½ teaspoon dried
1 bay leaf
3 sprigs of parsley
2 cups dry white wine
1¼ teaspoons salt
1 large red bell pepper
1 large yellow bell pepper
½ pound asparagus, trimmed and cut into
   ½-inch pieces

1¼ pounds medium shrimp
1 teaspoon olive oil
4 large shallots, minced (½ cup)
Small pinch of saffron threads
¾ cup drained, seeded, and chopped canned
   Italian peeled tomatoes
¼ cup heavy cream
½ teaspoon freshly ground black pepper
2 tablespoons minced fresh chives, chervil or
   parsley

In a large saucepan, combine the onion, leek, carrot, thyme, bay leaf, parsley, white wine, salt, and 5 cups of water. Bring to a boil over high heat. Reduce the heat to low and simmer the court bouillon for 30 minutes.

Meanwhile, roast the red and yellow bell peppers directly over a gas flame or under the broiler as close to the heat as possible, turning until charred all over, about 5 minutes. Enclose the peppers in a bag to steam for 10 minutes. Using a thin sharp knife, scrape the skin off the peppers and remove the core, seeds, and ribs. Cut the peppers into ½-inch dice and set aside.

In a medium saucepan of boiling salted water, cook the asparagus for 2 minutes. Drain and rinse under cold running water; drain well and set aside.

Return the court bouillon to a boil over high heat. Reduce the heat to moderate, add the shrimp and cook until opaque, about 5 minutes; remove with a slotted spoon and transfer to a large bowl. Set aside to cool. Boil the court bouillon over high heat until reduced to 4 cups, about 10 minutes. Cover to keep warm.

Peel and devein the shrimp, place in a bowl and cover with plastic wrap. In a food processor, grind the shrimp shells for 2 minutes in 2 batches, then add 1 cup of the hot court bouillon. Process until the mixture becomes reddish in color, about 3 minutes. Scrape the mixture into the remaining court bouillon and simmer over low heat for 20 minutes. Strain through a fine-mesh sieve (lined with cheesecloth if necessary), pressing down on the shells with the back of a wooden spoon to extract all the liquid. Discard the shells and vegetables.

In a medium saucepan, combine the olive oil and 2 teaspoons of water. Add the shallots and cook, covered, until soft and translucent, about 5 minutes. Add the saffron and tomatoes and cook, stirring, for 1 minute. Stir in the shrimp stock and heavy cream and bring to a boil over high heat. Reduce the heat to low and add the shrimp, red and yellow bell peppers, and asparagus. Cook until heated through, about 3 minutes. Season with the black pepper. Divide the ragout among 4 warm soup bowls. Garnish each serving with the minced herbs.

Variation: Crayfish Ragout, 249 calories per serving. This recipe works wonderfully with crayfish, although they are a little more work to clean and peel. If you have access to live crayfish, substitute 5 pounds for the shrimp and use 8 cups of water in the court bouillon. Cook the crayfish in 4 batches, transferring them to a bowl with a slotted spoon and letting the court bouillon return to a boil after each batch. To shell the crayfish, twist the tails from the heads and break off the end flippers. Using small kitchen scissors, cut down the middle of the inside tail shell. Grasp the sides of the tail shell between the index finger and thumb of each hand and break away from the meat. Grind the shells in 2 batches, then return all the ground shells to the work bowl and proceed with the recipe.

**4 Servings   262 Calories   27.0 gm Protein
9.2 gm Fat   18.6 gm Carbohydrate per Serving**

Seafood Filé Gumbo

This gumbo is roughly adapted from a recipe by K. Paul Prudhomme, the great chef in New Orleans. Its flavor is authentic and uninhibited. It is thickened with filé powder, a seasoning made of ground dried sassafras leaves, that is available in spice stores or specialty food markets. This gumbo departs radically from K. Paul's in the amount of fat used. The original recipe calls for three quarters of a cup of margarine, at 1,200 calories. This wild gumbo uses less than three tablespoons of margarine (following K. Paul's dictum that butter won't do) with no loss of flavor or texture that I could detect. It is a great recipe, especially for a crowd, for it can easily be doubled or tripled and gets better after sitting a day or two. The base, without the seafood, can be frozen and then reheated when desired with seafood poached in it just before serving. For a more fiery gumbo, increase the amount of hot pepper sauce and cayenne. Serve with half a cup of white or wild pecan rice per serving.

Seafood Filé Gumbo

1½ teaspoons sweet paprika
1 teaspoon salt
1 teaspoon cayenne pepper
½ teaspoon freshly ground white pepper
½ teaspoon freshly ground black pepper
½ teaspoon thyme
½ teaspoon oregano
2 bay leaves
2 tablespoons plus 2 teaspoons margarine or
   vegetable oil
1 large onion, chopped (2½ cups)
3 to 4 large celery ribs, chopped (2 cups)
3 medium green bell peppers, seeded and
   chopped (1½ cups)
2 medium red bell peppers, seeded and chopped
   (1 cup)
3 tablespoons filé powder
2 garlic cloves, minced
1½ teaspoons hot pepper sauce
2 cans (8 ounces each) tomato sauce
1 cup clam juice mixed with 1 cup of water
2½ pounds seafood, in any combination, such as
   1½ pounds peeled, deveined shrimp plus 1
   pound shucked oysters or 80 mussels, or 2
   pounds boned fish or seafood plus 40 mussels

In a small bowl, combine the paprika, salt, cayenne, white and black pepper, thyme, oregano, and bay leaves. Set this spice mixture aside.

In large heavy saucepan or flameproof casserole, heat the margarine over moderate heat. Add the onion, celery, and bell peppers. Cook, stirring constantly, until the onion is softened but not browned, about 5 minutes. Increase the heat to moderately high and stir in the filé powder, garlic, hot pepper sauce, and reserved spice mixture. Cook until fragrant, about 5 minutes, stirring constantly. Reduce the heat to moderate, add the tomato sauce, and cook, stirring constantly and scraping the bottom of the pan, for 5 minutes. Add the clam juice and 2 cups of water. Bring the gumbo to a boil, reduce the heat, and simmer, stirring occasionally, until the vegetables are tender and the sauce is slightly thickened, about 35 minutes. *(The gumbo base can be made in advance and frozen for up to 3 months. Simply thaw before proceeding with the recipe.)*

Stir in the fish and shellfish. Simmer until the fish is just cooked through and the shellfish have opened, about 4 minutes. Serve at once.

Variation: Chicken and Country Ham Gumbo, 250 calories per serving. Substitute 2 cans of chicken broth for the clam juice and water. Replace the seafood with 2 pounds skinless, boneless chicken breasts, sliced into 2-by-½-inch strips, and ¼ pound shredded country ham. Cook for 7 minutes, until the chicken is tender. Although unorthodox, 1 tablespoon of sour cream is delicious on the gumbo.

8 Servings   216 Calories   23.3 gm Protein
7.2 gm Fat   14.6 gm Carbohydrate per Serving

Shellfish Stew with Saffron

. . . .

This shellfish stew is an amalgam of memories: steamed clams boiled over a wood fire on the beach, fragrant bouillabaisse in the south of France, mussels cooked in white wine and garlic in New York's Little Italy. In this recipe, a variety of shellfish is cooked in white wine flavored with garlic, shallots, herbs, saffron, and fennel seeds to make a rich and satisfying stew. The optional teaspoon of heavy cream per serving enriches the broth and harmonizes the seafood flavors. Toasted thin slices of baguette spread with Hot Red Pepper and Saffron Sauce—a variation of the traditional accompaniments to bouillabaisse in France—adds further dimension and body to the stew. Four to five slices of the toast and two tablespoons of the sauce add just 132 calories.

. . . .

2 teaspoons extra-virgin olive oil
2 tablespoons minced shallots
1½ teaspoons minced garlic
¼ teaspoon minced fresh chile
¼ teaspoon thyme
Scant ¼ teaspoon fennel seeds
¼ teaspoon saffron threads
1 bay leaf
1 medium leek, white and pale green parts, julienned and cut into 3-inch lengths (3 ounces)
1 large carrot, julienned and cut into 3-inch lengths (3 ounces)
2 cups dry white wine
12 medium shrimp
20 Little Neck or Manila clams
8 large or 12 medium mussels, scrubbed and debearded
½ pound shelled sea or bay scallops, or 16 Singing Scallops in the shell
Pinch of salt
Freshly ground black pepper
¼ cup chopped Italian flat-leaf parsley

1 tablespoon plus 1 teaspoon heavy cream (optional)

In a large heavy saucepan, combine the olive oil, shallots, garlic, chile, thyme, fennel seeds, saffron, and bay leaf. Cook over moderately low heat, stirring occasionally, for 2 minutes. Cover, reduce the heat to low, and cook, stirring occasionally, until the shallots are translucent, about 4 minutes. Stir in the leek, carrot, and 2 tablespoons of water; cover and cook, stirring occasionally, until the vegetables wilt, about 4 minutes. Add the white wine and 2 cups of water. Increase the heat to moderate and bring the liquid to a boil. Reduce the heat slightly and simmer for 5 minutes.

Add the shrimp, clams, mussels, and scallops to the pan. Cover and simmer until the shellfish open, about 5 minutes. Stir in the salt, pepper to taste, parsley, and the cream if desired. Serve at once.

4 Servings   235 Calories   33.7 gm Protein
5.2 gm Fat   11.8 gm Carbohydrate per Serving

Pepper and Salt Shrimp

. . . .

There are times when my culinary imagination seems to languish. I am hard put to generate ideas or even to cook, and local markets offer little inspiration. My antidote is an excursion to Chinatown to wander through the exotic markets on my way to dinner. The vivid displays of a culture other than my own—live turtles and crabs, winter melons, lychees, mangoes, foot-long string beans—seem to shock me awake with their possibilities. This recipe is adapted from one I have enjoyed many times in Chinatown, usually at the end of one of these inspirational forays. It is utterly simple: the shrimp are stir-fried in their shells with a mixture of Szechuan peppercorns, sugar, and salt. They are satisfyingly spicy and aromatic without being hot. The shrimp can be served straight from the frying pan, to be peeled and eaten with the fingers.

. . . .

1 tablespoon Szechuan peppercorns*
1¼ teaspoons sugar
1 tablespoon plus 1 teaspoon coarse (kosher) salt
¼ teaspoon freshly ground black pepper
1 pound medium shrimp (26 to 30 shrimp),
  in their shells
2 tablespoons plus 2 teaspoons peanut oil
*Available at Oriental markets and specialty food
  stores

In a small heavy skillet, toast the Szechuan peppercorns over moderate heat, shaking the pan occasionally, until very fragrant, about 3 minutes. Transfer the peppercorns to a mortar or a blender and pulverize to a medium-coarse powder. Stir in the sugar, 1 teaspoon of the salt, and the black pepper. Set the seasoned salt aside.

In a large bowl, place the shrimp in 1 quart of water mixed with the remaining 1 tablespoon salt. Let soak for 2 minutes. Drain, rinse, and pat dry.

In a large heavy skillet (preferably cast iron) or a wok, heat 2 tablespoons of the peanut oil until very hot and rippling. Add the shrimp, reduce the heat to moderately high and stir-fry until the shrimp are pink, the shells are crisp and golden, and the meat is opaque at the thickest part, 2 to 3 minutes. With a slotted spoon, transfer the shrimp to a plate.

Add the remaining 2 teaspoons oil and the reserved seasoned salt to the pan and stir-fry for 10 seconds. Return the shrimp to the pan and stir-fry until coated with the seasonings, about 1 minute. Add ¼ cup of water to the pan and boil, stirring occasionally, until the shrimp are well coated and the sauce is reduced to 2 tablespoons, 1 to 2 minutes. Transfer to a heated platter, or serve the shrimp straight from the pan.

4 Servings   187 Calories   18.8 gm Protein
10.7 gm Fat   3.2 gm Carbohydrate per Serving

◄ Pepper and Salt Shrimp, Fresh Cucumber Pickle, and Cold, Spicy Sesame Noodles

Crab Cakes

. . . .

Even in the dead of winter, these rich crab cakes evoke summer and seashore. This recipe is, in effect, an amalgam of several classic American crab recipes, from Southern Deviled Crab to the traditional Maryland Crab Imperial. Highly spiced with sherry, curry, paprika, and pepper and containing very little binder, the true crab flavor is not obscured. Fat and calories are minimized by replacing the traditional egg yolks with whites, trimming the mayonnaise, and frying the cakes in a small amount of oil in a nonstick skillet. The cakes are moist inside with a golden crust outside. Serve with Roasted Yellow Pepper Sauce.

. . . .

1¼ ounces fresh white sandwich bread (about 1½ slices)

3 egg whites

1 tablespoon mayonnaise

1½ tablespoons fresh lemon juice

1½ teaspoons Worcestershire sauce

1 teaspoon dry sherry

3 drops hot pepper sauce

1¼ teaspoons paprika

¼ plus ⅛ teaspoon curry powder

¼ plus ⅛ teaspoon freshly ground black pepper

¼ plus ⅛ teaspoon ground mustard

Scant ¼ teaspoon ground allspice

Scant ¼ teaspoon cayenne pepper

3 tablespoons minced Italian flat-leaf parsley

1½ pounds fresh lump crabmeat, picked over

2 teaspoons olive oil

Place the white bread in a food processor and process to soft crumbs. Set aside.

In a medium bowl, combine the egg whites, mayonnaise, lemon juice, Worcestershire sauce, sherry, hot sauce, paprika, curry powder, black pepper, mustard, allspice, cayenne, and parsley. Add the crabmeat and bread crumbs and toss with a fork to combine, taking care not to break up the crabmeat lumps. Shape the crab mixture into twelve 2½- to 3-inch patties and place on a baking sheet lined with wax paper. Refrigerate for at least 20 minutes to dry out the patties slightly. *(The patties can be made up to 1 day ahead; cover with plastic wrap and refrigerate.)*

In a 10-inch nonstick skillet, heat 1 teaspoon of the olive oil over moderate heat. Add 6 of the crab patties and fry until golden brown, about 3 minutes on each side. Set aside in a warm oven while you fry the other 6 patties with the remaining teaspoon olive oil. Serve at once.

4 Servings   264 Calories   38.1 gm Protein
8.4 gm Fat   6.7 gm Carbohydrate per Serving

Meat and Poultry

Pork Loin Prosciutto

. . . .

It seems as if I spend a lot of time trying to figure out ways to make ancient or rustic cooking processes available to urban apartment dwellers. I developed a method of smoking fish (page 103) and grilling bread (page 171) over wood on a stove. Now I have figured out a way to cure meat at home. The following recipe results in a prosciutto that is beautifully textured and flavored.

I adore dry-cured hams like prosciutto and Smithfield because they have a flavor that is at once sweet, salty, nutty, and spicy, and because they are very low in calories. But I have found that beyond a few gourmet markets in America's larger cities, not many places carry good-quality prosciutto. For example, I have yet to find great prosciutto in Seattle, which I consider to be one of the great food cities in America. Of the dry-cured hams you *can* find, with the exception of the rare and expensive Prosciutto di Parma, almost all are cured with nitrites, which may pose a health risk.

This recipe is the result of many months of my working like some eccentric scientist. A stack of farm journals and charcuterie manuals, tomes on meat science, even an ancient Latin cookbook all agreed about the basic, quite simple theory. Salt and sugar actually cure the meat by drawing water out of the cells and literally starving bacteria to inactivity or death. The whole process is affected by many elements: the weight and texture of the meat, the proportion of salt and sugar used, the length and temperature of the cure. A constant, cool environment (in the past, the cellar) is crucial so that the meat won't spoil before it is fully cured. In this recipe, amounts of up to five pounds of pork—considerably less than a whole ham—are cured. After an initial five-day curing with salt, sugar, and spices, the ham is hung to dry from a rack in one's home refrigerator, which is normally the right temperature—about 40°F. There is no more work to do, for the transformation that takes place from this point on is the work of nature and time. The pork loin takes up only a corner of the fridge. The drying time is five weeks.

Special note: The safety of meat cured without nitrites is of concern to many people these days. Trichinosis is a particular threat from pork products. During the course of my research, conversations with meat scientists have convinced me of the safety of the following method. Today's high standards for raising and testing pigs have drastically reduced the chances of a commercially raised pig having trichinae parasites. I have made and enjoyed these prosciuttos many times without fear. However, you can take extra precaution by simply freezing the cured and dried prosciutto for about five days. Freezing destroys any toxic organisms. Defrost for about 24 hours in the refrigerator.

Pork Loin Prosciutto

. . . .

4½ pounds very fresh boneless pork loin, fat
    trimmed to ¼ inch, tied with kitchen string at
    2-inch intervals
5½ cups coarse (kosher) salt
⅓ cup (packed) dark brown sugar
¾ pound fresh fatback, thinly sliced
2 garlic cloves, halved
1½ tablespoons Cognac
¾ cup black peppercorns
2 teaspoons allspice berries (see Note)

Place a thermometer in the refrigerator (an
instant-reading thermometer works well). Adjust
the thermostat until the temperature reads 40° to
43°.

Place the pork loin, fat side down, in a ceramic
or glass casserole just large enough to fit the loin
or in a large plastic bag. Combine 5¼ cups of the
salt and the brown sugar. Cover the pork with
this mixture, mounding and patting it against
the sides and top of the loin. Cover the casserole
loosely with plastic wrap, or twist the bag so that
it is loosely closed to allow for breathing. In a
separate dish or plastic bag, layer the fatback
slices with the remaining ¼ cup salt; cover
loosely.

Refrigerate the pork loin and fatback separately
to cure for 5 days, turning the loin over once a
day and patting the curing mixture back up over
the meat each time. The salt will draw out liquid
from the meat to form a brine.

After 5 days, using a paper towel, brush off any
salt still clinging to the meat. Rub the meat all
over with the garlic halves. Sprinkle the Cognac
on top.

Cover the meaty side of the loin with the fatback slices, overlapping them slightly to leave a
1-inch-wide strip of meat exposed along each
side of the fatback. Tie with kitchen string at
2-inch intervals to secure the fat.

In a spice mill, or in a mortar with a pestle,
coarsely grind the peppercorns and allspice berries. Cover the pork evenly with this seasoning
mixture, pressing it into the meat.

Cut a rectangle of triple-layered cheesecloth,
10 inches longer than the length of the meat and
6 times its width. Spread out the cheesecloth on
a work surface and place the meat along its length
so that 5 inches of cloth extend at each short end
of the meat. Starting with a long side of the
cheesecloth, tightly roll up the loin jelly-roll fashion in the cheesecloth, patting on the seasoning
mixture as you go. Using kitchen string, tie
around the loin at 1-inch intervals. Twist the
short ends of the cheesecloth and tie each in a
knot, as close to the meat as possible. At one
end, securely tie two 16-inch lengths of string by
which to hang the meat.

Adjust the shelves of your refrigerator to allow
the loin to hang freely. Tie the loin to the higher
rack with the 16-inch strings so it will hang vertically, unobstructed, with 4 inches of free space
all around it. Let hang to dry for at least 5 weeks.

To test if the meat is cured, press it between
the thumb and middle fingers. It should feel
quite firm yet still somewhat resilient. If it feels
like rare steak, let it hang longer, checking every
2 days, until it tests done. When the prosciutto
feels cured, cut about ½ inch off one end of the
meat. Let the loin sit for 1 minute. Smell the inside cut of the meat; it should have a fresh and
sweet aroma. (**Special Advice:** *If the meat smells
sour or moldy, test again by cutting further. If the
meat has not been properly cured, it will smell bad.
Do not eat cured meat if it does not smell
appetizing.*)

To serve, cut the amount of prosciutto you
need into paper-thin slices. (*The prosciutto will
keep refrigerated for at least 2 months, becoming
denser as it dries. Cover the cut side of the remaining prosciutto with plastic wrap; leave the rest
uncovered.*)

Note: *For a different, more aromatic flavor, de-
crease the peppercorns to ½ cup and substitute ½
cup dried sage leaves for the allspice.*

Makes About 3¾ Pounds   65 Calories
8.1 gm Protein   3.0 gm Fat
1.0 gm Carbohydrate per Ounce

Country Terrine

· ·

I once found a photograph from the Thirties of French peasants picnicking by a river. With his back to the camera, each is occupied with his own plate of food, lost in thought in a kind of private calm. The men and women lounging on the grassy bank appear content and unselfconscious, though they are all very large. These wonderful-looking people would be at odds with today's notion of beauty and chided for their uninhibited indulgence and lack of self-discipline.

I love the photograph and long for such a time and such a freedom, but I know too much about the food they are eating. Terrines, for example, commonly contain up to 45 percent pork fat. My knowledge of saturated fat and my own vanity inhibit me now, and I don't eat pâté unless I know it's a great one. I wonder sometimes if I know too much for my own good.

For a long time, I wished for a terrine that was both healthy and delicious, one that I could enjoy fearlessly on my own summer picnics. So I put everything I knew about terrines to work and created a version without fat.

I used a *panade*, bread softened and mashed with milk, to form a binding moistening paste. I took care to grind the meat to an interesting texture, added some liquid to keep the pâté moist, a small amount of gelatin to give it stability, and garlic, juniper berries, and Calvados to lend a bold flavor. I cooked it slowly to avoid toughening the meat and weighted it with a brick to bind it.

In reality, my terrine is a meat loaf made with trickery and calculation. It's well flavored, coarsely textured, and

Country Terrine, Pickled Cherries, and Rillettes of Duck ➤

moist—far better than most mass-produced terrines I've eaten in this country.

Serve the terrine with grainy mustard, coarse salt, Pickled Cherries, or cornichons and good French bread. Thinly slicing a baguette on the diagonal will usually yield five or six slices per ounce. Prepare the terrine at least one day before serving to let the flavors mellow.

Country Terrine

. . . .

1¼ cups apple cider or unsweetened apple juice
1 envelope (¼ ounce) unflavored gelatin
6 slices of white sandwich bread (5½ ounces), torn into small pieces
½ cup low-fat milk
2 eggs
2 pounds trimmed boneless loin of pork, cut into 1-inch chunks
14 ounces trimmed boneless veal shoulder, cut into 1-inch chunks
1 cup (loosely packed) Italian flat-leaf parsley, minced
¼ cup finely chopped shallots
2 garlic cloves, minced
2 teaspoons juniper berries, finely chopped or crushed
2 teaspoons salt
2½ tablespoons Calvados
¾ teaspoon thyme
1½ teaspoons coarsely ground pepper
3 imported bay leaves

Preheat the oven to 250°. In a small saucepan, bring 1 cup of the cider to a boil over high heat. Boil until reduced to ¼ cup, 8 to 10 minutes.

Meanwhile, in a small bowl, sprinkle the gelatin over the remaining ¼ cup cider and let soften, about 5 minutes. Add the hot cider and set aside, stirring once or twice, until the gelatin is completely dissolved, about 2 minutes. Let cool.

Using a fork, mash together the bread and milk to make a paste. Blend in the eggs.

In a food processor, chop the pork and veal in small batches, turning the machine quickly on and off, until the meat is ground medium-fine. Transfer to a large bowl. Add the parsley, shallots, garlic, juniper berries, salt, Calvados, thyme, bread-egg mixture, gelatin mixture and 1 teaspoon of the pepper. Mix until well blended.

Spoon the mixture into a 9-by-5-inch (8 cup) terrine or loaf pan, pressing the meat down firmly and smoothing the top. Rap the terrine on a folded kitchen towel on the counter several times to eliminate any air pockets. Sprinkle the pâté with the remaining ½ teaspoon pepper and arrange the bay leaves on top. Cover the pan with a double thickness of heavy-duty aluminum foil and place in a roasting pan. Set in the oven and fill the roasting pan with enough boiling water to reach halfway up the sides of the terrine. Bake for about 2½ hours until a thermometer inserted into the center of the terrine measures 160°. Let cool to lukewarm, then remove from the water bath.

Press a piece of foil directly onto the top of the terrine and weight with a slightly smaller terrine pan filled with heavy cans (about 4 pounds). Refrigerate for at least 12 hours and up to 6 days.

To serve, pour off any ungelled liquid. Slice into 12 even slices.

12 Servings   248 Calories   26.2 gm Protein
10.3 gm Fat   10.7 gm Carbohydrate per Serving

Clove-and-Pepper-Cured Roast Pork

Every year, usually in the spring, I go down south to eat the kind of food I seldom eat in New York. I view it as an antidote to modern city living that shakes up my sometimes rigid ideas about eating. Southern food is a paradox to me, at once nurturing and unhealthy. It is delicious and comforting, yet rich and often full of ingredients I view with suspicion—cured ham, bacon fat, sugar.

Inspired by revelations from my yearly pilgrimages, I have tried my hand at reinterpreting some southern favorites, like Black-Eyed Peas and Buttermilk Coleslaw and roast pork, to limit the less healthy aspects of them without dampening their deliciousness.

In this recipe, lean pork tenderloins are marinated—for several hours or overnight—in a dry mixture of spices, sugar, and salt to cure the meat slightly. This yields the clove-and-pepper flavor of country ham—with little of the fat, salt, or bother. The tenderloins are delicious hot or cold.

1½ teaspoons sugar
1 teaspoon coarse (kosher) salt
1 teaspoon coarsely ground pepper
½ teaspoon ground coriander
½ teaspoon ground cloves
2 pork tenderloins (12 ounces each), trimmed of fat
1 teaspoon olive or vegetable oil
1 tablespoon maple syrup

In a small bowl, combine the sugar, salt, pepper, coriander, and cloves. Place the tenderloins in a shallow nonreactive dish and rub the spice mixture into the meat. Cover and refrigerate for at least 6 hours or overnight.

Preheat the oven to 375°. Tuck the thin "tail" end of each tenderloin under itself to form a roast of even thickness. Tie with kitchen string at 2-inch intervals and place on a rack in a roasting pan.

Brush each loin with ½ teaspoon of the olive oil. Roast for 20 minutes. Brush the loins with the maple syrup. Roast for 25 to 30 minutes longer, basting twice more with the juices in the pan, until a meat thermometer inserted in the center reads 155°. Remove from the oven and let rest for 5 to 10 minutes.

Brush the meat with the pan juices. Slice the tenderloins across the grain into ¼-inch-thick slices. Arrange 7 to 8 slices in a fan on each of 6 dinner plates.

6 Servings   147 Calories   23.8 gm Protein
3.6 gm Fat   3.5 gm Carbohydrate per Serving

Cassoulet

. . . .

D o I commit heresy in trying to create a low-calorie cassoulet, to reach for the cassoulet's effect on the spirit without its dulling effect on the body? My own memory of cassoulets past guiding me, and a theory that the beans might drink up a concentrate of flavorful meat juices instead of the traditional fat, I began. The recipe took days to develop; my kitchen was a sea of notes amid simmering pots of duck legs and beans. Heresy.

But then again, cassoulet is famous for the controversy that surrounds it: the authenticity of mutton or confit or various kinds of beans and whether it should have a crust. There are cassoulets made of lentils and chorizo, of preserved duck and fava beans, even of salt cod. Each is unique, molded out of the opinions and theories of its creators. Cassoulets are personal statements. As is the recipe that follows.

This cassoulet employs a ragout of duck and pork in lieu of confit, sausages, and bacon. The traditional pork rind remains for richness and body, and whole garlic cloves add the penetrating garlic flavor normally provided by garlic-flavored pork sausage. White beans, cooked in the same pot as the duck carcasses and flavorful aromatics, plump on the gelatinous stock as it is made. Like most cassoulets, this one takes time and love to prepare. It has a garlicky, creamy, complex flavor and is comforting, filling, and well worth the effort.

A traditional cassoulet has approximately 1,604 calories per serving. The one here has less than a third of that.

You do not use one whole duck breast in this recipe. Save it for another use, such as the Pan-Fried Duck Steak.

Cassoulet

. . . .

2 ducks (5 pounds each)
1½ pounds lean pork shoulder, trimmed of fat
   and cut into 1½-inch cubes
1 tablespoon plus ½ teaspoon coarse (kosher) salt
1 teaspoon freshly ground pepper
3 cups (1¼ pounds) dry white beans, such as
   Great Northern, navy, or cannellini, rinsed
   and picked over
½ pound fresh pork rind (see Note)
1 large onion, peeled and left whole, plus 1
   medium onion, coarsely chopped
5 whole cloves
18 garlic cloves
4 medium carrots, peeled and sliced
4 sprigs of fresh thyme
4 sprigs of parsley
2 bay leaves
1 cup dry white wine
1 can (14 ounces) Italian peeled tomatoes,
   seeded, and their liquid
1 cup fresh bread crumbs

Remove the breasts from the ducks with the bones intact; refrigerate or freeze one whole breast for another use. Remove the legs with the thighs connected from both birds (you should have 2¼ pounds of duck legs and breasts). Remove the skin from the breast, legs, carcasses, and necks; cut ½ pound of the skin into 1-inch pieces and reserve. Separate the drumsticks from the thighs and slice the duck breast crosswise in half. Cut the carcasses into 4-inch sections.

In a shallow casserole, combine the pork cubes and the duck breast and legs. Sprinkle with 1 teaspoon of the salt and ¼ teaspoon of the pepper; cover and refrigerate for 6 hours or overnight.

Place the beans in a bowl with cold water to cover by 2 inches; set aside to soak for at least 6 hours or overnight. Alternatively, bring a large saucepan of water to a boil. Add the beans and cook for 1 minute. Remove from the heat and let stand, covered, for 1 hour.

Put the duck skin in a small heavy saucepan with ¼ cup of water. Bring to a boil over high

heat. Reduce the heat and simmer until the fat is rendered and the water has evaporated, 10 to 15 minutes. Strain the fat into a bowl and let cool; discard the skin.

Using a sharp knife, shave off any white fat left on the pork rind and discard. Place the rind in a medium saucepan with enough cold water to cover and bring to a boil over moderately high heat. Reduce the heat to moderate and simmer until softened, about 4 minutes. Drain and rinse under cold running water. Cut the rind into ½-inch square pieces.

Drain the beans and transfer to a large heavy saucepan or flameproof casserole. Add enough cold water to cover by 1 inch, cover and bring to a boil over moderately high heat. Drain the beans and return to the saucepan. Place the duck carcasses and the pieces of pork rind on top of the beans. Stud the whole onion with the cloves and add to the pot along with 2 of the garlic cloves, half of the carrots, 2 sprigs of the thyme, 2 sprigs of the parsley, 1 bay leaf, enough cold water to cover, and 2 more teaspoons of the salt. Bring to a boil, reduce the heat to a simmer, and cook, skimming occasionally, until the beans are tender, about 1 hour and 15 minutes. Drain the beans, pork rind, garlic, and carrots into a colander set over a large bowl and reserve; reserve the cooking liquid. Discard the duck bones, onion, sprigs of herbs, and bay leaf.

In a large flameproof casserole, heat 2 teaspoons of the reserved duck fat over moderate heat. Add the chopped onion and the remaining carrots and cook until lightly browned, about 12 minutes. Transfer the vegetables to a bowl.

Add 2 more teaspoons of the duck fat to the casserole and heat over moderately high heat. Add the duck pieces and cook, turning, until lightly browned, about 4 minutes on each side; transfer to a platter. Add 2 more teaspoons of duck fat and the pork cubes to the casserole and cook, tossing, until browned all over, 5 to 7 minutes. Transfer to the platter with the duck.

Carefully blot any excess fat from the pan with

paper towels. Add the wine to the casserole and bring to a boil, scraping up any browned bits from the bottom of the pan. Add the tomatoes and their liquid, 8 of the garlic cloves, the remaining 2 sprigs of thyme and parsley, the remaining 1 bay leaf, and the cooked duck, pork, and vegetables. Pour the reserved bean liquid over the meat. Bring to a boil, reduce the heat to low, cover, and simmer, skimming occasionally, until the duck and vegetables are tender, about 1½ hours.

Drain the meat and vegetables into a large colander set over a bowl to catch the stock. Pour the stock into a large saucepan. Boil over high heat until reduced to 4¼ cups. Stir in ¼ teaspoon of the pepper and the remaining ½ teaspoon salt.

Preheat the oven to 275°. Cut 1 clove of garlic in half, rub it over the bottom and sides of a large casserole, preferably earthenware, and leave in the pot. Add one third of the beans–pork rind–vegetable mixture and season with ¼ teaspoon of the pepper. Arrange the duck and vegetables over the beans and cover with one third more of the

beans, the remaining ¼ teaspoon pepper, and the remaining 7 garlic cloves. Layer the pork over the beans and cover with the remaining beans. Ladle the duck stock over the cassoulet until the liquid just covers the beans. Sprinkle evenly with the bread crumbs.

Bake for 1 hour. Gently break the bread crumb crust with a large spoon and drizzle some of the meat juices over the crumbs. Continue to bake until the cassoulet is hot throughout and the top is golden brown, about 1 hour longer. *(The cooked cassoulet will keep for up to 1 week in the refrigerator.)*

Note: *If fresh pork rind is not available, substitute the rind from fatback (10 ounces of fatback yields 2 ounces of skin). Rinse the salt from the fatback and cut the rind away with a thin sharp knife. Be sure to remove every trace of fat. Proceed with blanching and cutting as above.*

10 Servings   489 Calories   38.3 gm Protein 17.6 gm Fat   44.6 gm Carbohydrate per Serving

. . . .

Carpaccio

A few years ago, about the time Arrigo Cipriani, son of the creator of the world-famous Harry's Bar in Venice, opened his restaurant in New York, carpaccio, lightly dressed, paper-thin slices of raw beef, began to receive a lot of attention in the press. Arrigo's father, Giuseppe, was reputed to have invented the dish. Harry's Bar was famous for it, and Arrigo was featuring it on the menu of his new restaurant Cipriani. Chic restaurants around town all got busy inventing their own version. Carpaccios appeared dressed with mayonnaise like the one at Cipriani, or with pestos, mustard sauces, and vinaigrettes flavored with pickles, capers, and herbs. I tried many of them, including a recipe containing more than 20 ingredients from a chef at Le

Cirque. Finally, I had to admit that the finest carpaccio in my book was the simplest—the way I had eaten it in Italy many times—dressed only with olive oil, lemon, pepper, and Parmesan cheese. Its effect is far greater than the sum of its ingredients.

Carpaccio is a very easy dish to make, and most of it can be done a couple of hours ahead of time. It is surprisingly rich and filling and makes a lovely main course for lunch or a late night supper. Serve it with an arugula salad and thin slices of crusty bread. Given its simplicity, the key to this recipe is to use the best ingredients possible, from prime beef to extra-virgin olive oil and parmigiano-reggiano cheese.

Carpaccio

¾ pound very lean boneless sirloin steak or New York strip steak
1 garlic clove, halved
2 teaspoons fresh lemon juice
Pinch of salt
1 tablespoon plus 1 teaspoon extra-virgin olive oil
1 ounce Parmesan cheese
Freshly ground pepper
About 12 green or purple basil leaves

Wrap the steak in plastic wrap and freeze until the meat is very firm, but not frozen, about 30 minutes. Place the meat on a work surface and using a thin sharp knife, preferably a salmon slicer, cut the steak against the grain as thinly as possible (each slice will weigh about ¾ ounce). Working with 1 slice of steak at a time, place the meat on the work surface and cover with a piece of plastic wrap. Using a meat pounder or the side of a heavy cleaver, pound until it is about ⅛ inch thick. Repeat with the remaining meat. Arrange an equal number of slices on each of four dinner plates. Cover each plate with plastic wrap and refrigerate. *(The beef can be prepared to this point up to 1 hour ahead.)*

Rub the cut side of one of the garlic halves over the inside of a small bowl. Add the lemon juice and salt. Spear both garlic halves on a dinner fork. Using this as a whisk, drizzle in the olive oil until the sauce thickens slightly. Set aside.

Using a mandoline, a slicer-julienner, or a truffle cutter, shave the Parmesan over a plate into paper-thin slices or simply grate the Parmesan cheese. Cover with plastic wrap until ready to serve. *(The cheese can be sliced up to 1 day ahead; refrigerate.)*

To serve, drizzle 1¼ teaspoons of the reserved dressing in a crisscross pattern across the beef on each plate. Season to taste with pepper. Divide the Parmesan evenly and scatter it randomly on each serving. Garnish each plate with several basil leaves.

Variation: The only embellishment that could improve this already perfect combination of flavors is a white truffle. Grate or thinly shave ½ to 1 ounce fresh truffle and toss over each serving.

4 Servings   212 Calories   20.2 gm Protein
13.4 gm Fat   2.5 gm Carbohydrate per Serving

Cajun Meat Loaf

. . . .

Louisiana chef K. Paul Prudhomme changed the way I view meat loaf. In 1984, he published a meat loaf recipe that employed sophisticated Cajun-style seasoning and yielded a moist loaf with a mild spiciness. It seemed to me it was what meat loaf should become, made even more American by original Cajun flavorings. Over the years, gradually adapting K. Paul's approach, I have varied and intensified the seasoning, replaced the green peppers with red to create a sweet creamy base for the spices and extra-lean meats, and used egg whites instead of egg yolks to reduce the fat. It is richly flavored, moist, and satisfying served warm or cold. If you prefer a spicier meat loaf, increase the hot pepper sauce and cayenne to taste.

. . . .

3 bay leaves
2 teaspoons salt
1½ teaspoons freshly ground black pepper
1½ teaspoons paprika
1¼ teaspoons ground cumin
1¼ teaspoons ground nutmeg
¾ teaspoon cayenne pepper
¾ teaspoon white pepper
½ teaspoon thyme
2 teaspoons olive oil
2 medium onions, coarsely chopped (1½ cups)
3 celery ribs, coarsely chopped (1¼ cups)

2 red bell peppers, coarsely chopped (1 cup)
1 medium chile (3 inches), minced
1 tablespoon minced garlic
1½ tablespoons Worcestershire sauce
About 1½ teaspoons hot pepper sauce
½ cup milk
½ cup tomato puree
2 teaspoons vinegar
1½ pounds lean ground beef
¾ pound lean ground pork
1 cup dry bread crumbs
3 egg whites

In a small bowl, combine the bay leaves, salt, black pepper, paprika, cumin, nutmeg, cayenne, white pepper, and thyme.

In a large heavy skillet, heat the oil over moderate heat. Add the onion, celery, red pepper, chile, garlic, Worcestershire and hot pepper sauces, and the spice mixture. Cook, stirring occasionally, until the mixture starts to stick to the bottom of the pan, about 6 minutes. Stir in the milk, tomato puree, and vinegar. Continue cooking, stirring occasionally, until the mixture is quite thick, about 12 minutes. Reduce the heat if necessary to prevent scorching. Remove the pan from the heat and set aside to cool.

Preheat the oven to 350°. Remove the bay leaves from the vegetable mixture. Add the beef, pork, bread crumbs, and egg whites; mix by hand until thoroughly combined. Scoop the mixture into the center of a 13-by-9-inch baking pan lined with foil. Shape into a loaf about 10 inches by 5 inches.

Bake the meat loaf for 25 minutes. Increase the oven temperature to 400° and cook for about 20 minutes longer or until a meat thermometer inserted in the center reads 150°. Let the meat loaf cool for at least 5 minutes. Blot up the fat in the pan with paper towels before slicing.

8 Servings   307 Calories   22.3 gm Protein
16.0 gm Fat   17.7 gm Carbohydrate per Serving

. . . .

Pot-Roasted Beef with Ancho Chiles and Sweet Spices

As comforting as traditional pot roast, this unusual variation has a subtly pungent flavor. The extraordinary sauce of dried ancho chiles, spices, and herbs is based on several traditional Mexican pot roast recipes, in particular Diana Kennedy's Carne Claveatada. The addition of a handful of dried currants, although unorthodox, lends a pleasant sweetness that enhances the complex flavors of the sauce. Serve with rice, noodles, or boiled potatoes.

Pot-Roasted Beef with Ancho Chiles and Sweet Spices

. . . .

6 large ancho chiles (about ¼ pound), stem,
    membranes and seeds removed, sliced
    lengthwise into 1-inch-wide strips (see Note)
8 garlic cloves
3 tablespoons red wine vinegar
1 tablespoon salt
1 teaspoon cinnamon
10 black peppercorns
¼ teaspoon thyme
¼ teaspoon marjoram
¼ teaspoon oregano
2 slices of bacon (2¼ ounces), sliced crosswise
    into ¼-inch pieces
4 pounds rump roast, trimmed of all fat
½ cup dried currants

Preheat the oven to 325°. In a large heavy skillet, toast the chile strips over moderate heat, turning occasionally with a spatula to prevent them from burning, until they begin to darken and smell pungent, about 3 minutes. Transfer to a medium bowl and cover with boiling water. Let soak for 20 minutes.

Meanwhile, in a blender or food processor, combine the garlic, vinegar, salt, cinnamon, peppercorns, thyme, marjoram, oregano, and 2½ cups of water. Drain the ancho chiles and add to the mixture. Blend at high speed until smooth, about 1 minute.

Place the bacon in a large flameproof casserole over moderately low heat. Cover and cook until the bacon is just beginning to brown, about 5 minutes. Add the beef and cook, uncovered, until browned, 3 to 4 minutes on each side. Remove the beef to a platter.

Strain off and discard the bacon fat. Return the bacon to the pan. Pour the chile mixture into the casserole and simmer, stirring constantly for 5 minutes. Return the beef to the casserole and spoon the chile sauce over it. Cover the casserole with a double thickness of aluminum foil and replace the lid to seal tightly.

Bake the pot roast for 1½ hours. Turn the meat over, baste with the sauce, and stir in the currants. Replace the foil and the lid and bake for 1½ hours longer or until the meat is very tender when pierced with a fork.

The meat slices best when chilled, so let cool to room temperature, then cover and refrigerate until chilled, about 2 hours. Skim off any fat that may have congealed on the top of the sauce. Remove the meat from the sauce. With a thin sharp knife, slice the meat into 10 slices, ¼ to ½ inch thick. Return the meat to the casserole and cook over low heat until warmed through. Pour the sauce into a measuring cup—you will have about 2½ cups. (Add a little water if the sauce is too thick or cook over moderate heat to reduce.) Serve each slice of meat with ¼ cup of the sauce. *(The pot roast will keep refrigerated for up to 5 days or frozen for up to 3 months.)*

Note: *Ancho chiles are large dried poblano chiles, available at Latin markets or the Mexican section of your supermarket.*

**10 Servings   266 Calories   34.0 gm Protein
9.6 gm Fat   11.7 gm Carbohydrate per Serving**

Pan-Fried Shell Steak with Madeira and Fennel

. . . .

Frying red meats in a well-seasoned pan with very little oil is an excellent low-calorie cooking method. Contact with the hot pan creates a surface crust on the meat that seals in juices. A minimum of oil is used for searing, then all the fat is discarded. The caramelized bits in the bottom of the pan become a flavorful base for a quickly made sauce, eliminating the need for a stock. In this recipe, fennel, garlic, and basil in a Madeira-and-red-wine reduction make a unique, richly flavored sauce that complements rare steak.

. . . .

1 teaspoon olive or peanut oil
2 boneless shell or strip steaks (8 ounces each) or four ¾-inch-thick beef medallions (4 ounces each)
½ cup Madeira, preferably Rainwater, or dry Marsala
½ cup dry red wine
2 teaspoons minced garlic
¾ teaspoon fennel seeds
1½ tablespoons tomato paste diluted in 1½ tablespoons water
½ serrano or jalapeño pepper, seeded and minced, or ¼ teaspoon crushed hot red pepper
Salt and freshly ground black pepper
2 tablespoons minced fresh basil

In a large heavy well-seasoned skillet (if you do not have a well-seasoned skillet, use a nonstick skillet), heat ½ teaspoon of the olive oil over moderate heat. When the oil is very hot but not smoking, arrange the steaks in the pan. Cook the steaks until seared brown, reducing the heat if necessary so that the oil does not burn, about 3 minutes. Add the remaining ½ teaspoon oil to the pan, turn over the steaks and cook to the de-sired doneness (2 to 3 minutes longer for rare, 4 minutes longer for medium). Transfer the steaks to a carving board.

Pour the fat from the pan and discard. Add the Madeira and red wine and increase the heat to high. Scrape the bottom of the pan with a wooden spoon to loosen the browned bits. Boil the wine for about 30 seconds. Add the garlic and fennel seeds and cook, stirring, for 30 seconds. Reduce the heat to moderately low and stir in the diluted tomato paste and the serrano pepper. Cook until the sauce is the consistency of thick cream and reduced to about ½ cup, about 4 minutes. Remove from the heat.

Using a sharp knife, slice the steaks into thin slices; season lightly with salt and pepper. Pour the steak juices, if any, into the sauce. Spoon about 2 tablespoons of sauce onto each of 4 warmed plates. Divide the steak slices equally and arrange in a fan over the sauce. Sprinkle the basil on top and serve at once.

4 Servings   212 Calories   23.5 gm Protein
9.7 gm Fat   6.3 gm Carbohydrate per Serving

Mechoui

. . . .

The traditional North African Berber *mechoui* is a whole lamb slowly spit-roasted as it is basted frequently with spiced butter. The meat is rendered crisp on the outside, meltingly tender and sweet inside. This recipe parlays the traditional *mechoui* spices—garlic, cumin, coriander, and paprika—into a highly unorthodox play on the original notion. Half of a leg of lamb is butterflied so that the spiced paste may penetrate the meat more completely; then it is grilled to medium-rare. This eliminates the need for the butter that the traditional slow-cooking method uses. Spiced Tomato Jam is a piquant counterpoint that amplifies the flavor of the spices. To prepare a whole leg of lamb, simply double the quantities and proceed as directed.

. . . .

1 tablespoon plus ¼ teaspoon coriander seeds
2 teaspoons cumin seed
2 teaspoons imported sweet paprika
½ teaspoon salt
¼ teaspoon sugar
5 to 6 garlic cloves, coarsely chopped
1 tablespoon plus 1 teaspoon olive oil
½ leg of lamb, from the shank end (3½ pounds), butterflied, fat trimmed

In a small skillet, toast the coriander and cumin until fragrant, about 2 minutes. Transfer to a blender, along with the paprika, salt, and sugar, and grind at high speed until the spices are reduced to a powder. Add the garlic, 1 tablespoon of the olive oil, and 1 tablespoon plus 2 teaspoons of water and blend to a thick paste.

Massage the spice paste into both sides of the lamb. Place on a platter, cover with plastic wrap, and refrigerate overnight or up to 24 hours.

Preheat the broiler or light a charcoal or wood grill. Blot the lamb dry with paper towels without wiping off all the spices. Rub the remaining 1 teaspoon oil into the lamb. Broil or grill the lamb on a hot rack for about 10 minutes on each side for medium-rare or until a meat thermometer inserted in the fleshiest part reads 130°. Let the lamb rest 10 to 15 minutes before carving the meat in wide diagonal slices across the grain.

6 to 8 Servings   281 Calories
39.4 gm Protein   11.9 gm Fat
2.3 gm Carbohydrate per 4-Ounce Serving

Rack of Lamb with Herbs of Provence

. . . .

In Greece, roasted or grilled lamb is always marinated in lots of lemon juice, olive oil, and wild herbs, particularly oregano. The resulting meat is succulent and richly flavored. In this recipe, a powerful mixture of Provençal herbs, including lavender, replaces the Greek herbs. The lemon juice tenderizes the lamb, and the combination of thyme, rosemary, savory, and lavender adds an unusual, slightly spicy, and floral note. The racks of lamb are roasted until rare, the meat is thinly sliced from the bone to create uniform portions, and the crisp rib bones are served alongside. A sauce of flavorful jus moistens the meat. Serve the lamb with White Beans with Garlic.

Dried lavender flowers can be purchased from herb stores or where potpourri is sold.

Have the butcher trim each rack of lamb; ask him to remove the chine bone and to French the rib bones. Have him wrap up all the trimmings—you will need them for the sauce.

Rack of Lamb with Herbs of Provence

. . . .

2 tablespoons fresh thyme plus 2 whole sprigs or
   1¼ teaspoons dried
1 tablespoon plus 2 teaspoons fresh rosemary or
   1¼ teaspoons dried, minced
1 tablespoon fresh savory or 2 teaspoons dried
½ teaspoon dried lavender flowers
3 garlic cloves
1 tablespoon extra-virgin olive oil
2 tablespoons fresh lemon juice
2 trimmed racks of lamb (about 13 ounces each),
   trimmings reserved
1 medium onion, unpeeled and quartered
3 leek greens from 1 leek, coarsely chopped
1 medium carrot, coarsely chopped
½ celery rib, coarsely chopped
½ cup dry white wine
1 imported bay leaf
Salt and freshly ground pepper

In a mortar with a pestle or in a blender, grind the 2 tablespoons fresh thyme (or ¾ teaspoon dried) with the rosemary, savory, lavender, and 1 garlic clove into a coarse paste. Gradually blend in 2 teaspoons of the olive oil and the lemon juice. In a shallow nonreactive dish, coat both racks of lamb with the marinade. Cover with plastic wrap and refrigerate for at least 6 hours or up to 1 day.

Meanwhile, prepare the sauce. Preheat the oven to 450°. In a medium nonreactive ovenproof skillet, combine the lamb trimmings, onion, leek, carrot, celery, and the remaining 2 garlic cloves and 1 teaspoon olive oil. Roast for 15 minutes, stirring once. Reduce the heat to 350° and roast, stirring occasionally, for 20 minutes longer, until the meat trimmings and vegetables are browned and the liquid in the pan is syrupy.

Place the pan over moderate heat and pour in the white wine; scrape with a wooden spoon to loosen the browned bits from the bottom of the pan. Add the thyme sprigs (or the remaining ½ teaspoon dried thyme), bay leaf, and 2 cups of water. Simmer for 1 hour. Pour the sauce through a fine-mesh strainer into a measuring cup, pressing with the back of a wooden spoon to extract all the juices. If you have more than 1 cup, return it to the skillet and cook longer to reduce the liquid. Let cool, then cover and refrigerate the sauce until you are ready to use it.

Preheat the oven to 450°. Remove the lamb from the marinade and pat dry with paper towels, leaving as many herbs as possible on the surface of the meat. Season lightly with salt and pepper. Place each rack of lamb meat side down on a rack in a roasting pan. Roast for about 15 minutes for medium-rare. Remove the lamb from the oven and let rest for 10 minutes before carving.

Meanwhile, remove the sauce from the refrigerator and spoon off and discard the congealed fat on the surface. Transfer the sauce to a small saucepan and warm over moderate heat until heated through. Season to taste with salt.

Using a long thin knife, slice each loin off the bone in 1 piece; it will look like a log. Cut the loins into thin slices and separate the ribs. Arrange an equal number of slices and ribs on each of 4 dinner plates. Pour a little of the sauce over the meat and pass the rest separately.

4 Servings   227 Calories   23.3 gm Protein
12.0 gm Fat   5.7 gm Carbohydrate per Serving

Rack of Lamb with Herbs of Provence and White Beans with Garlic ➤

Poule au Pot

. . . .

*P*oule au pot is the dish that inspired the French King Henry IV to wish that every peasant might have "a chicken in his pot every Sunday." Such a dish, in the 17th century, was a symbol of prosperity. *Poule au pot*, a whole chicken poached in stock with vegetables, is one of the classic dishes of provincial French cooking. It is said to be a variation of *pot au feu* and is as comforting and elegant in its simplicity. Variations of the dish are legion, as are legends of the almost mystical qualities it is said to possess if prepared by a truly great chef. The mystery is that such economical and unprepossessing elements achieve such perfection. La Mère Fillioux, a great chef of Lyon, is still remembered, long after her death, for her version, in which a Bresse chicken was poached with slices of truffle under its skin.

As easy as it is to make, one rarely finds *poule au pot* in America, I suspect because home cooks are put off by the necessity of having on hand a real chicken stock. To this end, I use the simplest method I know for making stock—my Chinese Chicken Stock—although a French chef would faint at the thought of it being used in a *poule au pot*. Store-bought canned broth just does not do the dish justice. A whole chicken, root vegetables, and herbs are poached in the stock, enriching and concentrating its flavor and lending it their own inimitable character.

I like to serve the *poule au pot* in large shallow soup bowls. A portion of chicken is surrounded by the colorful vegetables and moistened with the rich broth. Toasted slices of baguette spread with Garlic Sauce, similar to *aioli*, are wonderful served alongside to dunk in the broth. Accompany the dish with coarse salt.

Poule au Pot

. . . .

1 whole roasting chicken (2½ pounds), preferably free-range—rinsed and patted dry, neck reserved
1 quart Chinese Chicken Stock (page 244), or a premium store-bought (not canned) broth (see Introduction, page 21)
2 sprigs of fresh thyme
1 bay leaf
6 ounces baby carrots, scrubbed, green tops trimmed, or 6 ounces long thin carrots, peeled and sliced crosswise on a diagonal ½ inch thick
6 ounces baby turnips, scrubbed, green tops trimmed, or 6 ounces mature turnips, peeled and cut into ½-inch wedges
6 ounces leeks, white and tender green part only, sliced crosswise on a diagonal 1 inch thick
4 ounces parsnips, pared and sliced crosswise on a diagonal ½ inch thick

Put the neck in the cavity of the chicken. Truss the chicken by tying the drumsticks together with kitchen string. Place the chicken breast side down in a saucepan just large enough to hold it. Pour the chicken stock on top and add the thyme sprigs and bay leaf. Bring to a simmer over low heat, cover, and poach for 15 minutes. (Do not allow the stock to boil or the chicken will toughen.)

Turn the chicken breast side up. Nestle the carrots, turnips, leeks, and parsnips around the chicken, cover, and continue poaching for another 15 minutes or until the juices run clear when the thigh is pierced with a fork. Transfer the chicken to a serving platter and cover with foil to keep warm. Continue to simmer the vegetables and stock for 3 minutes longer, skimming off any fat that rises to the surface.

Remove the chicken skin and discard. Separate the wings from the breast. Carve the breast into thin slices. Separate the thigh from the leg. Divide the vegetables evenly among 4 warm shallow soup bowls. Divide the chicken evenly and place in the center of each bowl. Ladle some of the chicken broth over the chicken.

Variation: Poached Chicken with Truffles.
Before trussing the chicken, using your fingers, pry the skin from the breast and thighs without ripping it. Using a thin sharp knife, or a mandoline, cut ½ ounce truffle into 8 thin slices. Insert 2 under the skin of each breast and each thigh. Truss the chicken and wrap in plastic wrap. Refrigerate for about 1 hour to let the flavor of the truffle penetrate the chicken. Then proceed with the poaching as directed above.

**4 Servings   279 Calories   31.4 gm Protein
6.3 gm Fat   23.4 gm Carbohydrate per Serving**

Chicken with Forty Cloves of Garlic

When I first started cooking, the provincial French recipe "Chicken with Forty Cloves of Garlic" taught me my greatest lesson about garlic: that long, slow cooking renders it sweet and mild, and that cooked this way, great quantities may be eaten without the notorious after-effects. This recipe is derived from the classic but has a considerably greater amount of garlic and uses white wine rather than olive oil as the braising medium. The chicken, baked in a tightly sealed vessel, becomes moist, tender, and scented with garlic and herbs. The soft garlic cloves may be squeezed onto a slice of French bread, with a little of the pan juices to moisten it, for a sublime accompaniment. A salad is all that is needed to round out the meal.

The secret of the dish is to use a good free-range chicken and excellent fresh garlic with no sign of sprouting.

1 roasting chicken (3¾ pounds)
1 teaspoon salt
1 teaspoon freshly ground pepper
3 large heads of garlic, broken into cloves but
    not peeled, any excess white paper removed
8 sprigs of fresh thyme or 1 teaspoon dried
2 bay leaves
1¼ cups dry white wine
¼ cup minced Italian flat-leaf parsley

Preheat the oven to 350°. Using a thin sharp knife, cut the excess fat from the neck and hind cavity of the chicken and discard. Sprinkle the salt and pepper evenly on the inside and the outside of the chicken, rubbing it into the skin. Using toothpicks or trussing needles, pin the neck and hind cavities closed. Place the chicken breast side up on a rack in a large heavy casserole with a lid. Nestle the neck, giblets, garlic, thyme, and bay leaves around the chicken. Pour the wine on top. Cover the casserole with a double thickness of aluminum foil and place the lid over the foil.

Braise the chicken for 1½ hours or until the juices run clear when the thigh is pierced with a fork. Transfer the chicken and garlic cloves to a serving platter and keep warm. Discard the herbs and giblets. Pour the juices from the casserole into a measuring cup and let sit for 2 minutes. Using a spoon, carefully skim the fat from the surface and discard.

Remove the skin from the chicken and discard. Carve the chicken into 6 equal portions. Spoon 2 tablespoons of the juices over each portion. Scatter the cooked garlic cloves and the parsley on top. Pass the remaining sauce separately.

6 Servings   225 Calories   27.8 gm Protein
6.7 gm Fat   12.8 gm Carbohydrate per Serving

Chicken Pot Pie

. . . .

Some of the most peaceful times of my childhood were spent in the kitchen watching our housekeeper, Rosie Lee Robinson, prepare her chicken pot pie. It was a painstaking job involving many steps, from poaching the chicken and making a good strong broth that would be the base of the rich cream sauce to preparing the vegetables and making the crust. Rosie Lee made the work seem so effortless that it was only in trying to make a pot pie many years later that I realized what a labor of love hers had been. Her pot pie was the best I ever had, and the one against which I compare all others, although there are hundreds of different approaches to pot pie making. Her pastry was flaky, tender, and buttery. Her filling was rich, velvety, and subtle, fusing the simple elements of potato, peas, carrots, and chicken into one marvelous whole. Her pot pie gives new meaning to the expression "comfort food." In those days, nobody worried about fat and calories.

I never knew Rosie Lee's recipe. My pot pies have been a kind of divination, as I reach for the flavors and effect from those childhood memories. I have compared recipes found in old American cookbooks and embellished them with my own imagination.

No matter how you cut it, old-fashioned American pot pies are extremely fattening. A recipe from *The American Heritage Cookbook* calls for seven tablespoons of butter, six tablespoons of chicken fat, and one-half cup of heavy cream—over 300 calories in fat alone per serving.

This recipe makes a radical departure from the techniques of traditional pot pie making, in particular the flour-thickened cream sauce. My sauce is nothing more than a

Preheat the oven to 450°. Place the chicken parts skin side up in 1 layer in a roasting pan. Season with ½ teaspoon of the salt and some pepper. Bake the chicken until the juices run clear when pierced with a knife, about 30 minutes. Set aside to cool. When cool enough to handle, pull the skin off the chicken and discard. Pull the meat from the bones and cut into 1-inch chunks. Save the bones for stock or discard. Set aside 1½ pounds of the chicken meat and save the rest, if any, for another use.

If you are using fresh pearl onions, cut a criss-cross score in the root end of each onion. In a medium saucepan, place the onions and enough water to cover by 1 inch. Bring the water to a boil, reduce the heat to moderate, and cook until tender but not mushy, 5 to 7 minutes. Drain and transfer to a bowl of cold water to cool; drain again. Using your fingers or a small sharp knife, peel the onions, leaving enough of the root end so they don't fall apart. Set aside.

Bring a large pot of water to a boil. Add the carrots and cook until tender but not mushy, 5 to 7 minutes depending on their size. Using a slotted spoon, transfer the carrots to a bowl of cold water to stop the cooking. When cool, drain and set aside. Add the asparagus to the boiling water and cook until crisp tender, about 3 minutes. Drain and plunge the asparagus into a bowl of cold water to stop the cooking. When cool, drain and add to the carrots. *(The recipe can be prepared to this point up to 2 days ahead. Cover the chicken and vegetables separately and refrigerate.)*

To make the sauce, in a medium saucepan, combine the olive oil, butter, potato, celery root, parsnip, leek, garlic, thyme, sugar, the remaining ½ teaspoon salt, and ½ cup of water. Cover and simmer over moderate heat until the water is almost completely evaporated, about 15 minutes.

Add the chicken stock, bring to a simmer, and cook, covered, over moderate heat, until the vegetables are very tender, about 15 minutes longer. Discard the thyme branch.

Transfer the mixture to a food processor or blender and puree until perfectly smooth, about 1 minute. Season with freshly ground pepper to taste and set aside. *(The sauce can be prepared to this point and refrigerated up to 2 days ahead or frozen for up to 3 months.)*

Roll the Flaky Butter Pastry into a 14-inch circle. Using cookie cutters, cut out leaves, hearts, circles, or stars, or, using a large knife, cut the dough into wedges, strips, or squares. Cut the scraps of dough into small triangles or squares. Using a metal spatula, transfer the dough cutouts to a baking sheet, prick several times with a fork, and freeze for about 15 minutes. *(The pastry can be baked up to 3 days ahead; store well wrapped at room temperature and reheat in a warm oven at the last minute.)*

Preheat the oven to 375°. In a large casserole, combine the reserved chicken, onions, carrots, asparagus (or peas), and the sauce. Bake for 30 minutes or until just heated through. Bake the pastry for about 12 minutes or until golden.

Arrange the pastry cutouts over the top of the casserole. Or, to make individual pies, divide the filling evenly among 8 warm individual casseroles or shallow ovenproof soup bowls. Top each with an equal number of pastry cutouts. Garnish with fresh parsley if desired and serve at once.

Variation: Turkey Pot Pie. Substitute 1½ pounds cooked skinless boneless turkey for the chicken and proceed as directed.

8 servings   377 Calories   30.6 gm Protein
15.0 gm Fat   30.7 gm Carbohydrate per Serving

Coq au Vin

In the Fifties, *coq au vin* and chocolate mousse were the dishes my mother used to serve at her dinner parties. Along with little black dresses, these lent the party elegance and sophistication and assured its success. Apparently a lot of other people had the same idea, for both *coq au vin* and chocolate mousse suffered the same fate of becoming ordinary and so went out of fashion, underground as it were, for several decades. The fact is that *coq au vin*, in its many guises, is one of the glorious dishes of French cooking. It is elegant yet earthy fare. It appears to be making a comeback as jaded cooks rediscover the delicious treasure that was so unjustly discarded.

In this recipe, the chicken is skinned before it is cooked to keep the rich sauce as fat free (and low calorie) as possible. I have found that caramelized onions provide a flavor similar to the traditional sautéed salt pork at a great savings in calories and fat.

Serve this with Saffron Fettuccine, egg noodles or roasted new potatoes, dressed with the flavorful sauce rather than butter.

1 pound unpeeled white pearl onions

1 chicken (3½ pounds), preferably free-range,
   skinned and trimmed of fat

1 tablespoon plus 1 teaspoon all-purpose flour

3 ounces country ham

½ cup Cognac or Armagnac

1½ cups full-bodied dry red wine

¼ cup plus 2 tablespoons Madeira

¼ cup plus 2 tablespoons sherry

2¼ cups chicken stock (see Introduction,
   page 21)

1 tablespoon tomato paste

1 pound button mushrooms (if only large
   mushrooms are available, quarter them)

1½ teaspoons potato starch

1 tablespoon sugar

1 tablespoon Crème de Cassis

½ teaspoon or more red or white wine vinegar
   (optional)

Pinch of salt (optional)

Freshly ground white pepper

In a medium saucepan, bring the onions and enough cold water to cover to a boil. Boil for 1 minute. Drain the onions and place in a bowl of cold water to cool. Drain again, peel, and set aside.

Cut the chicken into eighths, separating the wings from the breasts and the thighs from the drumsticks. Reserve the back and the neck. Pat the chicken pieces dry with paper towels. Put the flour on a pie plate; roll the chicken in the flour and shake off the excess.

Trim the fat from the ham and cut the ham into ¼-inch dice. Set aside. In a large heavy skillet, preferably cast iron, cook 2 teaspoons (a scant ½ ounce) of the trimmed ham fat over moderately low heat until the fat is rendered, about 4 minutes. Add the chicken, in batches if necessary, and cook over moderate heat until all sides are golden brown. Tilt the pan and blot up the rendered fat with a paper towel. Pour the Cognac over the chicken and, using a long kitchen

match, ignite it and cook until the flames subside. Transfer the chicken to a large ovenproof casserole. Preheat the oven to 350°.

Add the red wine, Madeira, sherry, chicken stock, and tomato paste to the skillet, scraping up any browned bits in the pan. Bring the liquid to a boil over moderate heat and cook until the liquid has reduced by about one half, about 20 minutes. Add the chicken back and neck and the mushrooms to the skillet. Reduce the heat to low and simmer the sauce for 5 minutes longer.

Pour the sauce over the chicken in the casserole, making sure that the meaty parts are completely covered with liquid. Nestle the chicken back and neck and the mushrooms around the chicken parts. Bake uncovered for 25 to 30 minutes, until the chicken is tender.

In a small bowl, mix the potato starch with 3 tablespoons of cold water. Stir in ¼ cup of the hot sauce. Tip the casserole and pour the potato starch mixture into the liquid. Swirl the casserole to incorporate. Bake for 5 minutes longer.

In a medium skillet or saucepan, combine the reserved onions, the sugar and 1 tablespoon of water. Cook over moderate heat, shaking the pan frequently, until the onions are glazed and browned, about 10 minutes.

Remove the chicken back and neck from the casserole; discard. Add the onions and the reserved diced ham. Stir in the Cassis. Add the vinegar and salt if necessary to lift the flavors. Season to taste with the pepper. *(Coq au Vin may be made up to 2 days ahead and refrigerated. To reheat, bring just to the boiling point over low heat. Simmer, covered, until the chicken is heated through, about 5 to 10 minutes. If the sauce is too thin, mix 1 tablespoon potato starch with 3 tablespoons of water. Stir in ¼ cup of the hot sauce. Pour the mixture into the casserole and swirl to incorporate. Heat until the sauce re-thickens.)*

6 Servings   274 Calories   34.6 gm Protein
6.0 gm Fat   19.5 gm Carbohydrate per Serving

Roast Chicken with Lemon and Tarragon

. . . .

It used to be said that the test of a great cook was the way she roasted a chicken. Like an omelet, a great roast chicken might seem the simplest thing in the world, composed as it is of only a few elements. The rest is a matter of temperature and time. It is difficult by virtue of that simplicity, however, for the end result is impossible to disguise or fudge. There is no second chance for a badly roasted chicken—charred or under-browned skin and dry, tough flesh cannot be repaired. A successful roast chicken is as much a reflection of a cook's expertise as it is of her sensibility about food. This is simple food, with origins in the home and in the country, evoking Sunday dinners or bistro meals—not much fanfare or extravagance but good, satisfying, comforting food.

At restaurants I worked in years ago, chickens were invariably cloaked in softened butter before roasting and were always delicious. How could they not be? An uninhibited slather of butter almost guarantees that even a mediocre chicken will be moist and flavorful. But with my growing concern about calories and fat, chickens could no longer be roasted with a quarter pound of butter. Here was a cook's test for our leaner times: to produce a great roast chicken without butter or fat of any kind.

I came across the following method while reading Marcella Hazan's *More Classic Italian Cooking* in bed one evening. The chicken is roasted with a lemon in its cavity, which by some chemistry I don't understand produces a crisp skin, very moist, flavorful flesh, and abundant pan juices—in short, everything one could ask of a roast chicken, with no added fat. It is a great technique, for it always works and is easily embellished with garlic cloves and fresh herbs.

The other secret to a good roast chicken is to start with a farm bird rather than a mass-produced supermarket variety. The more natural the bird, the more flavor it will have, so I make it a point to know nearby sources of free-range chickens (they are even available in many supermarkets).

Because the delicious crisp skin of a roasted chicken contains an inordinate amount of fat, calories, and cholesterol, it almost defeats the purpose of this dish. If you cannot resist having it, bear in mind that an ounce, or one quarter, of the chicken's skin adds about 110 calories to a serving.

. . . .

½ teaspoon vegetable oil
1 roasting chicken (2½ pounds), rinsed and patted dry, neck and giblets reserved
1 teaspoon salt
1 teaspoon freshly ground pepper
10 fresh tarragon leaves or 1 teaspoon dried tarragon
1 large lemon (about 4 ounces), rinsed
2 shallots, peeled
2 tablespoons Madeira
2 tablespoons dry white wine

Preheat the oven to 350°. Line a shallow roasting pan with heavy-duty aluminum foil. Using your fingertips, lightly spread the oil over the foil to cover an area the size of the chicken.

With a thin sharp knife, cut the excess fat from the neck and hind cavities of the chicken and discard. Rub the chicken inside and out with the salt and pepper. Gently tuck the tarragon leaves under the skin—over the breast and near the thigh-drumstick joint. Prick the lemon about 25 times with the tines of a fork or a skewer and place in the cavity of the chicken. Using toothpicks or a threaded trussing needle, close the neck and hind cavities. Place the chicken breast side down on the oiled portion of the roasting pan. Nestle the neck, giblets, and shallots around the chicken. Roast for 15 minutes.

Taking care not to rip the skin, turn the bird breast side up. Roast for 20 minutes longer, then increase the oven temperature to 400°. Roast the chicken for 20 to 25 minutes longer, until the skin is brown and crisp and the juices run clear when the leg is pierced with a fork. Remove the trussing from the hind end. Transfer the chicken to a carving board, tilting it slightly as you lift it so the juices from the cavity run into the pan. Cover loosely with foil to keep warm.

Pour the pan juices into a small saucepan. Skim the fat off the surface. Add the neck, giblets, and shallots to the saucepan and place over moderate heat. Add the Madeira and white wine and simmer until the liquid is reduced slightly and the alcohol has burned off, skimming off any fat that rises to the surface, about 3 minutes. Discard the neck, giblets, and shallots.

Carve the chicken into 4 equal portions. Remove the skin (or serve half portions of skin, per headnote above). Pour any juices that have collected on the carving board into the gravy. For a lemony sauce, if desired, squeeze the lemon into the gravy. Spoon about 2 tablespoons of the gravy over each serving.

4 Servings   212 Calories   29.9 gm Protein
8.2 gm Fat   5.0 gm Carbohydrate per Serving

Roast Poussin with Cabbage and Pears

· ·

*P*oussins are baby chickens that weigh about one pound, yielding just enough meat for one serving. In this recipe, the skin is entirely removed and replaced with paper-thin slices of pancetta, the pepper-cured Italian bacon. As the fat in the pancetta renders in the high oven heat, it bastes and protects the flesh and provides a crisp, flavorful covering for the birds. The poussins are served on a bed of wilted savoy cabbage leaves with pears in a port wine pan sauce, a play on the classic treatment of game birds like pheasant or squab. The pancetta adds the element of gaminess to the tender poussin meat.

· ·

1 medium head of savoy cabbage (about 1½ pounds)

4 poussins (about 1 pound each), giblets reserved

¾ teaspoon salt

1 teaspoon freshly ground pepper

12 very thin slices of pancetta (3 ounces total)

4 shallots, finely chopped

¼ cup ruby port

1 cup dry white wine

2 medium Bosc pears—peeled, halved, cored, and sliced crosswise ¼ inch thick

6 juniper berries (optional)

Peel 12 to 16 whole leaves from the cabbage, to equal 14 ounces. Shave off the thick ribs from the back of each leaf. Bring a large pot of salted water to a boil. Add the cabbage leaves and boil until wilted, about 4 minutes. Drain, rinse under cold water until the cabbage is cool; drain and reserve. *(The cabbage may be prepared to this point up to 8 hours ahead; cover and refrigerate.)*

Preheat the oven to 425°. Rinse the poussins inside and out under cold running water and pat dry with paper towels. Cut off the neck and wing tips at the first joint and reserve. Using your fin-

gers and a pair of small scissors, remove the skin from the birds and discard. Sprinkle ⅛ teaspoon of the salt in the cavity of each bird. Sprinkle ⅛ teaspoon of the pepper over the outside of each bird. For each bird, place 1 slice of pancetta so that it completely covers the breast. Place 1 slice of pancetta over each drumstick. Secure the pancetta by tying kitchen string around the breast and legs of each bird.

Arrange the birds breast down in a large ovenproof skillet. Roast in the oven for 20 minutes. Turn the birds over. Roast for 20 to 25 minutes longer until the juices run clear when the thigh is pierced with a knife. Transfer the poussins to a platter and cover lightly with aluminum foil to keep warm.

Pour off the rendered fat in the skillet and discard. Add the shallots to the pan and cook over moderately high heat, stirring constantly, until they begin to wilt, about 30 seconds. Add the port and cook until reduced slightly, about 15 seconds. Add the white wine, pear slices, reserved cabbage leaves, juniper berries, if using, and the reserved giblets, neck, and wing tips. Cover, reduce the heat, and simmer until the cabbage is

Roast Poussin with Cabbage and Pears

tender and the wine is reduced by half, about 10 minutes. Add the remaining ¼ teaspoon salt and ½ teaspoon pepper. Remove from the heat and set aside.

Arrange 3 or 4 cabbage leaves on each of 4 dinner plates. Place 1 poussin and a quarter of the pear slices on the cabbage. Spoon about 2 tablespoons of the sauce on top and serve at once.

Variation: Roast Squab with Cabbage and Pears, 415 calories per serving. Since squab is an extremely rich and caloric meat, prepare only 2 birds and serve ½ bird per portion. Do not skin the birds or cover them with pancetta. Instead truss their legs with kitchen string. Heat a large skillet until very hot. Add the squabs breast side down. Cook over moderate heat, turning occasionally, until well browned all over, about 10 minutes. Transfer the squabs to a roasting pan and place in a preheated 425° oven. Roast until medium-rare, 15 to 20 minutes. While the squabs are roasting, proceed with the sauce as directed above.

Transfer the squabs to a carving board. Using a sharp knife, halve the squabs. Remove the wing tips, necks, and giblets from the skillet and discard. Using a rubber spatula, scrape the squab juices into the sauce, stir, and reheat.

**4 Servings   339 Calories   37.0 gm Protein
11.8 gm Fat   21.8 gm Carbohydrate per Serving**

. . . .

Turkey Marsala with Wild Mushrooms

. . . .

Although I had been hearing it for years, I was surprised to discover that thinly sliced and pounded turkey breast is actually a very good substitute for veal scaloppine. It seemed just too good to be true, for good quality veal scaloppine is incredibly costly these days and can be hard to come by properly cut. It is also very high in cholesterol. Turkey breasts, which are readily available in supermarkets, can be cooked any way that veal scaloppine can, and are, in fact, less vulnerable to drying out. The slight difference in flavor and texture is attenuated by the robust flavors of the rich Marsala and wild mushroom sauce in this recipe. Boiling down the Marsala by half burns off the alcohol and most of its calories, producing a flavorful stock that is further enriched by the flavor of the wild mushrooms. The turkey itself is extremely low in calories and cholesterol.

. . . .

1 ounce dried mushrooms, such as cèpes (porcinis) or morels
1 cup boiling water
1 pound turkey breast, thinly sliced
3 tablespoons all-purpose flour
1 teaspoon salt
1 teaspoon freshly ground pepper
1 tablespoon plus 1 teaspoon olive oil
1½ cups dry Marsala
¾ pound fresh wild mushrooms, such as shiitakes, Romans or cèpes (porcinis), sliced
1 teaspoon arrowroot or potato starch mixed with 2 teaspoons water
2 tablespoons minced Italian flat-leaf parsley or chervil (optional)

In a small bowl, combine the dried mushrooms and boiling water. Cover and set aside to let the mushrooms soften, about 15 minutes.

On a work surface, place 1 turkey slice, cover with plastic wrap, and pound it lightly with a meat pounder, the side of a heavy cleaver, or the bottom of a heavy skillet, until it is about ¼ inch thick. Repeat with the remaining turkey slices.

Spread the flour in a shallow pan. Lightly sprinkle the salt and pepper over both sides of each turkey slice. Dredge in the flour to coat all sides.

Using a slotted spoon, transfer the mushrooms from their liquid to a strainer and rinse them well. Squeeze out any excess water and chop coarsely. Set aside the mushrooms and their soaking liquid separately.

In a large heavy nonstick or cast-iron skillet, heat 1 teaspoon of the olive oil over moderate heat. When it is very hot, add enough turkey slices to cover the bottom of the pan in 1 layer. Cook the turkey until nicely browned, about 2 minutes on each side; transfer the slices to a platter. Repeat with the remaining oil and turkey slices.

Blot the fat from the pan with paper towels. Add the Marsala to the skillet. Pour ½ cup of the reserved mushroom soaking liquid (taking care not to disturb the sediment on the bottom of the bowl) into the skillet. Stir in the reserved dried mushrooms and the fresh mushrooms. Boil over high heat, stirring to scrape up browned bits from the bottom of the skillet, until the mushrooms are tender and the wine has reduced by half. Reduce the heat to moderately low, stir in the arrowroot mixture, and stir until the gravy thickens slightly. Return the turkey slices to the pan, coating them with the mushrooms and gravy, and heat through. Scatter the parsley, if desired, over the top. Serve at once.

4 Servings   272 Calories   29.7 gm Protein
6.8 gm Fat   23.2 gm Carbohydrate per Serving

Pan-Fried Duck Steaks

Duck, particularly the common Peking duck widely available in this country, is generally considered to be an extremely fattening meat. Over half of its calories and most of the fat are in the skin. Once that is removed, the remaining flesh has fewer calories than an equal amount of filet mignon.

Skinless, boneless duck breasts make richly flavored little steaks—each a perfect portion for one. Cooked rare or medium rare like a beef steak, the gamey flavor comes through. They need only be accompanied by a cool fruit sauce like Mango Salsa, and, if desired, a half cup of wild rice per serving. The duck steaks are also delicious served warm on a Mesclun Salad.

In the method below, the duck steaks are briefly marinated in a dry salt-and-spice mixture that tenderizes the meat and accentuates the duck's natural flavors. The steaks are then seared in a hot pan and thinly sliced, which adds visual appeal and further tenderizes the meat. Although the duck can be cooked in olive oil, the same amount of duck fat adds a great deal of rich duck flavor (which would normally be provided by the skin) with no increase in calories.

Boneless duck breasts are increasingly available in supermarkets. Simply remove and discard the skin (reserving some of the duck's fat) before beginning the recipe. It is often more economical to buy whole ducks and ask your butcher to cut them apart. The remainder of the duck—legs, thighs, and carcass—can be used to make the delicious Ragout of Duck Legs.

◄ Pan-Fried Duck Steak with Mango Salsa

Pan-Fried Duck Steaks

. . . .

1½ teaspoons coarse (kosher) salt
½ teaspoon black peppercorns
4 juniper berries
4 allspice berries
½ bay leaf, crumbled
¼ teaspoon thyme
⅛ teaspoon sugar
4 skinless, boneless duck breasts
    (about 4 ounces each)
1 teaspoon duck fat or olive oil
Freshly ground pepper

With a mortar and pestle, or in a spice grinder, coarsely crush the salt, peppercorns, juniper berries, allspice berries, bay leaf, thyme, and sugar. Place the duck breasts on a platter and rub ½ teaspoon of the spice mixture into each one. (Discard or save for another use any remaining

spice mixture.) Cover with plastic wrap and refrigerate for at least 4 hours or overnight.

About 20 minutes before cooking, remove the duck breasts from the refrigerator to return to room temperature. Pat dry with paper towels.

In a heavy medium skillet, heat the duck fat until melted and hot. Add the duck breasts and cook until the outside is brown but the meat feels springy to the touch, about 2 minutes on each side. Transfer the breasts to a cutting board. Using a thin sharp knife, slice each breast on a diagonal ⅛ inch thick. Arrange the slices of one breast on each of 4 hot dinner plates. Season with pepper to taste and serve at once.

4 Servings   161 Calories   20.8 gm Protein
7.8 gm Fat   .4 gm Carbohydrate per Serving

. . . .

Goose or Wild Duck Prosciutto

. . . .

This recipe is a variation of the method for Pork Loin Prosciutto. Since the meat is cured in much smaller quantities, it takes only two weeks to produce an exceptionally delicate, unctuous prosciutto. It can be served in any of the ways you would serve traditional prosciutto. Warmed briefly in a heavy frying pan, it is a cross between country ham, bacon, and pancetta and is wonderful for breakfast or lunch.

Ask your butcher to bone the goose or duck, leaving the skin on. You need to refrigerate the meat at a temperature of 40°F to 43°F. Place a thermometer (an instant-reading one works well) in your refrigerator and adjust the thermostat if necessary.

. . . .

2 tablespoons plus 2 teaspoons coarse
   (kosher) salt
1 teaspoon thyme
1 bay leaf
20 coriander seeds
20 black peppercorns
3 pounds very fresh boneless goose, mallard,
   or Muscovy duck legs and breast, with the
   skin on
Extra skin from the bird carcass, removed in as
   large a piece as possible, or 4 to 6 thin sheets
   of fresh fatback

In a mortar with a pestle, coarsely crush together the salt, thyme, bay leaf, coriander seeds, and peppercorns. Place the goose or duck, skin side down, along with the extra skin in a ceramic or glass dish or in a plastic bag. Rub the spice mixture into the meat and extra skin until each piece is completely coated. Cover loosely with plastic wrap, or twist the bag so that it is loosely closed to allow for breathing. Refrigerate the goose or duck to cure for 24 hours, turning the meat over once.

Using paper towels, pat all the meat dry. Roll the breasts and legs lengthwise, skin side outwards into sausage shapes, pressing tightly to remove any air pockets from the center of each roll. Place a strip of extra skin over any exposed meat, leaving a ¼-inch strip uncovered at the seam. Discard any remaining extra skin.

Cut a rectangle of triple-layered cheesecloth, 10 inches longer than the length of the meat and 6 times its width. Spread the cheesecloth on a work surface with one of the short sides nearest you. Place the meat in the middle of the cheesecloth parallel to this edge so that 5 inches of cloth extend at each end of the meat. Tightly roll the meat lengthwise in the cheesecloth to form a log. Tie with string at 1-inch intervals. Twist the ends of the cheesecloth and tie each in a knot, as close to the meat as possible. At one end tie two 16-inch lengths of string by which to hang the meat.

Adjust the shelves of your refrigerator (at a temperature of 40° to 43°) to allow the goose to hang freely. Tie the goose to the higher rack with the 16-inch strings so it will hang, vertically, unobstructed, with 4 inches of free space all around it; let hang this way for at least 2 weeks before cutting.

To test if the meat is cured, press it between the thumb and middle fingers. It should feel quite firm yet still somewhat resilient (if it feels like rare steak, it should be allowed to hang longer). Cut about ¼ inch off one end of the meat. Let the prosciutto sit for 1 minute. Smell the inside cut of the meat; it should have a fresh and sweet aroma. (Do not eat cured meat if it does not smell appetizing.)

To serve, discard the skin and cut the prosciutto into paper-thin slices. *(This prosciutto will keep for several weeks refrigerated, becoming denser as it dries. To keep after cutting, cover only the cut side with plastic wrap; leave the rest uncovered.)*

Makes About 2¼ Pounds   61 Calories
8.6 gm Protein   2.7 gm Fat
.1 gm Carbohydrate per Ounce

Ragout of Duck Legs

A single duck is best divided and used for two separate and very different preparations. The breasts should be cooked rare like a steak, for they tend to dry out when subjected to the longer cooking times that the tougher legs and thighs require. Contributing their flavor to the liquid in which they are cooked, these parts become tender and unctuous when subjected to moist slow heat.

In this ragout, the browned legs and thighs are slowly braised in a mixture of red wine, Cognac, and Madeira. Instead of making a separate stock, one cooks the carcass along with the meat to augment the rich duck flavor. The legs and thighs are cooked without their skin to avoid fat and calories.

This ragout is really a companion recipe to Pan-Fried Duck Steaks. Two whole ducks are broken down into their separate parts: the breasts to be used for the duck steaks and the legs, thighs, and one carcass for this ragout.

Have your butcher skin the ducks and remove the breasts and the legs with thighs attached. For this recipe, you will need one-quarter ounce of the thick white fat that surrounds the cavity opening. Reserve the breasts and the remaining fat for the Pan-Fried Duck Steaks (the parts can be frozen). Cut one carcass into five or six sections. The second carcass may be discarded or saved to make stock.

Any additional fat is skimmed from the sauce before serving. Pearl onions and chestnuts add richness and complexity. Serve the ragout with Roasted Polenta or ½ cup fresh noodles or pasta per person.

1½ teaspoons (¼ ounce) duck fat
1 duck carcass, cut into 5 or 6 sections
3 tablespoons all-purpose flour
4 duck legs with the thighs attached, skinned
2 tablespoons Cognac
4 to 5 shallots, chopped (2 ounces)
3 cups full-bodied dry red wine
¼ cup Rainwater Madeira
½ teaspoon salt
1 bay leaf
2 sprigs fresh thyme or ¼ teaspoon dried
7 garlic cloves, peeled
10 ounces fresh pearl onions, unpeeled, or 1 jar
   (8 ounces) pearl onions in water, rinsed
¼ pound whole peeled roasted chestnuts (about
   20) (see Note)
Freshly ground pepper
2 tablespoons minced Italian flat-leaf parsley
   (optional)

In a heavy medium casserole, heat the duck fat over moderate heat until most of the fat is melted, about 5 minutes. Add the carcass sections and cook, stirring occasionally, until browned, about 7 minutes. Transfer the carcass pieces to a platter.

Place the flour in a shallow bowl. Dredge the duck legs lightly in the flour, shaking to remove any excess. Add the legs to the casserole and cook until browned, about 5 minutes on each side. Pour in the Cognac and, using a long kitchen match, ignite the Cognac and cook until the flames subside. Transfer the duck legs to the platter with the carcass.

Add the shallots to the casserole, reduce the heat to low, and cook until lightly browned, about 1 minute. Stir in the remaining dredging flour. Slowly add ½ cup of the red wine, stirring constantly to form a paste. Gradually add the remaining 2½ cups wine and the Madeira. Increase the heat to moderate and boil the mixture for 5 minutes, stirring to scrape the browned bits up

from the bottom of the pan. Add the salt, bay leaf, thyme, and garlic. Arrange the duck legs in the casserole; nestle the carcass sections between them.

Place a piece of aluminum foil over the casserole and press the casserole lid down to form a tight seal. Simmer over low heat until the duck legs are tender, about 1½ hours. (Alternatively, bake in a preheated 300° oven.)

If you are using fresh pearl onions, cut a crisscross score in the root end of each onion. In a medium saucepan, place the onions and enough water to cover by 1 inch. Bring the water to a boil and cook the onions until tender but not mushy, 5 to 7 minutes. Drain and transfer to a bowl of cold water to cool; drain again. Using your fingers or a small sharp knife, peel the onions, leaving enough of the root ends so they don't fall apart. Set aside.

Transfer the duck legs to a platter and cover. Discard the carcass pieces. Pour the sauce into a medium measuring cup. Refrigerate or freeze until the fat rises to the surface, about 30 minutes. Skim off the fat.

Arrange the duck legs, chestnuts, and reserved onions (or jarred onions) in a heavy casserole to fit; pour the sauce over them. Bring to a simmer over moderately low heat. Cook until the duck legs are heated through, about 5 minutes. Season with pepper to taste. Garnish with the chopped parsley if desired.

Note: *I use bottled peeled roasted chestnuts, such as Minerve brand for this recipe to avoid the tedious task of roasting and peeling chestnuts. The chestnuts are vacuum-sealed in glass jars without any liquid and are firm and flavorful. They are available in the gourmet section of supermarkets and at specialty stores.*

**4 Servings   284 Calories   23.5 gm Protein
9.0 gm Fat   26.2 gm Carbohydrate per Serving**

Grilled Breaded Turkey Cutlets

I make these turkey cutlets when I am hankering for a breaded veal cutlet fried in olive oil like the one served at the Italian luncheonette around the corner. Turkey breast does an excellent job of mimicking the veal. The pounded cutlets are coated with bread crumbs mixed with grated Parmesan cheese and rosemary. They are grilled, rather than fried in oil, and this yields a lovely toasty crust and fewer calories. A little extra-virgin oil is drizzled on at the end for added flavor. Served on a bed of lightly dressed arugula, they make a perfect, simple lunch.

1 pound turkey breast, sliced ½ inch thick
¼ cup fine dry bread crumbs
¼ cup grated Parmesan cheese
1 teaspoon dried rosemary, crumbled
Freshly ground pepper
1 tablespoon plus 2 teaspoons extra-virgin
  olive oil
4 lemon wedges, for serving

Preheat the broiler. Place 1 turkey slice on a work surface, cover it with plastic wrap, and pound it lightly with a meat pounder, the side of a heavy cleaver, or the bottom of a heavy skillet, until it is about ¼ inch thick. Repeat with the remaining turkey slices.

In a shallow casserole, combine the bread crumbs, Parmesan, rosemary, and pepper. Brush both sides of the turkey slices with 1 tablespoon of the olive oil. Dredge the slices in the bread crumb mixture, patting it over them until they are completely coated.

Broil the turkey cutlets for about 1½ minutes, until the bread crumbs are brown and crisp. Turn the cutlets over and cook for 1 to 1½ minutes, until the second side is brown. Divide the turkey evenly among 4 warm plates and drizzle ½ teaspoon of the remaining olive oil over each serving. Garnish with a lemon wedge. Serve immediately.

4 Servings   222 Calories   29.9 gm Protein
8.6 gm Fat   5.0 gm Carbohydrate per Serving

Breads

Buckwheat Popovers

. . . .

*C*risp on the outside and crepe-like on the inside, popovers are nothing more than a unique quick bread made from crepe batter that pops—inflates with air—in its pan when subjected to high heat. Next to corn bread, they are about the easiest bread to whip up at a moment's notice. These popovers are lovely for dinner, lunch, or breakfast. The addition of buckwheat flour makes them a wonderful if rather unorthodox accompaniment to sour cream and caviar or smoked fish, as well as to a side of ham or eggs along with a sweet spread like the Pear Hazelnut Sauce. When day-old popovers are sliced and toasted they resemble a buttery French brioche. They can also be made with white flour only.

. . . .

¾ cup sifted all-purpose flour
¼ cup sifted buckwheat flour
1 tablespoon confectioners' sugar
½ teaspoon salt
¾ cup plus 2 tablespoons milk, at room
  temperature
3 eggs, at room temperature
1 tablespoon unsalted butter, melted

Preheat the oven to 400°. In a large bowl, sift together the all-purpose flour, buckwheat flour, sugar, and salt. Whisk in the milk. Add the eggs, one at a time, whisking well after each addition. The batter will be quite thin.

Place a popover pan, a ½-cup-capacity muffin tin, or ten ½-cup ovenproof custard cups arranged on a baking sheet in the oven and heat for 5 minutes. Remove and quickly brush the inside of each cup with the melted butter.

Fill each cup halfway with the batter and bake for 15 minutes; do not open the oven door. Reduce the temperature to 250° and bake for another 15 minutes, until the popovers are puffed and browned. Prick each popover to let the steam escape and bake for 5 minutes longer. Let cool briefly, then remove by running a knife around the rim and inverting the dish.

Variation: This recipe can easily be converted into a rough adaptation of something called "Bouncing Babies," which were billed as "big, fat popovers" in the 1953 edition of *The Joy of Cooking*. (The recipe has disappeared from more recent volumes.) The same batter is divided into 6 portions rather than 10 to produce huge, extravagant popovers that make a wonderful special-occasion breakfast. Proceed as directed in the recipe above, baking the popovers in 6 ovenproof soufflé dishes, about 3½ by 2 inches. Reduce the oven temperature to 350° rather than 250°. Makes 6 large popovers, 150 calories each.

Makes 10 Popovers   90 Calories
3.8 gm Protein   3.5 gm Fat
10.6 gm Carbohydrate Each

Buckwheat Popovers with sour cream and caviar ➤

Buckwheat-Beer Griddle Cakes

· ·

These easy-to-make griddle cakes are reminiscent of yeast-raised blini, owing to the amber beer in the batter. Like blini, they are wonderful with Double Sour Cream and caviar or smoked salmon for a luxurious brunch or late-night supper. They also go well with maple syrup, Pear Hazelnut Sauce and sautéed country ham for a rustic, old-fashioned breakfast. Or try them with Blueberry Caviar.

· ·

½ cup buckwheat flour
½ cup unbleached or all-purpose flour
1 teaspoon baking powder
½ teaspoon baking soda
½ teaspoon salt
1 cup plus 2 tablespoons buttermilk
⅓ cup amber beer
1 egg, beaten
1 tablespoon molasses
1 tablespoon plus 2 teaspoons melted unsalted
   butter

In a medium bowl, combine the buckwheat and unbleached flours, baking powder, baking soda, and salt. In a small bowl, beat together the buttermilk, beer, egg, molasses, and 2 teaspoons of the melted butter. Pour into the dry ingredients and whisk together until just combined.

Preheat a griddle or large nonstick skillet over moderate heat until a drop of water skitters on the surface. Brush lightly with some of the remaining melted butter. Drop the batter by heaping tablespoons onto the hot griddle, allowing each room to spread. Reduce the heat to moderately low. Cook until bubbles appear on the surface of the cakes, the batter looks dry, and the undersides are golden, 2 to 3 minutes. Flip the griddle cakes and cook until the undersides are browned, about 1 minute longer.

Continue with the remaining batter, brushing the griddle with more of the melted butter as necessary. Serve at once or, if desired, transfer each batch to a baking sheet lined with a kitchen towel and keep warm in a 200° oven while you cook the remaining cakes. Serve 6 griddle cakes per person.

6 Servings   142 Calories   5.0 gm Protein
4.8 gm Fat   20.1 gm Carbohydrate per Serving

Pan-Grilled Bread

. . . .

*C*rusty peasant bread grilled over a wood fire remains for me the simplest yet most pleasing accompaniment to a host of dishes, from stews to soups to composed salads. It is sublime on its own as an hors d'oeuvre with drinks. Since very few city-locked apartment dwellers have fireplaces, or the wherewithal to grill over wood, hearth-grilled bread might seem like a rather elitist fantasy. This very simple method for grilling bread, in a frying pan on the stovetop, recreates the flavor, texture, and satisfaction of the real thing without the necessity of a roaring fire. It also makes a great grilled cheese sandwich (see Variation 1 below).

. . . .

4 slices coarse peasant bread (1 ounce each)
1 tablespoon extra-virgin olive oil
⅛ teaspoon coarse (kosher) salt
½ tablespoon wood chips*
1 garlic clove, quartered (optional)
*See notes on wood chips under Divine
    Inspiration Pan-Smoked Salmon (page 103).

Brush 1 slice of bread on both sides with ¾ teaspoon of the olive oil. Repeat with the remaining bread slices and olive oil. Sprinkle each side with a pinch of the salt.

Place a large heavy skillet (preferably cast iron), fitted with a round rack, over moderate heat. When the pan is hot, sprinkle the wood chips over the bottom. When the chips begin to smoke, after about 5 minutes, arrange the bread on the rack, cover, and toast until golden, 3 to 4 minutes on each side. If desired, brush the bread with a piece of the cut garlic. Serve at once.

Variation 1: For a grilled cheese sandwich, at 237 calories per serving, arrange ½ ounce of crumbled ripe aged goat cheese or shredded Swiss mountain cheese, such as Appenzeller or Gruyère, on each slice of bread after the first side has been toasted. Cover and grill until the cheese is melted, about 2 minutes longer.

Variation 2: An Italian-style bruschetta—grilled bread topped with diced, seasoned fresh tomatoes—at 168 calories per serving, makes a lovely hors d'oeuvre or first course. Top each serving of pan-grilled bread with ¼ cup Cold Fresh Tomato Sauce (page 238).

4 Servings   137 Calories   3.9 gm Protein
2.6 gm Fat   24.0 gm Carbohydrate per Serving

Irish Brown Bread

. . . .

Although brown bread is a constant throughout Ireland, every cook has his or her own special recipe, purported to be the best and truest. Most recipes call for graham flour, a coarsely milled whole wheat flour not readily available in America. This recipe is a product of my mother's experiments with brown bread and her research into the differences between Irish and American flours during her 20 years in Ireland. It is an amalgam of much patient experimentation and recipes culled from Irish friends. A combination of whole wheat and unbleached flours with rolled oats and oat bran approximates the Irish flours, yielding a toothsome bread that is high in fiber, low in calories, and virtually fat free (so indulging in a teaspoon of fine sweet butter will do no serious damage).

Brown bread is a lovely accompaniment to smoked salmon, Pepper-Cured Gravlax, salads, and soups. This bread is also delicious toasted for breakfast or tea. Wrapped well, it freezes beautifully for up to three months.

Irish Brown Bread

. . . .

½ teaspoon vegetable oil
2⅓ cups whole wheat flour
1 cup all-purpose flour
⅓ cup rolled oats
⅓ cup oat bran
2 teaspoons dark brown sugar
1½ teaspoons salt
1 teaspoon baking powder
1 teaspoon baking soda
About 1¾ cups buttermilk

Preheat the oven to 400°. Brush ¼ teaspoon of the oil into each of two 8-by-4-inch loaf pans, coating the bottom and sides of the pans evenly.

In a bowl, stir together 2¼ cups of the whole wheat flour, the all-purpose flour, rolled oats, oat bran, brown sugar, salt, baking powder, and baking soda.

With a fork, stir in 1½ cups of the buttermilk. Add more buttermilk, little by little, just until the dough is soft but not too wet. (The amount of buttermilk needed will vary with the moisture content of the flour but should not exceed 1¾ cups.) Knead the dough in the bowl until all the flour is incorporated and the dough is smooth, about 2 minutes. If the dough is too wet, knead in a little of the remaining 4 teaspoons whole wheat flour, 1 teaspoon at a time.

Divide the dough into 2 equal portions and shape each into a log about the size of the loaf pans. Place a log of dough in each pan, patting down gently to fill the pans. With a thin sharp knife, cut 3 or 4 lengthwise slashes, ½ inch deep, in the top of the dough. (This allows the dough to expand evenly as it cooks.)

Bake the loaves for 30 to 35 minutes or until a cake tester inserted in the middle comes out clean and the bottoms of the loaves sound hollow when tapped. Remove the bread from the pans and place on a rack to cool.

To serve, slice 1 loaf into 18 thin slices. Serve 2 slices per person.

Variation: If desired, you can shape this bread into 2 freestanding traditional round loaves. Brush a baking sheet with ½ teaspoon vegetable oil, divide the dough, and shape into 2 rounds. Place on the baking sheet and, using a thin sharp knife, make 2 crisscrossing slashes on top of the loaf. Each loaf weighs approximately 18 ounces.

Makes Two 8-Inch Loaves   100 Calories
4.1 gm Protein   .9 gm Fat
20.1 gm Carbohydrate per 2-Ounce Serving

Crackling Corn Bread

*W*hen I was young, my mother, whose parents were Greek, evidenced an innate talent for such old-fashioned American classics as chicken pot pie, New England boiled dinner, and Lady Baltimore cake. She also made incredible corn bread in a black cast-iron skillet and served it with all manner of foods, from cool seafood salads at breezy summer luncheons to pork chops smothered in onions with applesauce in winter. Following her intuition, she used coarse yellow polenta cornmeal, which gave it a rich flavor and pleasant crackle. I learned at a tender age that the skillet and the coarsely ground meal were the keys to great corn bread.

This crackling skillet bread is quite different from my mother's, although based on that early lesson. It is delicious split and toasted for breakfast.

1 cup coarsely ground yellow cornmeal*
½ teaspoon salt
½ teaspoon baking soda
1 cup buttermilk
1 egg
2 teaspoons extra-virgin olive oil
*Available at some supermarkets and at specialty food stores

Preheat the oven to 450°. In a medium bowl, combine the cornmeal, salt, and baking soda. In a small bowl, beat together the buttermilk and egg. Pour the buttermilk mixture into the cornmeal and stir until combined. Do not overmix.

Heat a 10-inch cast-iron skillet or griddle in the oven for 5 minutes. When hot, swirl the olive oil into the pan. Spoon the batter into the pan and shake slightly to spread evenly. Bake until the bread is set and a knife inserted into the center comes out clean, about 10 minutes.

Let cool about 5 minutes before inverting the corn bread onto a wire rack. Serve warm or at room temperature.

Variations: Crackling Rosemary Corn Bread: Add 1 to 2 tablespoons fresh rosemary to the hot olive oil and carefully spoon the batter on top so the rosemary leaves form a pattern on the bottom of the corn bread. Or add 2 teaspoons dried crumbled rosemary to the buttermilk mixture. Proceed as directed.

Crackling Sage Corn Bread: Arrange 16 fresh sage leaves in the hot olive oil in the bottom of the skillet and spoon the batter carefully on top. Or add 2 teaspoons dried sage to the buttermilk mixture. Proceed as directed.

4 Servings   189 Calories   6.5 gm Protein
4.7 gm Fat   29.9 gm Carbohydrate per Serving

Nelly's Breakfast Apple Cake

*V*ery high in fiber and low in cholesterol, this tender apple cake made with oat bran is scented with cinnamon, nutmeg, hazelnut oil, and vanilla. Serve as is, or with a tablespoon of Yogurt Cheese or ricotta cheese for a healthy low-calorie breakfast.

2 cups less 2 tablespoons oat bran
½ cup plus 2 tablespoons unbleached flour
1¼ teaspoons cinnamon
2 teaspoons baking powder
¾ teaspoon baking soda
½ teaspoon salt
¼ teaspoon nutmeg
¼ cup dried currants
½ cup fresh orange juice
½ cup buttermilk
3 tablespoons molasses
3 egg whites
2 tablespoons hazelnut or vegetable oil
1 teaspoon vanilla extract
1 large Golden Delicious apple—peeled, cored, and cut into ¼-inch dice

Preheat the oven to 375°. Lightly grease an 8-inch square baking pan and set aside. In a medium bowl, combine the oat bran, flour, cinnamon, baking powder, baking soda, salt, and nutmeg. Stir with a wooden spoon to combine. Add the currants and toss well to coat.

In a small bowl, whisk together the orange juice, buttermilk, molasses, egg whites, oil, and vanilla. Add the diced apple. Stir into the dry ingredients until just combined.

Pour the batter into the prepared pan and bake for 35 minutes, checking halfway through and covering the cake with foil if it's browning too quickly. The cake is done when a cake tester inserted in the center comes out dry. Let the cake cool in the pan for 25 minutes. Run a knife around the edges of the pan and invert the cake onto a cooling rack. *(Wrapped well, the cake can be refrigerated for up to 1 week or frozen for up to 2 months.)* Serve at room temperature.

Variation: This batter can also be baked into muffins. Proceed as directed using 8 muffin cups (1-cup capacity). Bake for 30 minutes. Cool the muffins in their pan for 20 minutes before inverting onto a cooling rack.

**8 Servings   186 Calories   6.9 gm Protein
5.3 gm Fat   36.2 gm Carbohydrate per Serving**

Focaccia and Pizza

*N*owadays, focaccia and pizza take many forms, depending on the whim of their maker: there are no set rules as to either the thickness of the crusts or the flavorings that are applied to them. I make both my focaccia and pizza with a yeasty, chewy, thin crust because it is very satisfying, yet much lighter and less filling than the usual thicker crusts. Focaccias flavored simply with olive oil and herbs are the quintessential hors d'oeuvres. They are elemental and rustic and fill the house with the smell of baking bread. They are also an excellent accompaniment to a main meal, such as a hearty soup, stew, or warm salad. With the addition of more substantial items, like mozzarella and tomatoes, this versatile crust becomes a pizza—a little meal in itself when paired with a salad.

Traditionally, both focaccias and pizzas are drizzled with quite a bit of olive oil before baking. Here, the dough is brushed with a small amount of extra-virgin olive oil, baked, and, just before serving, brushed again with olive oil so that its flavor will hit the palate with the first bite, making it seem as if there is a lot more oil than there really is.

The following master recipe illustrates the basic method for forming and baking one seven-inch focaccia or pizza. A variety of toppings are listed at the end of the recipe, with cooking directions. If you wish to make several focaccias or pizzas, simply multiply the ingredients by that number.

I bake my focaccia on a pizza stone, which simulates the effect of baking in a brick oven, rendering the dough chewy and flavorful. If you don't have a pizza stone, a cast iron skillet works almost as well.

Focaccia and Pizza

. . . .

2 ounces Focaccia and Pizza Dough (one sixth of
    the recipe; page 180)
1 teaspoon all-purpose flour
¾ teaspoon extra-virgin olive oil
1 tablespoon fresh rosemary leaves or 1 teaspoon
    dried
Pinch of coarse (kosher) salt
Freshly ground pepper

Preheat the oven to 450°. Place a pizza stone or
cast-iron skillet in the oven to heat for at least 15
minutes.

Flatten the dough into a disk and roll out into
roughly a 7-inch circle, using the flour if necessary to keep it from sticking. Prick the dough
with a fork. Brush the dough with half the oil.
Scatter the rosemary evenly over the dough and
season with salt and pepper.

Using metal spatulas, transfer the dough round
to the pizza stone or skillet and bake. After 2
minutes, check the focaccia and, using a fork or
knife, prick any large air bubbles that may have
formed. Bake for about 5 minutes longer, until
the bubbles that form on the focaccia are golden
and the edges are browned. Remove the focaccia
from the oven and brush with the remaining oil.
Serve at once.

Garlic and Sage Focaccia
Tomato, Basil, and Mozzarella
Focaccia ➤

Variation: Parmesan and Pepper Focaccia,
197 calories per focaccia. Omit the rosemary and
proceed with the master recipe. Bake the focaccia
for about 4 minutes until the dough forms bubbles and is just beginning to brown. Scatter ¼
ounce grated or thinly shaved Parmesan cheese
on top. Bake for 1 minute longer, until the cheese
is melted. Brush with the remaining oil and serve.
Garlic and Sage Focaccia, 171 calories per focaccia. Omit the rosemary and arrange 16 to 20
sage leaves and 1 thinly sliced garlic clove on the
dough. Brush with half the olive oil. Season
lightly with salt and pepper, as above, and proceed
as directed.
Spiced Red Onion Focaccia, 185 calories per
focaccia. Brush the dough lightly with oil. Omit
the rosemary and arrange ¼ cup thinly sliced red

onion on top. Brush the onion rings lightly with
oil. Season with coarse salt, freshly ground pepper, and a pinch of ground coriander. Scatter
¼ teaspoon fennel seeds over the top. Proceed as
directed.
Tomato, Basil, and Mozzarella Pizza, 251 calories per pizza. Omit the rosemary and arrange
1 ounce thinly sliced mozzarella cheese on top of
the dough. Top with 8 fresh basil leaves and
3 thin slices of tomato or 5 cherry tomatoes cut
into quarters. Brush with half the oil. Sprinkle
1 tablespoon minced red onion or shallot on top.
Proceed as directed.

Makes 1 Individual 7-Inch Focaccia or Pizza
172 Calories   3.9 gm Protein   5.5 gm Fat
26.7 gm Carbohydrate Each

Focaccia and Pizza Dough

This basic dough will make six thin-crusted seven-inch focaccias or pizzas. It makes a chewy, crisp, and yeasty crust that is delicious with a variety of toppings. The dough can be wrapped in individual portions and frozen so that single focaccias or pizzas can conveniently be baked for a light lunch or to accompany cocktails. Let the dough thaw at room temperature for one hour before using. The dough can be refrigerated for up to four days. See Focaccia and Pizza for toppings.

½ cup lukewarm water (105° to 110°)
1¼ teaspoons active dry yeast
1½ cups unbleached all-purpose flour
1 teaspoon salt
2 teaspoons extra-virgin olive oil

Pour the lukewarm water into a small bowl. Sprinkle the yeast over it. Set aside for 5 minutes. Stir to dissolve completely.

Add the flour and salt to a food processor. With the motor running, pour in the yeast mixture and the olive oil. Process until the mixture is uniform: it either will have the texture of coarse meal or will gather into 1 or 2 balls near the blade. Gather the dough together and knead until smooth and elastic, about 6 minutes. Form the dough into a ball and place in a lightly oiled bowl. Brush the top of the dough lightly with oil. Cover the dough with a damp kitchen towel and set aside in a warm place until doubled in bulk, about 2 hours.

Punch down the dough and form into a log, about 2 inches in diameter, or divide into 6 equal portions. Wrap in plastic wrap until ready to use. *(The dough can be made and refrigerated up to 4 days ahead or frozen for up to 2 months.)*

Variation: Quick Focaccia Dough, 128 calories per serving. Although it does not have the yeasty flavor of the original, this method requires no kneading or rising. Omit the yeast and add 1½ teaspoons baking powder to the flour. Process the dough with hot water rather than lukewarm. Gather the dough into a ball, cover with plastic wrap, and let rest for 30 minutes before using.

6 Servings   130 Calories   3.6 gm Protein
1.9 gm Fat   24.2 gm Carbohydrate per Serving

Desserts

Simple Fruit Desserts

. . . .

On a warm midsummer's day many years ago, as we were wandering around Chinatown after lunch at a local restaurant, my sister and I bought some fresh lychees at a market we passed. We went into a nearby park and sat on a bench under the trees to eat our dessert. Peeling the thin russet-colored shells with our fingernails, we ate one after another, enthralled by the sensuous fruit and its perfume of roses, honey, and a faint indescribable spice. Those lychees were as perfect and simple a dessert as I will ever encounter.

The clarity of flavor of fresh fruit after a meal can be sublime and truly memorable, surprising by its very simplicity. Ripe and in their season, fruits offer sweetness without refined sugar. The ripening process concentrates the flavors as well as the natural sugars of the fruit. Their aromas are satisfying and refreshing. Fruits are naturally low in calories.

Even the most ordinary of market offerings can be transformed into a dessert of great delicacy with the addition of a little wine, liqueur, fresh herbs, a dusting of spices, a drizzle of orange or rose flower water, or simply another fruit. The possible combinations are endless. Since these additions are used in small amounts to add nuances of flavor that enhance or offset the fruit, they add only a few calories.

The following are some of my favorite ways of embellishing fruit. Each suggestion is for four people and may be easily multiplied to feed many. Because they are so low in calories, they can be enjoyed with one or two plain cookies, such as Lace Cookies.

Simple Fruit Desserts

Strawberries Dipped in Powdered Sugar, 75 calories per serving. Serve 4 cups of whole strawberries (stems on) with ¼ cup of confectioners' sugar to dip them into.

Pineapple with Kirsch, 71 calories per serving. Drizzle 1 tablespoon plus 1 teaspoon kirsch over 3 cups pineapple chunks. Garnish with 2 teaspoons slivered lime zest.

Peaches in Champagne, 95 calories per serving. Pour 1 cup Champagne over 2 cups sliced peaches and 1 cup blackberries.

Oranges with Flower Water, 85 calories per serving. Toss 4 cups orange sections with 2 teaspoons orange or rose flower water mixed with ¼ cup water. Dust lightly with cinnamon.

Kirsch with Fresh Cherries, 187 calories per serving. Serve a small cordial glass of kirsch (1 ounce) with 1 cup sweet ripe cherries per person.

Berries in Red Wine, 113 calories per serving. Toss 4 cups mixed raspberries and sliced strawberries with 1 tablespoon plus 1 teaspoon sugar. Marinate for 2 hours. Toss the berries with 1 cup fruity red wine, 1 tablespoon fresh lemon juice, 8 whole basil leaves, and a pinch of cinnamon.

Melon with Anisette, 80 calories per serving. Drizzle 1 teaspoon anisette mixed with ¼ cup water and 2 tablespoons plus 2 teaspoons confectioners' sugar over 4 cups canteloupe slices. Garnish with 1 tablespoon plus 1 teaspoon slivered lemon zest.

Melon with Crystallized Ginger, 86 calories per serving. Toss 4 cups honeydew, Persian, or Crenshaw melon with 3 tablespoons fresh lime juice and 2 tablespoons (1 ounce) slivered crystallized ginger.

Star Fruit with Raspberries, 67 calories per serving. Combine 2 cups sliced star fruit (carambola) or peeled Asian pear with 2 cups raspberries. Drizzle with 1 tablespoon plus 1 teaspoon Framboise.

Oranges with Irish Whisky, 141 calories per serving. In a small saucepan, simmer 1 cup water, ¼ cup sugar, 16 white peppercorns, and 1 vanilla bean, split and scraped, for 4 minutes. Add 1 tablespoon Irish whisky, Cognac, or bourbon and ¼ cup slivered lemon zest and simmer for 2 minutes. Spoon the syrup over 4 cups orange sections.

Berries in Buttermilk, 72 calories per serving. Pour 1 cup buttermilk over 2 cups mixed strawberries, raspberries, blackberries, and blueberries. Drizzle 2 teaspoons honey and ¼ cup chopped fresh basil on top.

Fruit with Passion Fruit Sauce, about 18 calories per serving of passion fruit. The pulp of passion fruit with its intense perfume of pineapple, orange, and banana makes a lovely sauce for a variety of fruits. Simply slice 4 passion fruit in half and spoon out the pulp. Toss with 4 cups fresh berries or sliced peaches, apricots, mangoes, or papaya, in any combination.

Oven-Poached Pears or Peaches with Currants, 134 calories per serving. Peel, halve, and core 4 pears or peaches and arrange the halves in a baking dish. Pour ½ cup Gewürztraminer wine over the fruit and sprinkle 1 tablespoon sugar, 1 tablespoon slivered orange zest, and 1 split vanilla bean on top. Cover tightly and bake for 30 to 45 minutes or until the fruit is tender. For each serving, spoon 2 pear halves and some syrup into a soup bowl and sprinkle ¼ cup fresh currants or blackberries on top.

Fruit and Cheese

· ·

In France, cheese is often served prior to or in lieu of dessert. In good restaurants, a tray of the day's offerings is presented to the diner, who may choose one or several. The portions that are served are small by American standards, probably totaling not much more than an ounce. In this amount, the cheese is not meant to be filling, but to act more as a flavorful, piquant end to the meal and something with which to enjoy the last glass of wine. Cheeses are high in calories and fat. The French know instinctively to enjoy them in moderation. The cheeses are served ripe and at room temperature so that their flavor and texture may be fully appreciated.

If handled judiciously, fruit and cheese in combination can be a glorious and relatively low-calorie end to a meal. An ounce of Roquefort and a ripe pear, for example, are less than 200 calories. There are hundreds of cheeses to choose from, each with its own unique pleasure to offer—from a Brin d'amour, the Corsican sheep's milk cheese, to a handmade goat's cheese from Washington State's Okanogan region. With cheese, as with all the taboo foods, the trick is simply to watch the quantity you eat, for it is easy to keep shaving off slivers of a delicious cheese until you have consumed hundreds of calories without noticing. Cheeses average about 100 calories per ounce, with the softer cheeses being slightly less and the harder cheeses, such as Parmesan, slightly more. Figure that one ounce of cheese plus one cup of fruit will average less than 200 calories per serving for dessert.

What follows are some of my personal favorites in matching fruit and cheese.

Fruit and Cheese

. . . .

Ripe pears marry well with the more assertive, nutlike flavors of blue-veined cheeses, such as Roquefort, Stilton, and Gorgonzola, as well as with parmigiano-reggiano, aged Gouda, and the herb-coated aged goat and sheep's milk cheeses, such as Brin d'amour.

Fresh cheeses, such as mild goat or ricotta cheese (considerably fewer calories, at 45 per ounce), are wonderful with soft, perfumed fruits, such as berries, peaches, nectarines, cherries, figs, pineapple, and papaya.

Triple crème cheeses, such as Explorateur, St. André, the Italian Robiola, and soft-ripening goat cheeses, such as Caprella, are lovely with berries, cherries, figs, and peaches.

Muscat grapes have an affinity for creamy Italian Taleggio and Bel Paese.

◄ Ripe pears with Brin d'amour cheese

Warm Cherries with Zabaglione

The combination of warm fresh cherries with zabaglione is a revelation for those who have never encountered it. The idea for this splendid dessert came about through joint inspiration, as my friend Margot Wellington and I were cooking one summer evening at her house on Long Island. The creation of that dessert is among my dearest memories and a reminder of the reason I love to cook. Margot and I sat looking at a bowl of ripe cherries we had bought at a farm stand, wondering what to do with them. The idea seemed to hit us both at the same time, like that flash of intuition that scientists often describe. Motivated by its promise, we cooked in tandem at the huge restaurant stove in a kind of dance—I the cherries, she the zabaglione. Then she, her husband, Albert, and I sat in the twilight, eating the fragrant cherries in their warm sauce, wondering why we had never thought of it before, and marveling at what our farm stand cherries had become.

Although this dessert is very rich, it is also very low in calories, for zabaglione—egg yolks beaten with Marsala and a little sugar—is really made up of a great deal of air, and the summer cherries are sweet and fragrant enough to need only a small amount of honey.

There are several well-designed cherry pitters on the market that can pit a pound of cherries in just a few minutes. It is not entirely necessary, however, since the French often serve unpitted cherries in dessert—a warning to your guests is all that is necessary.

3 cups fresh sweet cherries (about 60 cherries)
2 tablespoons plus 2 teaspoons honey
1 vanilla bean, split
3 egg yolks
2 tablespoons sugar
⅓ cup dry Marsala

Pit the cherries if desired. In a medium saucepan, combine the cherries, honey, and 2 tablespoons of water. Scrape the seeds from the vanilla bean into the pan and add the bean. Cook over moderate heat until the cherries release their juices, about 2 minutes. Uncover and cook over high heat until the cherries are tender, about 2 minutes longer. Remove from the heat and set aside, covered, at room temperature for up to 3 hours; reheat before serving if necessary. Discard the vanilla bean.

In a double boiler over simmering water, combine the egg yolks and sugar. Whisk until pale yellow, warm, and creamy, about 4 minutes.

Add the Marsala and beat vigorously until the zabaglione is hot and thickened enough to mound softly. Serve at once with the cherries or set aside, covered, for up to 2 hours.

Variations: For those who can't or don't wish to serve the cherries, the classic combination of zabaglione with fresh summer strawberries or raspberries is wonderful. The zabaglione alone is 99 calories per serving; add 45 calories for a cup of strawberries and 61 calories for a cup of raspberries.

**4 Servings   226 Calories   3.4 gm Protein
5.2 gm Fat   38.6 gm Carbohydrate per Serving**

Prunes Poached in Red Wine

Although one would never imagine it before tasting them, prunes poached in red wine are transformed into a sublime dessert with a lovely flavor evocative of wild raspberries. It is classically made with red burgundy, but less expensive wines that are robust and fruity work well. Each serving may be topped with one tablespoon stirred sour cream.

1 cup dry red wine
3 tablespoons sugar
1 strip of orange zest (1 by 3 inches) plus slivered
   zest, for garnish
½ vanilla bean, split and scraped
8 ounces pitted prunes

In a small nonreactive saucepan, combine the wine, sugar, orange zest strip, vanilla bean and scrapings, and 1 cup of water. Bring to a boil over moderately high heat, then reduce the heat to moderately low and simmer for 5 minutes. Add the prunes and simmer until they are very tender but not falling apart and the syrup has thickened slightly, about 15 minutes. Serve the prunes with their syrup chilled or at room temperature, garnished with the slivered orange zest.

**4 Servings   177 Calories   1.6 gm Protein
.3 gm Fat   46.0 gm Carbohydrate per Serving**

Alain Senderen's Salade de Fruit Exotique

. . . .

One of my most vivid memories of food is of a tropical fruit salad I had many years ago in Paris at Alain Senderen's restaurant l'Archestrate. Perhaps it was the fact that it was Thanksgiving Day and my last day in Paris, perhaps it was the effect of the wine we had at lunch that etched it so indelibly in my mind. Perhaps it was that the salad itself became the symbol of the entire lunch, a kind of enchantment. It was called Salade de Fruit Exotique. The fruits were nothing more than kiwi, pineapple, and mango. They were macerated in a delicate and hauntingly flavored syrup scented with vanilla, clove, coriander, lemon, lime, mint, and ginger that transformed the fruits into a lush, unforgettable dessert.

This is an ideal fruit salad for winter because the tropical fruits are available year-round and ripen naturally. The riper and more fragrant the fruit, the better the salad will be.

. . . .

2 tablespoons plus 2 teaspoons sugar
½ vanilla bean, split
3 coriander seeds
1 whole clove
¼ teaspoon five-spice powder*
Zest of 1 lime
Zest of ½ lemon
½ teaspoon chopped fresh ginger

1 sprig of fresh mint (optional)
1 tablespoon fresh lime juice
1 pineapple
1 mango
2 large kiwis
2 passion fruits
*Available at Asian markets and in the spice
    section of some supermarkets

Alain Senderen's Salade de Fruit Exotique

In a small saucepan, combine 1½ cups of water with the sugar, vanilla bean, coriander seeds, clove, five-spice powder, lime and lemon zests, ginger, and mint, if using. Simmer over moderate heat for 10 minutes. Set aside to cool. Then stir in the lime juice. *(The syrup may be made up to a week ahead and refrigerated.)*

Slice off the top and the rind from the pineapple; quarter it lengthwise. Reserve 3 of the quarters for another use. Slice 1 of the quarters crosswise ⅛ inch thick. Using a sharp paring knife, peel the mango and slice lengthwise, parallel to the pit on both sides, into disks ⅛ inch thick. Slice each mango disk in half lengthwise.

Peel the kiwis and halve lengthwise. Cut each half lengthwise into thin wedges.

Divide the fruit evenly and arrange in each of 4 shallow soup bowls, overlapping the slices to form a decorative pattern. Strain the reserved syrup and divide equally among the 4 servings. Cover with plastic wrap and refrigerate for at least 1 or up to 4 hours. Just before serving, halve the passion fruits crosswise. Using a teaspoon, scoop the pulp out of each half onto the fruit in each bowl.

**4 Servings   147 Calories   1.2 gm Protein
.7 gm Fat   37.0 gm Carbohydrate per Serving**

· · · · · · · · · ·

Gratin of Raspberries

This is one of my favorite desserts, for it is at once incredibly easy to make and very elegant. It is adapted from a recipe Jeremiah Tower called, without explanation, Russian Raspberry Gratin. I would love to know the true origins of this dessert, for it is rare that one finds a dessert that is so simple and so good. It is very rich and full of contrasting textures, as sugar caramelizes over sour cream to form a fine, crackly veil. The perfume of the fresh raspberries is released by being heated. All of this complexity with only three ingredients, for under 200 calories.

The recipe can be doubled or tripled to serve more people. It can be made in a single large gratin dish rather than in individual dishes.

. . . .

1 cup (about ½ pint) fresh raspberries or
  blackberries
½ cup sour cream
2 tablespoons plus 2 teaspoons dark brown sugar

Preheat the broiler. Arrange ½ cup of the berries in each of two 5½-inch gratin dishes or 4-inch soufflé dishes. Stir the sour cream to liquify it slightly and spread ¼ cup over each dish of berries, leaving a ring of berries uncovered around

the edge of the dish. Sieve 1 tablespoon plus 1 teaspoon of the brown sugar over each, mounding it slightly in the middle.

Place the dishes under the broiler about 3 to 4 inches from the heat source. Broil just until the sugar bubbles and begins to caramelize but do not let it burn. Serve at once.

2 Servings   222 Calories   2.4 gm Protein
12.4 gm Fat   27.3 gm Carbohydrate per Serving

. . . .

Blueberry Caviar

. . . .

This is another wonderfully simple and delicious invention of my friend Margot Wellington. Fresh blueberries are simply thrown into a hot pan with some sweet butter and sugar just long enough to glaze and warm them and for their fragrance to release. The first time she made the caviar, Margot ate it rolled into a warm buckwheat crepe, and so called it Blueberry Caviar in honor of the classic combination of blinis and caviar. It is sublime on just about anything, from Buckwheat-Beer Griddle Cakes to sorbets, ice milks, ice creams, even fresh ricotta cheese. The caviar is also spectacular on store-bought passion fruit sorbet.

. . . .

1½ teaspoons unsalted butter
1 pint (2 cups) fresh blueberries
1 tablespoon sugar

In a heavy medium skillet, heat the butter over moderate heat until hot and bubbly. Increase the heat to high and toss in the blueberries and sugar. Working quickly, shake the pan vigorously, tossing the blueberries with the butter and sugar

until completely coated and slightly softened. Serve at once.

Variation: This method works equally well for raspberries. Substitute 1 pint raspberries for the blueberries.

4 Servings   65 Calories   .5 gm Protein
1.7 gm Fat   13.3 gm Carbohydrate per Serving

Phyllo Pear Tart with Fried Raspberries

. . . .

Every year I invent a "birthday cake" for my friend Chris. It is a labor of love with no constraints, so I let myself take liberties with the definition of birthday cake and with my own notions of dessert and celebration. More often than not, my cake somehow ends up as a pie or a tart, for my sensibilities veer toward the concentrated flavors of fresh fruit and the visual possibilities of pastry.

I created this Phyllo Pear Tart for my dear friend, who is as thin as a rail and has never considered counting a calorie in his life. I put all the wonderful flavors I could think of into it: caramelized pastry, pears baked in a fragrant syrup, warm raspberries in a thin shell of sugar. Yet despite all this indulgence, this sensual dessert is still incredibly low in calories.

Only three sheets of phyllo, as thin as tissue paper, are needed to create a dramatic free-form shell for the fruit. They are laid into a pie plate and crumpled slightly, then brushed with butter, sprinkled with sugar, and baked until golden. The shell is filled with pears and warm raspberries, cooked separately. When the pastry is cut, the thin sheets of pastry shatter, making a wonderful, rather messy effect.

For those who wish to gild the lily, Chantilly Cream may be passed separately.

Phyllo Pear Tart with Fried Raspberries and Chantilly Cream ➤

Phyllo Pear Tart with Fried Raspberries

. . . .

Phyllo pastry

Pears baked with Sauternes and vanilla

1 tablespoon plus 2½ teaspoons unsalted butter
3 sheets of phyllo dough
2 tablespoons sugar
2 large or 3 medium pears (1 pound)—peeled, halved, and cored
½ cup sweet dessert wine, such as Muscat de Beaumes de Venise, Sauternes, or Barsac
½ vanilla bean, split
1 cup raspberries

Preheat the oven to 375°. In a small saucepan, melt 1½ tablespoons of the butter over low heat. Skim off the solids from the top. Spoon 1 tablespoon of the clear yellow liquid into a small bowl, leaving behind the whey at the bottom of the pan.

Lightly brush a 10-inch pie plate with some of the clarified butter and place it on a cookie sheet. Working with both hands, gently drape 1 sheet of the phyllo dough over the pie plate; lightly press in the dough to line the plate, leaving the edges overhanging. Brush the sheet lightly with more of the clarified butter. Place another sheet of phyllo on top of the first so that it covers more of the pie plate than is covered by the first phyllo sheet. Brush lightly with more of the butter. Repeat with the third sheet of phyllo. Roll and fold the edges of the three sheets loosely under themselves to form a ruffled edge that resembles crumpled tissue paper. Brush the ruffled edges and the center of the shell with the remaining clarified butter. Sprinkle the edges of the dough with 1 teaspoon of the sugar. Bake the shell for about 5 minutes or until golden. Set aside to cool.

Arrange the pear halves in another pie plate or baking dish. Pour the wine over the fruit. Scrape the seeds from the vanilla bean into the wine and nestle the bean among the pears. Cover with foil and bake, brushing the pears occasionally with the wine, for 30 to 40 minutes, until the pears

are tender. If the wine is evaporating too quickly, add a little warm water to the baking dish.

Sprinkle the pears with 1 tablespoon more of the sugar. Bake uncovered, brushing the pears frequently with the syrup, 10 to 15 minutes longer, until the pears are glazed and golden. Set aside to cool.

Just before serving, arrange the pear halves in a pinwheel in the center of the phyllo shell. In a heavy medium skillet, heat the remaining 1 teaspoon butter over moderate heat until hot and bubbly. Increase the heat to high and toss in the raspberries and the remaining 2 teaspoons sugar. Working quickly, shake the pan vigorously until the raspberries are completely coated. Spoon the raspberries around the pear in the tart shell and serve at once.

**4 Servings   211 Calories   2.4 gm Protein
6.0 gm Fat   39.2 gm Carbohydrate per Serving**

. . . .

Pineapple Upside-Down Cake

I had not eaten or even thought about pineapple upside-down cake since I was a kid, until a recent trip to West Virginia. An extraordinary and original meal at the house of my friends Irene and Mary began with real old-fashioneds; proceeded with Chinese food, hot yeast rolls, and beans from the garden boiled with slab bacon; and ended with pineapple upside-down cake for dessert. That meal is a memory I conjure occasionally when I'm feeling low. The cake, powerfully brown-sugared and buttered, became a challenge to recreate in low-calorie terms. It is a testament to my own obsessiveness, for it took many tries to make it work.

This recipe represents a totally revised version of the traditional one, which called for two cups of sugar and half a cup or more of butter. Here, sugar and butter in judicious amounts yield a butter caramel. The cake is an orange-and-vanilla-scented *genoise*. Fresh pineapple makes all the difference. The result is a dazzling cake for grown-ups who long for the lost pleasures of childhood.

Pineapple Upside-Down Cake

1 tablespoon plus 1 teaspoon unsalted butter
½ cup plus 1 tablespoon dark brown sugar
4 slices (½ inch thick) of fresh pineapple, or 6
    unsweetened canned slices, drained
3 large eggs, at room temperature
Pinch of salt
1½ teaspoons vanilla extract
1 teaspoon grated orange zest
½ cup sifted all-purpose flour

Preheat the oven to 375°. In a 9-inch ovenproof skillet, melt the butter with 3½ tablespoons of the brown sugar over moderate heat, stirring constantly, until bubbly, about 3 minutes. Arrange 3 fresh pineapple slices in the skillet (or 5 canned), overlapping if necessary. Cut the remaining slice in thirds. Place the pieces in gaps between the whole slices.

Cook the pineapple over moderate heat until the juices are released, about 5 minutes. Continue cooking, turning several times, until the fruit is tender and the juices have reduced to a syrupy brown caramel, about 10 minutes longer. Remove the skillet from the heat.

In a medium mixer bowl, beat the eggs with the remaining 5½ tablespoons brown sugar and the salt at high speed until tripled in volume, 7 to 10 minutes. Drizzle in the vanilla, add the orange zest, and continue beating until well combined, about 1 minute longer.

Sift half of the flour over the batter. Fold in until just combined. Then sift on and fold in the remaining flour. Pour the batter over the pineapple slices in the skillet.

Bake for 18 minutes, or until the cake is golden brown and a skewer inserted in the center comes out clean. Let the cake cool on a rack for 5 to 7 minutes. Run a knife around the edge to loosen the cake, then invert onto a serving plate. With a rubber spatula, scrape any caramel that may be clinging to the bottom of the skillet and drizzle it over the top.

6 Servings   194 Calories   4.3 gm Protein
5.3 gm Fat   32.6 gm Carbohydrate per Serving

Deep-Dish Rosewater Apple Pie

For years I made my apple pies the way my mother made hers: with green apples, lemon, and cinnamon. As simple as it was, it had a tart, concentrated flavor that was perfect. I had never tasted anything to make me try otherwise until I came across a Shaker recipe called Rosewater Apple Pie, from Eldress Bertha Lindsay at the Shaker Village in Canterbury, New Hampshire. It is a perfect example of the brilliance of Shaker cooking, for the two flavoring elements, rosewater and a breath of nutmeg, marry with the apples in a subtle and totally unexpected way. I have served it to the most straitlaced apple pie aficionados, who have raved about the freshness and delicacy of this pie.

The sugar has been dramatically cut back from the original recipe. Since the pie is made in a deep casserole or pan, I have forgone a bottom crust, which would only get soggy and add calories. I have kept a top crust of short, flaky pastry. Since the pie is quite low in calories, it can be accompanied by Chantilly Cream, vanilla ice milk, or frozen yogurt, if desired.

I usually make this pie in a straight-sided two-quart oval French porcelain gratin dish or in a two-quart casserole. It can also be made in a 9- or 10-inch round skillet, gratin, or copper sauté pan.

Deep-Dish Rosewater Apple Pie

. . . .

3 pounds tart green apples, such as Granny
   Smith (about 7 large apples)—peeled, cored,
   and sliced ⅛ inch thick
⅓ cup sugar
¼ teaspoon freshly grated nutmeg
1 tablespoon rosewater
1 teaspoon fresh lemon juice
Pinch of salt
1 teaspoon cold butter, cut into small pieces
Flaky Butter Pastry (page 222)
1 tablespoon confectioners' sugar

Place the apple slices in a 2-quart oval gratin
dish, about 13 by 9 by 2 inches. In a small bowl,
stir together the sugar and nutmeg. Sprinkle it
over the apples and toss well.

In a small bowl, combine the rosewater, lemon
juice, salt, and 1 tablespoon of water. Sprinkle
this mixture over the apples and toss to coat.
Distribute the apples evenly over the casserole
without pressing them down. Dot the apples with
the butter.

On a lightly floured work surface, roll the
pastry 2 inches larger than the diameter of the
baking dish. Roll the pastry gently back over the

rolling pin and place it over the apples, so that
the edge overhangs the lip equally on all sides.
Fold the overhanging edge of the pastry under itself all around the pan. Gently lift the edge of the
pastry and, using a pastry brush dipped in water,
moisten the lip of the pan. Using a fork, crimp
the edges of the pastry to the pan. Prick the top
of the pasty at 2-inch intervals with a fork or cut
decorative air vents with a thin sharp knife. Refrigerate the pie for about 15 minutes to firm up
the crust. Meanwhile, preheat the oven to 350°.

Bake the pie for 45 to 50 minutes, until golden
brown. If the crust begins to brown too quickly,
cover it lightly with a piece of aluminum foil. Let
cool slightly. Just before serving, sift the confectioners' sugar over the crust.

Variation: To make my mother's original
cinnamon-and-lemon-scented pie, replace the
rosewater, nutmeg, and water with 1½ teaspoons
cinnamon and increase the lemon juice to 2
tablespoons.

8 Servings   244 Calories   2.1 gm Protein
7.9 gm Fat   43.3 gm Carbohydrate per Serving

. . . .

Sorbets

. . . .

*W*hen their flavors are pure and they are freshly made,
sorbets are crystalline essences of flavor at the end
of a rich meal. While intense, sorbets should be refreshing
and light. Chantilly Cream may be served alongside for true
indulgence, lifting the sorbet into the realm of ice cream.

I use two very simple methods for making sorbet at
home. The first does not even require an ice cream maker.
Soft-fleshed fruits are sliced, frozen, and then pureed in a

food processor with some liqueur or eau de vie and a little honey if necessary. In the second method, a sweet-flavored liquid is made first, either from fruit juices or espresso. It is then frozen in an ice cream maker. These methods work equally well. Sorbet is best eaten within a day after it is made, since its flavor diminishes with time.

. . . .

Method One

Strawbery Sorbet

2 pints of strawberries, hulled
1 tablespoon honey
1 teaspoon orange liqueur, such as Triple Sec or
    Grand Marnier (optional)

Place the berries on a cookie sheet, cover with plastic wrap, and freeze until solid. In a food processor, process until reduced to the texture of coarse meal, stopping frequently to scrape down the sides, (if the fruit is too hard to process, allow it to soften for 1 or 2 minutes before continuing). Add the honey and liqueur and process until fairly firm. Serve at once or transfer to a serving bowl, cover with plastic wrap, and freeze up to 1 day ahead.

Variation: Pear Sorbet, 128 calories per serving. Peel and core 6 ripe Bartlett or Comice pears (1¾ pounds). Slice into chunks and toss with 1 tablespoon fresh lemon juice. Freeze and puree as directed with 1 teaspoon Poire William and 1 tablespoon honey.

　Peach Sorbet, 73 calories per serving. Peel and pit 4 large ripe peaches (1½ pounds). Slice into 1-inch chunks. Toss with 1 tablespoon fresh lemon juice. Freeze and puree as directed with 1 tablespoon honey.

4 Servings　　64 Calories　1.0 gm Protein
.6 gm Fat　15.6 gm Carbohydrate per Serving

Method Two

Espresso Sorbet

⅓ cup superfine sugar
4 cups warm strong espresso
½ cup whipped cream (optional)
Cinnamon, for dusting (optional)

In a medium stainless steel bowl, add the sugar to the espresso and stir until dissolved. Let cool to room temperature. Refrigerate until very cold, about 1 hour, or freeze for 15 to 20 minutes.

　Transfer the mixture to an ice cream maker and freeze according to the manufacturer's instructions. To serve, divide the sorbet evenly among 4 dessert bowls. If desired, spoon 2 tablespoons whipped cream over each serving and dust lightly with cinnamon.

Variation: Grapefruit Cassis Sorbet, 135 calories per serving. Combine 3 cups fresh pink grapefruit juice and ¼ cup plus 1 tablespoon cassis (black currant) syrup. Transfer to an ice cream maker and freeze according to the manufacturer's instructions.

　Escoffier's Melon Sorbet, 108 calories per serving. In a food processor, puree 4 cups ripe honeydew melon chunks with ¾ cup fresh orange juice, ¼ cup fresh lemon juice, 2½ tablespoons superfine sugar, and 1½ teaspoons orange flower water. Transfer to an ice cream maker and freeze according to the manufacturer's instructions.

4 Servings　　71 Calories　.4 gm Protein
.0 gm Fat　17.8 gm Carbohydrate per Serving

Fresh Ginger Gingerbread

Every once in a while I feel like baking late at night, motivated by a hankering for a warm slice of a plain, old-fashioned cake that fills the house with its aroma. Gingerbread is the cake I usually end up baking. It took me some time to devise a gingerbread that I could happily have as a late-night indulgence, for more traditional recipes are extremely liberal with molasses and butter, often upward of 500 calories per slice. This lightened version has all the elements of an old-fashioned gingerbread, including molasses, mustard, and a host of spices, as well as strong coffee and grated fresh ginger. It relies on buttermilk for tenderness and richness as well as for leavening, in league with baking soda. Hazelnut Pear Sauce or Chantilly Cream is a delicious accompaniment.

3 tablespoons plus ½ teaspoon unsalted butter, softened
1½ cups sifted all-purpose flour
3 tablespoons (packed) dark brown sugar
1 large egg
¼ cup plus 2 tablespoons unsulphured molasses
3 tablespoons grated fresh ginger
2 tablespoons strong brewed coffee
1 teaspoon vanilla extract
1 teaspoon baking soda
1 teaspoon ground ginger
½ teaspoon cinnamon
½ teaspoon ground mustard
⅛ teaspoon ground cardamom
Pinch of salt
½ cup buttermilk
1 tablespoon confectioners' sugar

Preheat the oven to 350°. With your fingers, rub an 8-inch round cake pan with ½ teaspoon of the butter. Dust the pan with 1 teaspoon of the flour and set aside.

In a large bowl, using a mixer or a wooden spoon, beat the remaining 3 tablespoons butter and the brown sugar until light and fluffy. Add the egg, molasses, fresh ginger, coffee, and vanilla and beat well to combine.

Sift together the remaining flour, the baking soda, ground ginger, cinnamon, mustard, cardamom, and salt. Add the dry ingredients alternately with the buttermilk to the molasses mixture, beating well after each addition.

Pour the batter into the prepared pan. Bake for about ½ hour until a knife inserted in the center comes out clean. Cool the cake on a wire rack for about 10 minutes. Run a knife around the edges of the pan and invert onto the rack. Let cool completely. Transfer the cake bottom side up onto a plate. Sift the confectioners' sugar over the top.

6 Servings   268 Calories   4.8 gm Protein
7.4 gm Fat   45.3 gm Carbohydrate per Serving

Chocolate Chestnut Truffles

. . . .

Does anyone really think about the fact that a single chocolate truffle from a traditional French recipe, say by Fernand Point or Alice B. Toklas, contains upwards of 85 calories worth of egg yolks, butter, cream, sugar, and chocolate? It is a reality we choose to ignore or excuse, for there is nothing as satisfying as a fine chocolate truffle. The diet versions fail to convince us that balls of ground prunes flavored with cocoa powder or other such unlikely combinations will do the trick. Like the wild black truffle, people have tried in vain to fabricate one—until recently. About the time two scientists in California successfully produced real truffles in their laboratory, I finally figured out a way to make a worthy low-calorie chocolate truffle at home. The question had been in the back of my mind for years, how do you achieve the effect of all those forbidden ingredients—the density and richness and intensity—in some other, low-calorie way? What would be the medium that would provide the unctuous texture? Suddenly, quietly, one day the obvious answer came to me.

I remembered a chocolate cake I used to make when I was a caterer. That cake was as dense and rich as a truffle, and chestnut puree had been the main ingredient. Chestnuts were the answer. They are essentially a finely textured starch, closer to a potato than to a nut, for they are very low in fat. Their flavor combines beautifully with chocolate and Cognac. In my experiments, I found that either bottled peeled whole roasted chestnuts or canned chestnut puree worked well, were easy to find, and obviated the tedious work of peeling chestnuts. Both varieties are produced by the French company Minerve and are available at some supermarkets and most specialty food stores.

In my recipe, the chestnuts are cooked in milk until very tender, then pureed with melted chocolate and corn syrup, which provides the silkiness attributed to the high-fat butter and egg yolk of a traditional truffle. My truffles—dense, melting, and perfumed with Cognac—have fewer than half the calories of a classic recipe. They will keep for several weeks refrigerated in a tightly covered plastic container.

The better the chocolate you use, the better the truffle will be. I recommend using an imported semisweet chocolate, such as Callebaut.

Chocolate Chestnut Truffles

. . . .

¼ pound (18 to 20) peeled whole roasted
  chestnuts (see Note)
½ cup milk
⅓ vanilla bean, split
2½ ounces semisweet chocolate, coarsely
  chopped
1 tablespoon light corn syrup
2 to 3 teaspoons Cognac or Armagnac
Pinch of salt
1 tablespoon plus 2 teaspoons cocoa powder

In a small heavy saucepan, combine the chestnuts and ½ cup of water. Cover and simmer over very low heat until the water is evaporated but the chestnuts are still moist, about 15 minutes.

Stir in the milk. Scrape the seeds from the vanilla bean into the mixture and add the bean. Cover and simmer over very low heat until the chestnuts are very tender and the milk has reduced slightly, about 15 minutes. Remove the pan from the heat, stir in the chocolate, cover, and set aside to melt, stirring occasionally, until the chocolate is creamy, about 3 to 4 minutes. Discard the vanilla bean.

In a food processor, combine the chocolate-chestnut mixture and the corn syrup; process, scraping down the sides occasionally, until the mixture is perfectly smooth, about 2 minutes. Add the Cognac to taste and the salt and process for 1 minute longer. Transfer the truffle mixture to a bowl, cover, and refrigerate until firm.

Place the cocoa powder in a medium bowl. Scoop up 2 teaspoonfuls of the truffle mixture and roll into a rough ball with your fingers. Repeat with the remaining truffle mixture. Working with a few at a time, toss the truffles in the bowl of cocoa. Transfer to a plate as they are finished, then sift any remaining cocoa over them. (The truffles will keep refrigerated for several weeks in a tightly sealed container. If the truffles absorb the cocoa, sift a little more over them prior to serving.)

Note: If peeled whole chestnuts are not available, canned unsweetened chestnut puree may be substituted. Truffles will have a slightly softer texture. In a small heavy saucepan, combine ½ cup (4 ounces) chestnut puree and 6 tablespoons milk. Add the vanilla scrapings and bean and proceed with the recipe.

Makes 20 Truffles   35 Calories   .52 gm
Protein   1.6 gm Fat   4.9 gm Carbohydrate Each

Banana Soufflé

These individual soufflés look like a great deal more than they are in terms of calories. Although they are extremely simple to make and virtually foolproof—with a base of pureed bananas and egg yolks—they are as creamy, rich, and dramatic as a traditional cream sauce–based soufflé. Using very ripe, fragrant bananas keeps sugar (and calories) to a minimum. If desired, two tablespoons of Pear-Hazelnut Sauce may be spooned into the center of each hot soufflé just before serving, for a contrasting texture and flavor.

½ teaspoon vegetable oil
2 very ripe medium bananas, cut into 1-inch chunks
2 teaspoons fresh lemon juice
2 teaspoons Pear William
1 teaspoon vanilla extract
4 eggs, separated, at room temperature
3 tablespoons plus 1 teaspoon sugar
Pinch of cream of tartar

Preheat the oven to 450°. Brush four 1½-cup soufflé dishes lightly with the oil.

In a food processor, puree the bananas with the lemon juice, Pear William, and vanilla until smooth. Add the egg yolks and 1 teaspoon of the sugar; process to blend thoroughly. Scrape the banana base into a medium bowl.

In a mixer bowl, beat the egg whites with the cream of tartar at high speed until stiff peaks form. With the mixer on, sprinkle the remaining 3 tablespoons sugar onto the whites and continue beating until glossy. Fold the egg whites into the banana base.

Spoon into the prepared dishes—the mixture will mound to the top. Run your thumb around the inside rims to form a ¼-inch groove in the mixture; this will help the soufflés rise evenly.

Set the dishes on a baking sheet and bake the soufflés for 7 minutes. Reduce the heat to 425° and bake for 7 minutes longer or until puffed and browned. Serve immediately.

4 Servings   174 Calories   6.8 gm Protein
5.3 gm Fat   25.6 gm Carbohydrate per Serving

Lace Cookies

. . . .

𝒜mong the many American cookbooks I have collected, my favorite is the *Mennonite Community Cookbook* by Mary Emma Showalter. Mrs. Showalter painstakingly collected hundreds of recipes from women in the Mennonite community throughout the United States. The name of the contributor follows each recipe, as was once the style in American cookbooks. These names are signposts of a way of life, a unique culture that made its home in rural America: Mrs. Ephraim Delp, Luella Shoup, Ruth Slaymaker, Tillie Mae Hamilton. One is signed simply "A Sister, Lancaster, Pa."

This recipe is adapted from one attributed to "Mrs. L. Strong, Waterloo, Ont., Can." The cookies are fragile and lacy, for the rolled oats are held together only by a light crunchy glaze of butter and sugar. The orange flower water is my own addition, for it intensifies the buttery flavor.

The cookies are a wonderful accompaniment to Simple Fruit Desserts and Sorbets. I also like to dip them in strong espresso.

. . . .

2½ teaspoons unsalted butter, softened
¼ cup plus 3 tablespoons sugar
1 egg
1 teaspoon vanilla extract
½ teaspoon orange flower water (optional)
1¼ cups old-fashioned rolled oats
1 teaspoon double-acting baking powder
¼ teaspoon salt

Preheat the oven to 375°. Grease 2 large baking sheets with ¼ teaspoon each of the butter and set aside.

In a medium bowl, beat the remaining 2 teaspoons butter and the sugar together until light and fluffy, about 5 minutes. Add the egg, vanilla, and orange flower water and beat until light and fluffy, about 6 minutes.

In a separate bowl, combine the oats, baking powder, and salt. Stir the dry ingredients into the wet ingredients until blended.

Drop 12 mounded teaspoonfuls of the batter about 2 inches apart onto each cookie sheet. Bake in the lower third of the oven for 10 minutes or until the edges are browned and the centers are golden. Using a thin metal spatula, quickly transfer the cookies to a wire rack to cool completely. *(The cookies can be made up to 2 weeks ahead; store in airtight tins at room temperature.)*

**Makes 24 Cookies   37 Calories   .9 gm
Protein   .8 gm Fat   6.5 gm Carbohydrate Each**

Hazelnut Espresso Genoise

. . . .

This Hazelnut Espresso Genoise resembles a cake I had in France years ago. Without icing, it is delicate, elegant in its austerity, and intensely perfumed with roasted hazelnuts. With a cup of espresso, it is a sublime end to a long afternoon lunch.

This cake employs one of my favorite tricks in low-calorie cooking—using a nut oil as a flavoring to replace nuts, which are among the most caloric foods. In this recipe it takes only two teaspoons of hazelnut oil (80 calories) to achieve the flavor of one cup of whole hazelnuts (852 calories). It is essential to use the best hazelnut oil you can find, since the more scented the flavor of the oil, the better the cake will be (see Introduction, page 13).

. . . .

¼ cup plus 2 tablespoons all-purpose flour
½ teaspoon baking powder
2 eggs, at room temperature
3 tablespoons (packed) dark brown sugar
2 teaspoons instant espresso powder
Pinch of salt
½ teaspoon vanilla extract
2 teaspoons hazelnut oil
1 tablespoon Frangelico (hazelnut) liqueur
1½ teaspoons confectioners' sugar

Preheat the oven to 350°. Spray an 8-inch-square cake pan with nonstick cooking spray. Coat the bottom and sides with flour and tap out any excess.

In a small bowl, sift together the flour and baking powder.

In a medium bowl, combine the eggs, brown sugar, espresso, and salt. Using an electric hand mixer, beat at high speed until the mixture is almost tripled in volume and forms a ribbon when the beaters are lifted from the bowl, about 5 minutes. Beat in the vanilla.

Sift the flour mixture over the batter and fold in 2 or 3 times. Add the hazelnut oil and continue folding until the flour is completely incorporated. Pour the batter into the prepared pan and bake until a cake tester inserted into the center of the cake comes out clean, about 12 minutes.

Let the cake cool in the pan for 10 minutes. Invert onto a rack and let cool completely. Transfer to a platter.

In a small bowl, combine the Frangelico and 1 tablespoon of water. Brush the mixture over the top of the cake. Just before serving, sift the confectioners' sugar around the edge of the cake.

4 Servings   158 Calories   4.3 gm Protein
5.2 gm Fat   21.6 gm Carbohydrate per Serving

Espresso Crème Brûlée

At last count, a serving of crème brûlée weighed in at an extraordinary 570 calories. This lightened version gives the illusion of richness at a little less than half the calories. I have had raves about this dessert from serious food purists, who scorn the idea of ever limiting calories, not to mention in a classic like crème brûlée. Freshly ground espresso and a vanilla bean infused in the hot milk, with a small amount of cream added, give the dish an intense coffee flavor and a silky texture associated with full cream custards.

¼ cup plus 2 tablespoons (packed) dark brown
   sugar
2½ cups milk
½ cup freshly ground espresso
1 vanilla bean, split
2 whole eggs
3 egg yolks
¼ cup plus 2 tablespoons granulated sugar
¼ cup plus 2 tablespoons heavy cream

Preheat the oven to 200°. Spread the brown sugar on a baking sheet and bake until dry, about 12 minutes. Let the sugar cool slightly, then press through a sieve into a small bowl and set aside. Increase the oven temperature to 300°.

In a medium saucepan, bring the milk to a boil over moderately high heat. Remove from the heat and stir in the espresso and the vanilla bean. Cover and let steep for 10 minutes.

Line a fine sieve with a double thickness of dampened paper towel or cheesecloth and set over a bowl. Remove the vanilla bean and slowly pour the milk through the strainer, stirring up the coffee grounds with a wooden spoon so the milk will filter through. Fold the edges of the towel over the coffee grounds and press to extract all the milk. Scrape the seeds from the vanilla bean into the milk.

In a medium bowl, stir together the whole eggs, egg yolks, granulated sugar, and cream until blended. Stir in the infused milk and strain the mixture into a pitcher or large measuring cup. Skim any bubbles from the surface.

Place six ½-cup ramekins in a baking pan and fill with the custard. Place the baking pan in the oven and pour in enough warm water to reach halfway up the sides of the ramekins. Cover the ramekins loosely with foil and bake for 1 hour or until the custards are firm around the edges; they may still wobble in the center but will set when chilled.

Remove the ramekins from the water bath and let cool. Cover and refrigerate until cold, at least 3 hours. (The custards can be prepared to this point up to 2 days ahead. Cover with plastic and refrigerate. If moisture collects on top, blot with paper towels before proceeding.)

Preheat the broiler. Set the ramekins on a baking sheet. Sprinkle 1 tablespoon of the reserved brown sugar over the top of each custard in an even layer. Broil the custards as close to the heat as possible until the sugar is caramelized, 30 seconds to 2 minutes. Let cool and serve immediately or refrigerate, uncovered, for up to 3 hours.

6 Servings   272 Calories   7.3 gm Protein
13.1 gm Fat   31.9 gm Carbohydrate per Serving

Chocolate Pudding

. . . .

Chocolate pudding—unsophisticated, comforting, re-
calling the pre–chocolate mousse days of corny Sunday chicken dinners with mashed potatoes, peas, and
carrots—is the object of many Americans' secret hanker-
ings. This is a rich chocolate pudding, creamier than usual,
with an intense chocolate flavor.

. . . .

2 cups low-fat milk
2 tablespoons cornstarch
3 tablespoons sugar
2 tablespoons unsweetened cocoa powder
1 tablespoon instant espresso powder
Pinch of salt
1 ounce (1 square) unsweetened chocolate
½ teaspoon vanilla extract
½ teaspoon hazelnut or walnut oil

In a small bowl, stir together ¼ cup of the milk
and the cornstarch until combined. In a heavy
medium saucepan, combine the remaining 1¾
cups milk, the sugar, cocoa powder, espresso powder, salt, and unsweetened chocolate. Place over
moderate heat and stir occasionally until the
chocolate is melted.

Reduce the heat to low. Whisk in the cornstarch mixture and cook, stirring frequently, until
very thick and barely boiling, about 10 minutes.
Remove from the heat and stir in the vanilla and
hazelnut oil. Pour into individual ½-cup custard
cups. Cover with plastic wrap—touching the surface if you do not want a skin to form—and refrigerate for at least 2 hours or until completely
set. (This pudding can be made a couple of days
ahead and refrigerated.)

4 Servings   164 Calories   5.4 gm Protein
7.2 gm Fat   22.7 gm Carbohydrate per Serving

Shaker Lemon Meringue Bread Pudding

. . . .

This very unusual bread pudding is roughly adapted from Ronald Johnson's *American Table*. The bread slices are reduced to bread crumbs rather than left whole, as is common. They become part of a fine, lemony custard. The topping is a tart meringue. Creating a dessert out of the practical necessity of using stale bread and leftover egg whites is pure Shaker. By Johnson's description this lovely pudding is "all balance and proportion."

. . . .

4 slices of firm-textured white bread
2 cups milk
2 strips of lemon zest
1 vanilla bean, split
⅓ cup plus 2 tablespoons sugar
1 tablespoon unsalted butter, softened
3 eggs, separated
1 tablespoon plus 2 teaspoons grated lemon zest
   (from about 2 lemons)
1 egg white
Pinch of cream of tartar
3 tablespoons fresh lemon juice, strained

Preheat the oven to 250°. Spray a 1½-quart soufflé dish or ovenproof casserole with nonstick cooking spray.

Set the bread on a cookie sheet and bake until dry but still slightly soft in the center, about 20 minutes. Transfer the bread to a food processor and process until the crumbs are medium sized. Increase the oven temperature to 350°.

In a medium saucepan, combine the milk, lemon zest, and vanilla bean. Bring to a boil over moderate heat. Remove from the heat, cover, and let cool for 20 minutes. Strain the milk into a bowl. Scrape the seeds from the vanilla bean into the milk and stir in the bread crumbs.

In a medium bowl, blend ⅓ cup of the sugar with the butter. Mix in the egg yolks and the grated lemon zest. Add the milk–bread crumb mixture and stir well to combine. Pour into the prepared soufflé dish. Set the dish in a pan filled with enough warm water to reach halfway up the sides and bake for 20 to 25 minutes, until the pudding is set.

In a medium bowl, beat all 4 egg whites with an electric mixer until foamy. Add the cream of tartar and beat until soft peaks form. Gradually beat in the remaining 2 tablespoons sugar until stiff. Drizzle in the lemon juice and beat until the whites are firm and silky, about 30 seconds. Spoon the meringue over the warm pudding, mounding it to form peaks. Bake until the peaks are golden brown, about 15 minutes. Serve warm or cold.

6 Servings   221 Calories   8.1 gm Protein
7.7 gm Fat   30.0 gm Carbohydrate per Serving

Truffle Sabayon

. . . .

Truffles are truly mysterious. They grow underground, at the base of oak trees, it is said. Female pigs and dogs are used to root them out, for nobody knows exactly where they are hidden. They are a fungus, and yet they are one of the most coveted and precious foods in the world. Their aroma and flavor is indescribable—repugnant to a few, sublime to many. Some consider them an aphrodisiac. They are fiercely expensive.

But they are actually quite economical. A little goes a long way. Their fragrance permeates whatever they are close to. A truffle kept in a jar with some eggs overnight will permeate the shells with its essence and flavor the eggs. The eggs will taste of truffle without having been cooked with it. The truffle can be used for another dish.

The idea for this recipe came about while I was experimenting with truffle dishes with two chef friends. We had pooled our resources to buy a pound, so that we could, for once in our lives, have enough truffles to cook in any way we wanted, to indulge our imaginations. This recipe might seem bizarre upon first reading, for it uses a truffle in a dessert rather than in a more usual savory preparation. It is sublime and intoxicating. Similar to a warm Italian zabaglione, the dessert is made with Madeira and perfumed with pounded truffle. Pounding the truffle into a paste beforehand and gently cooking it in the sabayon releases the intense perfume of the truffle so that only a small amount is needed. The flavor is further intensified if the eggs are "truffled" first, as described above. The effect is overwhelming: pure truffle in a heady delicious froth.

Although extremely rich, sabayons are generally very low in calories because they are, in effect, mostly air. One egg yolk per person is beaten with about two teaspoons of sugar and a little Madeira until it increases many times in volume. This dessert is for very special occasions.

½ ounce fresh black truffle
3 tablespoons sugar
4 egg yolks
¼ cup plus 2 tablespoons Rainwater Madeira

Place the truffle in a mortar. With a pestle, pound into a paste. Add the sugar and continue pounding until the mixture is well blended.

In a double boiler over simmering water, combine the egg yolks and truffle sugar. Whisk until pale yellow, warm, and creamy, about 4 minutes.

Add the Madeira and beat vigorously until the sabayon is hot and thick enough to mound softly, about 7 minutes. Serve at once.

4 Servings   107 Calories   2.9 gm Protein
5.1 gm Fat   12.4 gm Carbohydrate per Serving

Prune and Armagnac Ice Cream

This extraordinary ice cream was inspired by the wonderful flavors of prunes preserved in Armagnac from southwestern France. One would never guess it contains no cream. It owes its rich, silky texture to the natural creaminess of a prune puree that is frozen with a whipped milk custard. The alcohol contributes further to the smooth texture by inhibiting freezing. It is pure luxury.

15 pitted prunes (6 ounces)
¼ cup sugar
⅓ cup Armagnac
2¾ cups milk
1 vanilla bean, split
3 egg yolks
1 whole egg

In a small nonaluminum saucepan, combine the prunes with 2 tablespoons of the sugar and ¼ cup of water. Bring to a boil over moderately high heat. Reduce the heat to moderate and simmer until the sugar dissolves, about 5 minutes. Remove from the heat and let cool, then stir in the Armagnac. Cover and macerate overnight at room temperature.

In a medium saucepan, scald the milk with the vanilla bean. Remove from the heat, cover, and set aside.

In a heatproof bowl, beat the egg yolks with the whole egg and the remaining 2 tablespoons sugar until the mixture is thick and forms a rib-bon when the beaters are lifted, 8 to 10 minutes. Stir in the hot milk. Return the mixture to the saucepan and cook over moderate heat, stirring constantly, until the custard is thick enough to coat a spoon, about 10 minutes; do not let boil. Strain the custard into a medium bowl. Scrape the seeds from the vanilla bean into the custard. Let cool, then cover and refrigerate overnight. *(The recipe can be prepared to this point up to 2 days ahead.)*

In a food processor, puree the prunes with half of their syrup until smooth. Transfer to a small bowl. Add the custard and the remaining syrup to the processor and process until thick and frothy, about 2 minutes. Add the pureed prunes and process until just combined. Pour into an ice cream maker and freeze according to the manufacturer's instructions. Allow ⅔ cup per serving.

6 Servings   244 Calories   6.8 gm Protein
7.3 gm Fat   31.6 gm Carbohydrate per Serving

Mango Ice Cream

$\mathcal{B}$ecause ripe mangoes, like peaches and papaya, have a creamy, silky texture when pureed, they are the ideal medium for low-calorie ice creams and frozen desserts. They provide the smooth texture that quantities of cream and egg yolks normally achieve. In this quickly made ice cream, the fruit chunks are frozen, then pureed in a food processor with a small amount of cream and some buttermilk, resulting in a rich, flavorful ice cream. It reminds me of the tropical-flavored ice cream I buy from a stand in New York's Chinatown. After dinner there, it's the perfect accompaniment to a walk through the exotic neighborhood on a warm spring night.

The ice cream is best made just prior to serving but may also be made ahead and frozen. The riper the fruit, the better the texture and flavor of this ice cream will be.

3 medium ripe mangoes, (12 ounces each), peeled
3 tablespoons heavy cream
⅓ cup buttermilk
2 tablespoons fresh lime juice
1 tablespoon superfine sugar

Using a thin sharp knife, slice the fruit from the sides of the mango pits and scrape off any remaining flesh. Cut the fruit into ¼- to ½-inch dice. (You should have 4½ cups of fruit.) Spread the mango on a nonstick baking sheet and freeze for 1 hour or longer.

Break apart the frozen pieces of fruit and place in a food processor. Process until the consistency resembles coarse meal, stopping frequently to scrape down the sides. (If the fruit is too hard to process, allow it to soften for 1 to 2 minutes before continuing.)

Add the heavy cream, buttermilk, lime juice, and sugar. Process, scraping down the sides of the bowl frequently, to a creamy puree the consistency of medium-soft ice cream. (It does not

have to be completely smooth; a few chunks of fruit add a nice texture.) Serve at once or transfer to a serving bowl, cover, and freeze until ready to serve. If the ice cream becomes frozen solid, place it in the refrigerator for about 30 minutes to soften.

Variation: This method also works well using peaches, papaya, and kiwi. Substitute 2¼ pounds ripe fruit for the mangoes.

This ice cream can also be made in an ice cream maker. Peel and slice the fruit as directed in the recipe above but do not freeze. Reserve ½ cup of the fruit. In a food processor, process the remaining 4 cups of fruit to a thick puree. Add the heavy cream, buttermilk, lime juice, and sugar and process until smooth. Stir in the reserved fruit. Transfer to an ice cream maker and freeze according to the manufacturer's instructions.

4 Servings   175 Calories   1.8 gm Protein
4.8 gm Fat   35.0 gm Carbohydrate per Serving

Rich Cream

. . . .

Whipped cream is undoubtedly the single element that can bring an otherwise incomplete dessert to fruition and add greatly to the sense of indulgence. I have spent a lot of time experimenting with low-calorie whipped cream alternatives. My favorite is Chantilly Cream, which is true whipped cream lightened with meringue. This recipe is my version of a low-fat dessert cream. It has nearly the consistency and flavor of softly whipped cream, although it is somewhat denser. It takes well to the addition of any flavoring one would use in ordinary whipped cream: a few drops of liqueur or brandy or a dusting of ground cinnamon.

Very simply, a low-fat salt-free cottage cheese is pureed perfectly smooth. Small amounts of sour cream, heavy cream, vanilla, and sugar are added for flavoring and to provide the richness present in real whipped cream. A half cup of Rich Cream contains only three grams of fat, as compared with 24 grams in one half cup of regular whipped cream.

. . . .

1 cup no-salt low-fat (1%) cottage cheese
2 teaspoons superfine sugar
¼ teaspoon vanilla extract
2 teaspoons sour cream
2 teaspoons heavy cream

In a food processor, puree the cottage cheese, sugar, and vanilla until perfectly smooth, about 1 minute. Scrape the mixture into a small bowl. Using a rubber spatula, fold in the sour cream and heavy cream. Serve as is or flavor as suggested below. Cover and refrigerate until ready to use. *(This cream will keep for about 1 week.)*

Variations: To flavor Rich Cream, stir in ½ to 1 teaspoon of any liqueur that will complement the main dessert. Framboise and eau-de-vie de poire are my favorites to serve with fruit desserts. Fold in ¼ teaspoon of ground cinnamon for a delicious accompaniment to chocolate and coffee desserts.

Raspberry Cream, 16 calories per tablespoon. Stir 3 to 4 tablespoons strained raspberry puree, 1 to 2 teaspoons sugar, ½ teaspoon framboise, and ½ teaspoon fresh lemon juice into 1 cup Rich Cream. This vividly colored cream is lovely with fresh or poached fruit or alongside plain cakes.

**Makes 1 Cup   53 Calories   6.4 gm Protein
1.6 gm Fat   3.0 gm Carbohydrate per ¼ Cup**

Chantilly Cream

There is nothing like the flavor of real whipped cream. The general formula for whipped cream is that one tablespoon of heavy cream expands to two tablespoons of whipped cream. This recipe manages to increase the volume of whipped cream further by blending it with a light meringue, yielding a lovely, ethereal cream which can embellish a simple fruit dessert. So if you must have whipped cream, this recipe gives you the most for your money.

¼ cup heavy cream
1 egg white
Pinch of cream of tartar
2 teaspoons superfine sugar

In a chilled bowl, beat the cream until stiff peaks form, about 2 minutes. Refrigerate. Wash and dry the beaters or the whisk.

In a clean, dry bowl, combine the egg white and cream of tartar. Beat at high speed until soft peaks form, about 2 minutes. Gradually sprinkle the sugar on top and beat until stiff peaks form. Do not overbeat. Using a rubber spatula, fold the whites into the whipped cream. Refrigerate until ready to serve. *(The cream can be made up to 1 hour before serving.)*

**Makes 1 Cup   64 Calories   1.2 gm Protein
5.5 gm Fat   2.6 gm Carbohydrate per ¼ Cup**

Flaky Butter Pastry

. . . .

*𝒰*nlike most low-calorie pastry doughs, this pastry is made with sweet butter rather than margarine. It is the result of a great deal of experimentation to create a flaky, buttery dough without the compromise in flavor and texture that margarine affords for the same number of calories. The recipe calls for the smallest amount of butter possible. Sour cream makes the crust tender and melting. The recipe yields half a pound of dough, enough for one 10-inch pie shell or eight one-ounce portions. Any dough that is not used immediately may be frozen.

. . . .

1 cup unbleached flour
1 teaspoon sugar
½ teaspoon salt
4 tablespoons unsalted butter, softened
3 tablespoons sour cream

Place the flour in a mound on a work surface. Sprinkle the sugar and salt over it. Place the butter on top of the flour. Using a pinching motion with your fingers, mix the butter into the flour; rub the butter and flour between the palms of both hands until the mixture is the texture of coarse meal.

Spoon the sour cream and 1½ teaspoons of cold water on top of the mixture. Using a fork, stir the meal into the sour cream and mash together to roughly incorporate. With your hands, press the mixture into a ball, gathering up any loose particles remaining on the counter. With the palm of one hand, slide the dough forward about 8 inches along the counter so that you are practically smearing it. Gather the dough into a

ball and repeat the smearing once more. Gather the dough into a ball again, flatten slightly and wrap in plastic wrap. Refrigerate for 1 hour before rolling. *(The dough will keep refrigerated for 4 to 5 days and can be frozen for up to 3 months.)*

To roll the dough, sprinkle the work surface lightly with flour. Roll out the dough to the desired diameter or according to instructions given in a recipe. Transfer the dough to a cookie sheet, prick several times with a fork, and freeze for about 15 minutes.

To prebake the pie shell, fit the dough evenly into a pie or tart pan and bake in a preheated 375° oven for about 12 minutes or until golden brown. Cool before filling and serving. *(The pastry may be baked up to 3 days ahead and crisped in a warm oven at the last minute.)*

Makes Enough for a 10-Inch Pie Shell Serving Eight   121 Calories   1.8 gm Protein 7.0 gm Fat   12.7 gm Carbohydrate per Serving

Sauces and Condiments

Roasted Yellow Pepper Sauce

Quick to make, this deep yellow sauce has a mellow, sweet, and smoky flavor that is a perfect foil for spicy recipes like Crab Cakes and grilled seafood. It is also delicious as a spread for sandwiches with cold meats, chicken, fresh mozzarella, or goat cheese.

2 medium yellow bell peppers
¾ teaspoon Champagne vinegar or white wine vinegar
¼ teaspoon finely minced garlic
Pinch of salt
Freshly ground black pepper
3 tablespoons sour cream, stirred

Roast the bell peppers directly over a gas flame or under the broiler as close to the heat as possible, turning until charred all over, about 5 minutes. Enclose the peppers in a bag to steam for 10 minutes. Using a thin sharp knife, scrape the skin off the peppers, rinse, and remove the core, seeds, and ribs.

In a food processor or blender, combine the peppers, vinegar, garlic, salt, and black pepper to taste. Process until the mixture is a fine puree, scraping down the sides occasionally, about 1½ minutes. Transfer to a small bowl. Using a rubber spatula, fold in the sour cream. Adjust the seasoning, cover, and refrigerate until ready to serve. (The Pepper Sauce will keep for about 4 days.)

Makes About ¾ Cup   11 Calories
.2 gm Protein   .8 gm Fat
.8 gm Carbohydrate per Tablespoon

◄ Crab Cakes, Buttermilk Slaw, Roasted Yellow Pepper Sauce, with ripe summer tomatoes and herbs

Hot Red Pepper and Saffron Sauce

Rouille is the traditional Provençal sauce that accompanies fish soup. It is usually spooned onto slices of toasted baguette or stirred into the soup at the last moment. Made with garlic, hot chile, saffron, and often roasted red pepper, it is mounted with extra-virgin olive oil to achieve a mayonnaise-like consistency.

This low-calorie version has the complex, robust flavor of a traditional *rouille*, but a lighter texture. The base for the assertive flavorings is sour cream, which provides a fine creaminess with just enough fat to mimic the original and still produce only half the calories. A small amount of olive oil is stirred in, but not completely incorporated, at the last minute to further evoke the traditional flavors and effect.

Serve the *rouille* with Shellfish Stew. It is also wonderful with cold poached lobster or shrimp and with grilled salmon.

1 red or yellow pepper
1 small hot chile, such as serrano or jalapeño, seeded and chopped
2 garlic cloves
¾ teaspoon balsamic vinegar
¼ teaspoon saffron threads
¼ teaspoon salt
Freshly ground pepper
½ cup sour cream, stirred
1 tablespoon extra-virgin olive oil

Roast the bell pepper directly over a gas flame or under a broiler as close to the heat as possible, turning until charred all over, about 5 minutes. Enclose the pepper in a bag to steam for 10 minutes. Using a thin sharp knife, scrape the skin off the pepper, rinse, and remove the core, seeds, and ribs.

In a food processor, combine the roasted pepper, chile, garlic, vinegar, saffron, salt, and pepper. Process, scraping down the bowl occasionally, until the mixture is reduced to a fine puree, about 2 minutes. Transfer to a small bowl.

Using a rubber spatula, fold in the sour cream. Drizzle the olive oil over the *rouille* and stir with a spoon several times until just partly combined. Cover and refrigerate until ready to serve. *(The recipe can be made up to 2 hours before serving.)*

**Makes 1 Cup   25 Calories   .3 gm Protein
2.4 gm Fat   .7 gm Carbohydrate per Tablespoon**

Garlic Sauce

. . . .

Along with *rouille* (see Hot Red Pepper and Saffron Sauce), *aioli* is another great Provençal sauce. It is, in essence, a powerful garlic mayonnaise, rich with egg yolks and extra-virgin olive oil. Made in the traditional way in a marble mortar with a wooden pestle, a true *aioli* is silky, thick, redolent with garlic and olive oil, and, as cook and author Richard Olney so aptly described it, "voluptuously oily." You should never think of calories when you are eating *aioli* for it has far too many of them.

The following sauce takes the Provençal *aioli* as its inspiration. Perfumed with fine olive oil, this is a pungent garlic sauce for everyday consumption, for it contains only one third the calories of a true *aioli*. As in the Hot Red Pepper and Saffron Sauce, sour cream is the medium for the garlic and olive oil, providing a fine, creamy texture with a minimum amount of fat. It may be served in any number of ways: as an accompaniment to cold vegetables and seafood, on sandwiches, as in the Lobster and Corn Bread Sandwich, and on croutons to accompany the Poule au Pot.

Use the freshest, firmest garlic possible. If your garlic has sprouted, slice each clove in half and remove the green sprout with a paring knife to avoid a bitter flavor.

. . . .

½ cup sour cream
1 tablespoon extra-virgin olive oil
1 or 2 garlic cloves
⅛ teaspoon salt
Freshly ground pepper

In a small bowl, whisk together the sour cream and olive oil until blended.

Using a large knife, mince together the garlic and salt, mashing and scraping with the side of the knife until the mixture forms a puree. (Or crush the garlic through a press and mix with the salt.) Stir the garlic paste into the sour cream mixture. Season with pepper to taste. Cover and refrigerate until ready to use. *(The* aioli *will keep for up to 3 days.)*

Makes About ½ Cup   47 Calories
.5 gm Protein   4.7 gm Fat
.8 gm Carbohydrate per Tablespoon

Gewürztraminer Butter Sauce

In the classic French white butter sauce, *beurre blanc*, quantities of cold butter are emulsified in a concentrated reduction of vinegar and shallots. This divine sauce has an extraordinary number of calories—about 100 per tablespoon. In this recipe, I have reworked the basic premise of a *beurre blanc* to create a lighter sauce with a buttery flavor and silky texture at a fraction of the calories. The wine and shallot are reduced slightly and mounted with only a small amount of butter that is stabilized with a pinch of potato starch. Using a spicy wine like Gewürztraminer adds a piquant and somewhat floral quality to the sauce. It is lovely with delicate poached seafood, such as sole, salmon, or scallops.

⅛ teaspoon potato starch
½ cup spicy white wine, preferably
    Gewürztraminer
1 tablespoon minced shallot
2 tablespoons cold unsalted butter
1 tablespoon minced fresh chives, basil, Italian
    flat-leaf parsley, and chervil in any
    combination
Pinch of salt
Freshly ground white pepper
½ teaspoon Champagne vinegar or white wine
    vinegar (optional)

In small bowl, combine the potato starch and 1 teaspoon of the wine. In a small saucepan, boil the remaining wine and shallot together for 1 minute to burn off the alcohol. Stir a little of the hot wine into the potato starch mixture to heat it slightly. Then stir the potato starch into the saucepan. Boil for 15 seconds. Add the cold butter in one lump to the saucepan and boil it vigorously until it is melted and the sauce is thickened slightly. Stir in the herbs, salt, pepper, and the vinegar if desired. Serve at once.

Makes ½ Cup   34 Calories
.1 gm Protein   2.8 gm Fat
2.0 gm Carbohydrate per Tablespoon

Mango Salsa

This salsa, flavored with onion, chile, coriander, and basil, is cooked ever so slightly to mellow the taste and texture and still retain its freshness. It is a versatile accompaniment to roasted or grilled poultry, game, pork, and seafood.

¼ cup minced red onion
½ teaspoon minced chile, such as jalapeño or serrano
¼ teaspoon extra-virgin olive oil
1 cup diced fresh mango
2 tablespoons fresh lime juice
2 tablespoons chopped fresh coriander
2 teaspoons chopped fresh basil

In a small nonreactive saucepan, cook the onion and chile in the oil over moderate heat until the onion is soft and just beginning to brown, about 5 minutes.

Reduce the heat to low and add the mango. Cook, stirring frequently, until the mango begins to release some of its juices and softens slightly without losing its shape. Remove from the heat and stir in the lime juice, coriander, and basil. Serve warm or chilled. *(This salsa will keep, refrigerated, for up to 4 days.)*

Makes 1 Cup   36 Calories   .4 gm Protein
.4 gm Fat   8.6 gm Carbohydrate per ¼ Cup

Spiced Tomato Jam

This is a rich, sweet concentrate of tomatoes, cooked with the flavors of a Moroccan tagine: ginger, saffron, and cinnamon. It should be eaten like a chutney as an accompaniment to rich meats, such as Lamb Mechoui, Pan-Fried Duck Steaks, hamburgers, or roast chicken. Because of the assertive flavoring of the recipe, good-quality imported canned plum tomatoes work quite well if truly ripe tomatoes are not available.

1¼ pounds very ripe tomatoes, peeled and seeded, or 1 can (35 ounces) Italian peeled tomatoes, drained and seeded (2 cups), coarsely chopped
¼ cup grated onion
1 garlic clove, minced or crushed through a press
Pinch of saffron threads, crushed
1 tablespoon tomato paste
2 teaspoons honey
⅛ teaspoon freshly grated or ground ginger
½ teaspoon cinnamon
3 to 4 tablespoons chopped fresh coriander

In a heavy medium skillet, combine the tomatoes, onion, garlic, and saffron. Cook over moderate heat, stirring frequently, until the liquid has evaporated and the tomatoes thicken and dry out, about 15 minutes. Stir in the tomato paste, honey, ginger, and cinnamon and cook until the mixture has the consistency of a thick chunky chutney-like paste, about 5 minutes longer. Stir in the coriander to taste *(The jam will keep refrigerated about 1 week.)*

Makes About 1 Cup   11 Calories   .3 gm Protein   .1 gm Fat   2.6 gm Carbohydrate per Tablespoon

Pickled Cherries

The first time I had pickled cherries with a terrine was at the quintessential bistro in Lyon, La Mère Brazier. A slice of the *terrine maison* was served with little bowls of the wonderful cherries and grainy mustard, coarse salt, fresh pepper, and very good crusty bread—not a cornichon in sight. It was a revelation: the sweet perfume of the cherry embodied in a tart, mellow pickle, just the right contrast for the rich meat. The cherries are also a fine accompaniment to other cold meats, particularly pork and chicken. They can be eaten 24 hours after they are made and will keep indefinitely.

1 cup balsamic vinegar
3 tablespoons (packed) dark brown sugar
1 strip of lemon zest (1 by 2 inches)
1 cinnamon stick
6 whole cloves
4 allspice berries
2 juniper berries
¾ pound ripe cherries, rinsed, stems intact

In a medium nonreactive saucepan, combine the vinegar, brown sugar, lemon zest, cinnamon, cloves, allspice, juniper berries, and ½ cup of water. Bring to a boil. Reduce the heat to medium and simmer, uncovered, until reduced slightly, about 10 minutes.

Prick each cherry several times with a needle. Add the cherries to the saucepan, cover, and remove from the heat. Set aside to steep for 15 minutes. Uncover and let cool to lukewarm, about 30 minutes. Transfer the cherries and cooking liquid to a 1½-pint jar and set aside at room temperature for at least 24 hours before eating. Refrigerate for longer storage.

Makes About 1½ Pints   About 31 Calories .4 gm Protein   .3 gm Fat   7.3 gm Carbohydrate per 5 Pickled Cherries

Fresh Cucumber Pickle

These Japanese-style cucumbers provide a cool, refreshing counterpoint to Cold Spicy Sesame Noodles, as well as to grilled shrimp, tuna, and pork. Black sesame seeds are available at Japanese specialty and health food stores.

¼ cup rice wine vinegar
2 teaspoons superfine sugar
1 large, unpeeled European cucumber, halved crosswise and cut into thin strips or thinly sliced crosswise (about 2 cups)
1 teaspoon black or toasted white sesame seeds

In a small bowl, combine the vinegar and sugar. Add the cucumber slices and toss to coat. Cover and refrigerate for at least 1 hour before serving. *(The pickle will keep for up to 3 days.)* Sprinkle ¼ teaspoon sesame seeds over each serving.

4 Servings   21 Calories   .4 gm Protein .4 gm Fat   4.3 gm Carbohydrate per Serving

Pear Hazelnut Sauce

· ·

This rich, delicate pear puree is perfumed with hazelnut oil to give it a subtle flavor of roasted nuts without the calories or coarse texture. Serve it as a dessert sauce with Fresh Ginger Gingerbread or Banana Soufflé. It is also a delicious accompaniment to breakfast breads, pancakes, ham, or sausage as well as pork and game.

· ·

4 very ripe medium Anjou pears (about 7 ounces
    each)—peeled, cored, and cut into ½-inch dice
1 tablespoon fresh lemon juice
1 tablespoon honey
1 cinnamon stick
½ vanilla bean, split
½ teaspoon hazelnut oil

In a medium saucepan, combine the pears, lemon juice, honey, cinnamon, and 2 tablespoons of water. Scrape the seeds from the vanilla bean into the pan and add the bean. Cover and cook over moderate heat until the pears have released their juices, about 5 minutes.

Reduce the heat to low, uncover, and simmer until the pears are very tender and the liquid is reduced to ¼ cup, about 4 minutes. Discard the cinnamon stick and vanilla bean. In a food processor, puree the pears and liquid until smooth, about 1 minute. Serve warm or chilled. *(The sauce will keep for 1 week, covered, in the refrigerator.)*

**Make 1½ Cups   22 Calories   .1 gm Protein
.2 gm Fat   5.4 gm Carbohydrate per Tablespoon**

Flavored Oils

. . . .

Like vinegars, oil can be infused with a number of flavorings to make pungent oils that are used as condiments. A drizzle of scented oil can be used in lieu of a sauce, for example. A half teaspoon of chive or basil oil is wonderful for seasoning grilled fish, a serving of mashed potatoes, or even a simple steamed vegetable.

The possibilities for flavors are endless and include, besides those mentioned above, such fresh herbs as oregano, sage, and rosemary, singly or in combination, as well as garlic, chiles, lemon zest, horseradish, roasted red pepper, and black truffles. The method is simple. Macerate the chosen flavoring in the oil with a little salt in a cool, dark place until it has scented the oil, usually about one week. Then strain the oil into a clean glass jar and refrigerate for use at a moment's notice.

For a quickly made flavored oil, combine the oil, salt, and flavoring in a food processor. Process for two minutes. Let the mixture stand for at least six hours. Strain before using.

The oils will keep refrigerated for several months. Flavored oil has the same calorie count as regular oil: 40 calories per teaspoon.

The following amounts will flavor one cup extra-virgin olive oil mixed with one quarter teaspoon salt. The amounts can be doubled or tripled.

. . . .

Fennel Oil: 2 tablespoons crushed fennel seeds

Herb Oil: ½ cup fresh sage, thyme, rosemary, basil, or oregano leaves, or snipped fresh chives

Orange and Hot Chile Oil: 3 strips orange zest and 3 sliced fresh jalapeño or serrano chiles

Garlic Oil: 10 garlic cloves, peeled and bruised

Roasted Pepper Oil: 1 peeled seeded roasted red or yellow bell pepper, coarsely chopped

Truffle Oil: 4 or 5 thin slices fresh black truffle (do not strain)

Ancho Chile Oil: 2 ancho chiles, seeded and torn into 1-inch pieces

Flavored Vinegars

· ·

Good-quality vinegars can easily be flavored by steeping fruits, herbs, flowers, and spices in the vinegar for several weeks. The vinegar takes up the flavor essence but not the calories of whatever is steeping. Flavored vinegars can be used whenever you would use vinegar. They are particularly interesting in salad dressings, marinades, and sauces. Guided by your imagination and taste, you can choose endless flavorings and uses.

I generally use Champagne vinegar as a steeping vinegar because it is mild and less acidic than wine vinegars are and because its pleasing flavor marries well with a variety of elements.

The vinegars can be made directly in the jar in which you will store them. (The fruits or herbs left steeping in the jar are wonderful to look at.) Simply put the flavoring agent in a quart jar and fill it with vinegar. Cork lightly. Let the vinegars steep for at least three weeks before using. They will keep indefinitely. The following represents only a few of the possibilities for flavoring vinegars.

· ·

Gooseberry Vinegar: 1½ cups gooseberries, pricked several times with a pin or halved, sprinkled with 1½ teaspoons superfine sugar

Tarragon or Thyme Vinegar: 10 to 12 large branches of thyme or tarragon

Shallot and Lemon Vinegar: 6 or 8 peeled bruised shallots and two 2-inch strips of lemon zest

Raspberry or Blackberry Vinegar: 2 cups fresh berries, sprinkled with 1 teaspoon superfine sugar

Pear Vinegar: 2 medium peeled halved pears sprinkled with 1½ teaspoons superfine sugar

Fennel Vinegar: 1 fresh fennel stalk and 1 tablespoon fennel seed

Flower Vinegar: 2 cups fresh unsprayed rose petals or nasturtium blossoms

Gooseberry Vinegar ➤

Roquefort Dressing

. . . .

*B*ottled blue cheese dressing averages about 70 calories per tablespoon. Reduced-calorie dressings, although often very low in calories, contain an array of questionable ingredients including artificial flavors, lots of sodium, and a host of chemical additives. My alternative is made with real Roquefort cheese and scented with sherry vinegar and walnut oil. It is slightly thinner than the old-fashioned thick "blue cheese dressing," but for my money, the flavor is much better.

. . . .

2 ounces Roquefort cheese or other crumbly aged
   blue cheese, at room temperature
1 cup buttermilk
¾ teaspoon sherry vinegar
½ teaspoon walnut oil
Freshly ground pepper

In a food processor or blender, combine the cheese, buttermilk, vinegar, and oil. Process for about 1 minute until smooth and creamy. Transfer to a jar and stir in pepper to taste. *(The dressing will keep for about 1 week refrigerated.)*

Variation: Goat Cheese Dressing. Follow the recipe using 2 ounces aged goat cheese, such as Bucheron.

Makes 1 Cup   **20 Calories**   **1.3 gm Protein**
1.4 gm Fat   **.8 gm Carbohydrate per Tablespoon**

Garlic Cream Dressing

This garlicky dressing is excellent on simple salads of cold steamed baby vegetables, asparagus, artichoke bottoms, or sliced tomatoes.

¼ cup sour cream
¼ cup milk
1 teaspoon sherry vinegar
1 teaspoon walnut oil
½ garlic clove, finely minced
⅛ teaspoon salt
Freshly ground pepper
1 tablespoon minced fresh parsley or chervil

In a small bowl, whisk together the sour cream and milk. Whisk in the vinegar and let sit for 1 minute to thicken. Whisk in the oil, garlic, salt, pepper, and parsley. Cover and refrigerate for at least an hour before serving.

Makes About ½ Cup   26 Calories
.5 gm Protein   2.3 gm Fat
.7 gm Carbohydrate per Tablespoon

Champagne Vinaigrette

This is a delicate, rather elemental vinaigrette that is good on a variety of milder greens, Mesclun Salad, and cold spring vegetables. Use only high-quality fruity olive oil.

1 shallot, minced
Pinch of salt
Pinch of sugar
1½ tablespoons Champagne vinegar
¼ cup plus 2 tablespoons extra-virgin olive oil
Freshly ground pepper

In a small bowl, combine the shallot, salt, sugar, and vinegar. Stir to dissolve the salt and sugar. Gradually whisk in the olive oil and pepper to taste.

Variation: For a more robust and sweetly flavored vinaigrette, substitute ¼ cup plus 2 tablespoons balsamic vinegar for the Champagne vinegar and omit the sugar.

Or add 2 tablespoons minced fresh herbs, such as coriander, basil, Italian flat-leaf parsley, chervil, or chives.

Makes About ½ Cup   30 Calories
.0 gm Protein   3.5 gm Fat
.1 gm Carbohydrate per Teaspoon

Cold Fresh Tomato Sauce

· ·

I rank this as one of the all-time great sauces. It is extremely simple to make, and is sublime on a host of foods from grilled bread—as in bruschetta—to grilled seafood to pasta, whether a simple fresh fettuccine or a stuffed ravioli. The perfume of the fresh herbs that are used is released on contact with heat for an explosion of intense herbal flavor. This sauce is best when made just before serving. It depends on one using vine-ripened tomatoes, preferably in the height of summer. Occasionally in the winter I will come across decent tomatoes from Holland or Israel, or local hot-house varieties, with which to make this sauce, a hopeful reminder of lush summer days to come.

· ·

1 pound ripe tomatoes
¼ cup minced shallots
2 tablespoons balsamic vinegar
⅓ cup chopped fresh basil
2 tablespoons mixed minced herbs, such as
   thyme, tarragon, coriander, fennel tops, or
   Italian flat-leaf parsley, in any combination
Freshly ground pepper
1 tablespoon extra-virgin olive oil

Spear one of the tomatoes with a two-pronged kitchen fork. Hold the tomato over a burner at high heat, turning the tomato slowly as the skin blisters and splits, about 30 seconds. Repeat with the remaining tomatoes. Slip the skins off the tomatoes and discard. Halve the tomatoes crosswise, squeeze them to remove the seeds, and core them. Dice the tomatoes and transfer to a medium bowl.

Stir in the shallot, vinegar, basil, mixed herbs, and pepper to taste. Drizzle the olive oil over the top.

Makes 2 Cups   31 Calories   .7 gm Protein
1.9 gm Fat   2.7 gm Carbohydrate per ¼ Cup

Pasta with Cold Fresh Tomato Sauce ➤

Hazelnut or Walnut Oil Dressing

This dressing, made either with hazelnut or walnut oil, is good on greens with strong presence and slightly bitter flavor, such as Belgian endive, arugula, and Italian chicories (including radicchio). It also is delicious on fennel, oranges, pears, artichoke bottoms, parsnips, and roasted onions. Serve at room temperature or warmed in a small saucepan to slightly wilt the greens.

Pinch of salt
2½ tablespoons balsamic vinegar
¼ cup plus 2 tablespoons hazelnut or walnut oil
Freshly ground pepper

In a small bowl, stir together the salt and vinegar until the salt is dissolved. Gradually whisk in the oil and pepper to taste.

Variation: Add 2 teaspoons slivered orange or tangerine zest.

Or, replace the balsamic vinegar with 1½ tablespoons sherry vinegar plus 1 tablespoon dry sherry. Add 1 teaspoon minced shallots, a pinch of sugar, and 1 tablespoon minced fresh tarragon.

Makes ½ Cup   30 Calories   .0 gm Protein
3.4 gm Fat   .1 gm Carbohydrate per Teaspoon

Warm Rosemary Balsamic Dressing

In this recipe, rosemary is sautéed in olive oil, then finished with sweet balsamic vinegar. The dressing is poured hot over the lettuce to wilt it slightly. Surprisingly, milder-flavored lettuces, such as Bibb, hearts of romaine, and Boston, work well. This dressing is also good on warm steamed root vegetables, such as potatoes, parsnips, and turnips, as well as on grilled fish.

. . . .

1 tablespoon plus 2 teaspoons extra-virgin olive
   oil
1 large garlic clove, quartered lengthwise
1 teaspoon fresh rosemary or ½ teaspoon dried
1½ tablespoons balsamic vinegar
Pinch of salt
Freshly ground pepper

In a small skillet, combine the olive oil, garlic,
and rosemary. Cook over moderate heat until the

garlic is just beginning to brown. Remove from
the heat and pour in the balsamic vinegar, taking
care to stand back, since the mixture will splut-
ter. Stir in the salt and pepper to taste. Serve
warm.

4 Servings   53 Calories
.1 gm Protein 5.9 gm Fat
.6 gm Carbohydrate per Serving

. . . .

Russian Dressing

. . . .

The average deli Russian dressing contains about 230 calories for a three tablespoon serving. In this tangy version, buttermilk and only a minimal amount of sour cream replace the usual mayonnaise to cut three quarters of the fat and calories. This dressing is wonderful on old-fashioned salads like hearts of romaine or iceberg, on sliced tomatoes, or on turkey or roast beef sandwiches.

. . . .

½ cup buttermilk
3 tablespoons sour cream
1½ tablespoons tomato paste
1 tablespoon minced shallot
1 teaspoon grainy mustard
½ teaspoon prepared white horseradish, drained
¼ teaspoon Worcestershire sauce
¼ teaspoon sugar

In a small bowl, whisk together all the ingredients. Cover and refrigerate for at least 1 hour to
let the flavors meld. *(The dressing will keep for up
to 4 days.)*

Makes ¾ Cup   15 Calories   .6 gm Protein
.9 gm Fat   1.3 gm Carbohydrate per Tablespoon

Double Sour Cream

In my experiments with low-calorie recipes, I have found that sour cream used judiciously can do a lot for creamy texture and flavor, at about two thirds the calories of heavy cream—just 31 calories per tablespoon. Taken one step further in this recipe, sour cream is blended with buttermilk to produce a delicious sour cream with even fewer calories. Like crème fraîche, it thickens naturally overnight. It lasts several weeks refrigerated. Use it as you would regular sour cream. It is also delicious with fresh berries and cooked fruit desserts.

¾ **cup sour cream**
¾ **cup buttermilk**

The day before serving, in a medium bowl, whisk together the sour cream and buttermilk until blended. Cover with plastic wrap and refrigerate overnight.

**Makes 1½ Cups   18 Calories   .5 gm Protein
1.6 gm Fat   .7 gm Carbohydrate per Tablespoon**

Yogurt Cheese

This easy-to-make low-calorie spread tastes like a subtly tangy cream cheese. Yogurt cheese is usually made with nonfat yogurt which results in a cheese that is very acidic and tart. I use whole-milk yogurt—at only one more calorie a tablespoon—for a mild sweetly flavored yogurt cheese. It is great with all kinds of breakfast breads, from bagels to pancakes. It is also delicious with fresh fruit and a sprinkling of brown sugar on top.

1 quart whole-milk plain yogurt

Line a large colander or conical strainer with 3 layers of cheesecloth and place over a bowl. Spoon the yogurt into the cheesecloth and lightly cover the bowl with plastic wrap. Refrigerate for at least 6 hours or overnight. The liquid will drain from the yogurt, causing it to thicken like cream cheese. Discard the liquid. Transfer the cheese to a clean jar or bowl, cover, and refrigerate for up to 3 weeks.

Makes 1¾ Cups   20 Calories   1.1 gm Protein
1.0 gm Fat   1.5 gm Carbohydrate per Tablespoon

Homemade "Margarine"

*M*argarine has always been taboo in my mind. The hydrogenated fats and chemicals of which it is composed pose potential risks that far outweigh the benefit of reduced cholesterol. The flavor, though claiming to be just like butter, comes nowhere near the real thing for virtually the same number of calories. I'd rather eat small amounts of real, unsalted butter than this unsatisfying substitute—until I tasted this recipe for homemade "margarine."

Created by my sister in response to her need to lower her cholesterol, this recipe rolls the virtues of butter and margarine into one. It is made by blending extra-virgin olive oil with butter. It has a wonderful flavor, half the saturated fat of butter, and none of the chemicals used in commercial margarines. It can also be made with a neutrally flavored oil, such as canola, to more closely imitate whole butter.

1 stick (4 ounces) unsalted butter, softened
¾ cup extra-virgin olive oil
¾ teaspoon salt

In a small bowl, whisk together all the ingredients until completely blended and liquid. (Or puree in a food processor.) Transfer to a container, cover, and refrigerate. *(The margarine will keep for up to 2 weeks, refrigerated, and frozen for up to 3 months.)* The margarine will firm up as it chills.

Makes About 1¼ Cups   38 Calories
.0 gm Protein   4.3 gm Fat
.0 gm Carbohydrate per Teaspoon

Chinese Chicken Stock

. . . . , ...

I like this Chinese-style chicken stock because it is so easy to make, requiring only about three hours of unattended cooking. It has a clean, fresh flavor with just scallions and ginger added during cooking. I make it with chicken legs and thighs, which are cheap, readily available, and meaty enough to yield a lot of flavor. If you wish, you can also use an equal amount of stockpiled chicken bones and trimmings.

. . . .

3 pounds chicken legs and thighs, skinned
2 scallions, cut into 2-inch lengths
4 quarter-size slices of fresh ginger
¼ teaspoon Szechuan peppercorns (optional)
½ teaspoon salt

Using a meat cleaver, hack each leg and thigh into 3 or 4 pieces. Lightly smash the scallions and ginger with the broad side of the cleaver.

In a large heavy saucepan, place the chicken pieces and enough cold water to cover by about 3 inches. Bring the water to a simmer over moderate heat. Reduce the heat to moderately low to maintain a simmer. Using a large shallow spoon, skim off the gray scum on the surface of the water. Keep skimming until the liquid is almost clear, about 5 minutes.

Add the ginger, scallions, and peppercorns, if desired. Simmer the stock over moderately low heat for 3 hours until the liquid is reduced by half. Do not stir or shake up the stock and do not let it boil.

Set a fine-mesh strainer, china cap, or cheesecloth-lined colander over a bowl. Ladle the stock into the strainer. Then transfer the bones into the strainer to drain. Pour any stock left in the pot through the strainer. Discard the bones. Stir the salt into the stock.

Freeze the stock for about 20 minutes until the fat rises to the surface and congeals. Skim off the fat with a spoon. If you want a more concentrated flavor, pour the stock into a saucepan and simmer to reduce it. *(The stock will keep refrigerated for 3 days and frozen for several months.)*

Makes About 1 Quart   40 Calories
.5 gm Protein   1.8 gm Fat
5.2 gm Carbohydrate per Cup

o   o   o

Menus
Conversion Chart
Acknowledgments
Index

o   o   o

Some Very American Suppers

CLOVE-AND-PEPPER-CURED ROAST PORK
WARM BLACK-EYED PEAS WITH ONIONS AND BACON
BUTTERMILK SLAW
PINEAPPLE UPSIDE-DOWN CAKE

CRAB CAKES WITH ROASTED YELLOW PEPPER SAUCE
CORN, TOMATO, AND VIDALIA ONION SALAD
DEEP-DISH ROSEWATER APPLE PIE

SEAFOOD FILÉ GUMBO
WHITE OR WILD PECAN RICE
SHAKER LEMON MERINGUE BREAD PUDDING

A Very Special Sunday Brunch

BUCKWHEAT POPOVERS
RUSSIAN CAVIAR
DOUBLE SOUR CREAM
CHAMPAGNE

A Sampling of Hors d'Oeuvres to Make a Light Supper

....

CHEESE STRAWS

RILLETTES OF DUCK

SKORDALIA

SMOKED SALMON TARTARE

FRESH FENNEL AND THINLY SLICED BAGUETTE

FOCACCIA

A Picnic

....

COUNTRY TERRINE

PICKLED CHERRIES

THINLY SLICED BAGUETTE

ROASTED PEPPERS WITH CARAMELIZED GARLIC

FRESH RASPBERRIES AND BLACKBERRIES

LACE COOKIES

Four Seasonal Menus

. . . .

FALL

ARTICHOKE BOTTOMS AND CHICORY WITH
WARM WALNUT DRESSING

WILD MUSHROOM RAGOUT WITH ROASTED POLENTA

TRUFFLE SABAYON

WINTER

GARLIC-FRIED GREENS

CASSOULET

FRESH PINEAPPLE WITH KIRSCH

CHOCOLATE CHESTNUT TRUFFLES

SPRING

Mesclun Salad

Crayfish Ragout

Rosemary Focaccia

Hazelnut Espresso Genoise

SUMMER

Treviso and Belgian Endive Salad with

Walnut Oil Dressing

Roasted Garlic

Pan-Grilled Bread

Goat Cheese

Warm Cherries with Zabaglione

Conversion Chart

. . . .

Butter
Some confusion may arise over the measuring of butter and other hard fats. In the United States, butter is generally sold in a one-pound package, which contains four equal "sticks." The wrapper on each stick is marked to show tablespoons, so the cook can cut the stick according to the quantity required. The equivalent weights are:

1 stick = 115 g/4 oz
1 tablespoon = 15 g/½ oz

Cheese
In some of the recipes in this book, lower-fat cheese is used. To enable you to substitute an equivalent British cheese, these are the fat contents:

American part-skim mozzarella: 16% fat
American part-skim ricotta: 7.9% fat
Remember to take any differences in fat content into account when consulting the nutritional information for each recipe.

Flour
American all-purpose flour is milled from a mixture of hard and soft wheats, whereas British plain flour is made mainly from soft wheat. To achieve a near equivalent to American all-purpose flour, use half British plain flour and half strong bread flour.

American cake flour is made from soft wheat and can be replaced by British plain flour alone.

Sugar
In the recipes in this book, if sugar is called for it is assumed to be granulated, unless otherwise specified. American granulated sugar is finer than British granulated, closer to caster sugar, so British cooks should use caster sugar throughout.

Yeast and Gelatine
Quantities of dried yeast (called active dry yeast in the United States) are usually given in number of packages. Each of these packages contains 7 g/¼ oz of yeast, which is equivalent to a scant tablespoon.

Quantities of unflavoured powdered gelatine are usually given in envelopes, each of which contains 7 g/¼ oz (about 1 tablespoon).

Ingredients and Equipment Glossary
British English and American English are not always the same, particularly in the kitchen. The following ingredients and equipment used in this book are pretty much the same on both sides of the Atlantic, but just have different names.

AMERICAN	BRITISH
apple cider	non-alcoholic sweet-tart apple juice
arugula	rocket
baking soda	bicarbonate of soda
beef medallions	beef tournedos
beans (dried)—lima, navy, Great Northern	dried white (haricot) beans
Belgian endive	chicory
bell pepper	sweet pepper (capsicum)
Bibb and Boston lettuce	soft-leaved, round lettuce
broiler/to broil	grill/to grill
celery rib	celery stick
celery root	celeriac
cheesecloth	muslin
chile	chilli
confectioners' sugar	icing sugar
cookie cutter	biscuit or pastry cutter
cookie sheet	baking sheet
cornstarch	cornflour
cracker	savoury (i.e. cheese) biscuit
crushed hot red pepper	dried crushed red chilli
eggplant	aubergine
fatback	pork back fat
fava bean	broad bean
ground beef/pork	minced beef/pork
hard cider	cider (alcoholic)
heavy cream (37.6% fat)	whipping cream (35–40% fat)
hot pepper sauce	Tabasco sauce
kitchen towel	tea towel

CONVERSION CHART

AMERICAN	BRITISH
light corn syrup	(no equivalent but can use golden syrup)
low-fat milk	semi-skimmed milk
muffin tin	deep bun tin
parchment paper	non-stick baking paper
peanut oil	groundnut oil
pearl onion	button or baby onion
pork tenderloin	pork fillet
rack of lamb	best end of neck joint
romaine lettuce	cos lettuce
Romano cheese	pecorino cheese
scallion	spring onion
semisweet chocolate	plain chocolate
shell or strip steak	sirloin steak
shrimp	prawn (varying in size)
skillet	frying pan
squab	young pigeon
superfine sugar	use caster sugar
tomato puree	sieved tomatoes or pasatta
unsweetened chocolate	bitter *chocolat pâtissier*
vanilla bean	vanilla pod
whole milk	homogenized milk
zucchini	courgette

Volume Equivalents

These are not exact equivalents for the American cups and spoons, but have been rounded up or down slightly to make measuring easier.

AMERICAN MEASURES	METRIC	IMPERIAL
¼ t	1.25 ml	
½ t	2.5 ml	
1 t	5 ml	
½ T (1½ t)	7.5 ml	
1 T (3 t)	15 ml	
¼ cup (4 T)	60 ml	2 fl oz
⅓ cup (5 T)	75 ml	2½ fl oz
½ cup (8 T)	125 ml	4 fl oz
⅔ cup (10 T)	150 ml	5 fl oz (¼ pint)
¾ cup (12 T)	175 ml	6 fl oz
1 cup (16 T)	250 ml	8 fl oz
1¼ cups	300 ml	10 fl oz (½ pint)
1½ cups	350 ml	12 fl oz
1 pint (2 cups)	500 ml	16 fl oz
1 quart (4 cups)	1 litre	1¾ pints

Weight Equivalents

The metric weights given in this chart are not exact equivalents, but have been rounded up or down slightly to make measuring easier.

AVOIRDUPOIS	METRIC
¼ oz	7 g
½ oz	15 g
1 oz	30 g
2 oz	60 g
3 oz	90 g
4 oz	115 g
5 oz	150 g
6 oz	175 g
7 oz	200 g
8 oz (½ lb)	225 g
9 oz	250 g
10 oz	300 g
11 oz	325 g
12 oz	350 g
13 oz	375 g
14 oz	400 g
15 oz	425 g
1 lb	450 g
1 lb 2 oz	500 g
1½ lb	750 g
2 lb	900 g
2¼ lb	1 kg
3 lb	1.4 kg
4 lb	1.8 kg
4½ lb	2 kg

Oven Temperatures

In the recipes in this book, only Fahrenheit temperatures have been given. Consult this chart for the Centigrade and gas mark equivalents.

OVEN	°F	°C	GAS MARK
very cool	250–275	130–140	½–1
cool	300	150	2
warm	325	170	3
moderate	350	180	4
moderately hot	375	190	5
	400	200	6
hot	425	220	7
very hot	450	230	8
	475	250	9

Acknowledgments

. . . .

I only now understand the ubiquitous phrase—"without whom this book would never have been written"—always seen on acknowledgment pages. Though hackneyed, it is nevertheless completely true and really an understatement. Though it bears one person's name on the cover, a book becomes a collaboration of many generous people who each gave a part of themselves to its creation. I could write pages of thanks to the many people who have contributed their time, support and talent to this book and still not include everyone, or thank them adequately. I am honored to have worked with them.

My thanks to Leslie Stoker, my editor, for her enthusiasm, thoughtfulness, and great good sense; to my copy editor Pamela Mitchell, whose extraordinary patience, sensitivity, and support at my weakest moments made painstaking work a pleasure; and to my agent, Elise Goodman, who urged me to write this book, and then helped me to find a way to do it.

I am grateful to the entire team who came together to create the beautiful photographs in this book: photographer Maria Robledo for her unique sense of space and light; prop stylist Anita Calero for her inimitable style and the use of her personal collections; studio assistants Ann Iaison and Beatriz Martins who made long working days run smoothly; my assistant Dari Birnel who supported us all with her humor and comforting lunches, and who helped me negotiate the long hours and a sea of details.

Thanks to the dear friends who generously lent their personal collections for the photographs in this book: David Barrett, Tom Fallon, Mary and Howard Rower, Hannah Milman, and Jeffrey Miller.

Lynne Hill provided the nutritional information for each recipe, on a very tight deadline. My sincere thanks for her fine work and wise counsel.

I am grateful to the staff at Balducci's, especially Charlie Balducci and Gino Roselli, for their help in finding the best ingredients for my recipes and photographs.

Special thanks to Lee Haiken, who took a chance years ago and gave me my start in writing and styling. And to my friends at *Food & Wine* Magazine, who entrusted me with a monthly column on low-calorie cooking, which was the precursor to this book.

Thank you to the friends and family who gave me unrelenting encouragement and love during the sometimes difficult process of writing this book.

And finally, many thanks to all the cooks I have met over the years who shared their recipes, invited me to their tables and kitchens, and gave me many memories to write about and cherish.

Index

. . . .

Page numbers in *italic* indicate photographs.

Designed by Jim Wageman

Composed in Bernhard Modern and Antique Open by
Trufont Typographers, Inc., Hicksville, New York

Printed and bound by
Toppan Printing Company, Ltd.,
Tokyo, Japan